FREEBIRDS

The Lynyrd Skynyrd Story

Marley Brant

BILLBOARD BOOKS

an imprint of Watson-Guptill Publications

New York, New York

Dedication

To Ronnie, Allen, Dean, Leon, Steve, and Cassie, who will never be forgotten.

And to the survivors, who will never forget.

For Thumper

and for my mom, Gladys Wall Olmstead

Pages 2-3: Steve Gaines, Ronnie VanZant, Allen Collins, Gary Rossington, Leon Wilkeson.
Photo by Chuck Pulin/Star File

Copyright © 2002 Marley Brant
ISBN: 0-8230-8321-7

First published in 2002 in New York by Billboard Books,
an imprint of Watson-Guptill Publications, a division of VNU Business Media Inc.
770 Broadway
New York, New York 10003
www.watsonguptill.com

LIBRARY OF CONGRESS CATALOGING IN PUBLICATION DATA
The CIP data for this title is on file with the Library of Congress.

Printed in the United States

First printing, 2002
3 4 5 6 7 8 9 / 08 07 06 05 04 03 02

Senior Editor: Bob Nirkind
Editor: Margaret Sobel
Production Manager: Hector Campbell
Designer: Leah Lococo

Acknowledgments

To know the story of Lynyrd Skynyrd is to live, however parenthetically, among the joy of the music, the pain of the airplane crash, and everything in between. For those of us who called members of the band, friends, and for those of us who knew these fascinating music makers only through their songs and live appearances, the end of the original band came too quickly. The music continues to live on, some classic, some new and exciting, some mundane reissues. There are those who believe that the music died in 1977, and others who believe that Skynyrd's unique contribution to rock-and-roll will keep the music eternally alive. One thing is certain: everybody has an opinion about Lynyrd Skynyrd's music. Skynyrd is one of a kind and their remarkable stamp on our music can never be dismissed, forgotten, or ignored. Regardless of how we personally feel about the band, for the most part, the songs have touched our souls and live in our hearts. It is unlikely there will ever be another experience like that of Skynyrd and we are grateful that they have shared their music with us. With that in mind, I offer my deepest thanks to the members of Lynyrd Skynyrd. The gift of the music is not taken for granted.

So many people participated in this study of Lynyrd Skynyrd as well as its predecessor, *Southern Rockers*. I thank you all: Buddy Buie, Dave Bruegger, Tim Bruegger, Cha Cha Bruegger, Jeff Carlisi, Danny Chauncey, Charlie Daniels, Charlie Faubion, Marta Hall, Randall Hall, Paul Hornsby, Judy VanZant Jenness, Harriett Kilpatrick, Al Kooper, Ed King, Dru Lombar, Jim Dandy Mangrum, George McCorkle, Rickey Medlocke, Rodney Mills, Kathie Montgomery, Brian Nash, Mary Nash, Willie Olmstead, Billy Powell, Artimus Pyle, Kerri Hampton Pyle, Teresa Gaines Rapp, Hughie Thomasson, Donnie Van Zant, Johnny Van-Zant, Lacy Van-Zant, Melody VanZant, Leon Wilkeson, and all the fans who shared their memories and love of the music.

Thanks to Judy VanZant Jenness, Kerri and Artimus Pyle, Teresa Gaines Rapp, Ed King, Bob Johnson, Jeff Carlisi, Brian and Mary Nash, Harriett Kilpatrick, Mike Hausmann, John and Robin Eastwood, Bob "Slim" Rader, and Randall and Marta Hall for their photos.

Thanks to Dean Kilpatrick for being the inspiration behind this project. "You're one-of-a-kind, buddy."

Thank you always to Jesus for the opportunities and to my family for their never-ending support of my endeavors. My thanks to Billboard Books for the interest in this book and my terrific senior editor, Bob Nirkind, for his perseverance. Thanks also to editor Margaret Sobel. Billboard Books is a class act and I appreciate and respect their professionalism.

Some of you readers may find a date or name out of sync with the story or recall a different version of the story being told. Tracking Lynyrd Skynyrd wasn't easy and the people involved in the various tales or events remembered them differently from one another. It was challenging to sort it all out and bring it together. It wasn't all sunshine and roses and there were misses as well as hits. The band reminds me of that little ditty my mother used to say to me: "When they were good, they were very, very good. And when they were bad, they were awful." I can only be hopeful that the essence of Skynyrd shines through this intricate story so that you can judge Lynyrd Skynyrd for yourself.

Almost about the time this book was going to press we received the very sad news that Leon "Thumper" Wilkeson had passed away. Leon loved Lynyrd Skynyrd so very much and surely gave his heart and soul to the band. He was a terrific person—full of love, wit, poetry, fun, loyalty, and, of course, his music. He will be missed by so many and he will be missed by me.

MARLEY BRANT
Atlanta, Georgia

Author's Note: The name Van Zant has been spelled to reflect the desired spelling of the individual Van Zants.

Contents

1

Beginnings

JACKSONVILLE, FLORIDA, is similar in many ways to almost any other seaboard metropolis. Although waterfronts will always have their share of lovers and muggers, in recent years a major renovation of the waterfront along the St. John's River has brought a yuppie affluence to the Jacksonville of old. Jacksonville has widespread appeal to a variety of industry and tourism interests. It is a vital American city, with a vibrant social scene. That scene was in its infancy in the 1970s and has continued to develop into the new century.

For reasons difficult to determine, in the seventies a coterie of musical talent from this coastal environment erupted and flowed throughout the music world. The Allman Brothers Band's roots were somewhat based in this southern city, as were those of Blackfoot, Grinderswitch, .38 Special, and a band of ostensible misfits that called themselves Lynyrd Skynyrd. What was it about Jacksonville that bred so worthy a group of longhaired musical rebels? "I think the water or something," says Blackfoot and future Skynyrd guitarist Rickey Medlocke. "I used to ask my dad this stuff. 'Dad, there are a lot of bands here. What is it down here?' We really attributed it to Florida being a very transient state. Jacksonville [is a] big Navy town. You got Mayport, you got the Naval Air Station, Cecil Field, you got all these big naval bases there. So, first of all, you got a lot of people that lived in the military. You had the Jacksonville shipyards that brought in a lot of families. Jacksonville was a blue-collar kind of town. I believe it was because of all these roots [in country and bluegrass music] that just happened to be in and around the north Florida/south Georgia area, and it went all the way up into Nashville. The Allman Brothers were from Daytona [and later Jacksonville], and Dickey Betts and all them guys were from Sarasota. You had the Outlaws like Hughie and all of 'em . . . they came out of Tampa. Lynyrd Skynyrd comes out of Jacksonville, Blackfoot comes out of Jacksonville, the Allmans hung out in and around Jacksonville, Grinderswitch, all these bands. There were a lot of 'em. Wet Willie was from around the south Georgia, north Florida area. And I attribute it to all the transients that came in around [that] area."

Skynyrd's current lead vocalist Johnny Van-Zant says he doesn't know why so many rock bands came out of Jacksonville. "Maybe nothing else to do," he laughs. "That or jail. Just a bunch of good people got together and played music. I think it just got on a roll, kind of like the Seattle scene."

The fact that these bands started out attempting to plant their feet in New York and California's musical monopoly created a certain camaraderie that also reinforced the Jacksonville influence. "We used to loan each other gear and stuff like that, and help each other out, man," says Medlocke. "Whereas today I don't see that. It's like me, me, me, you know what I mean? Like a self-indulgence thing."

Back in the sixties, many of the people who lived in Jacksonville found the small city fairly routine and uninspiring. It was primarily a naval city, complete with bases, harbors, and the associated small industry that the military usually brings with it. Jacksonville was a transient city, yes, but the communities within it consisted of a variety of societies. There were the "Navy people," the thousands who toiled to make a living from the analogous industry, those who coordinated the city's commerce, and more than a handful of refugees from the Old South, looking to hang on to that age-old culture while accepting that, indeed, things were definitely changing. Jacksonville was growing and with that growth came many transformations.

At the onset of the sixties, it was too early in the game to determine just what those changes were going to be and how they would affect Jacksonville. So the everyday life of the average blue-collar Jacksonvillian, for the most part, just continued as it always had. For the average male, you got up, went to work, hung out, and went to bed. If you were lucky, you laughed with friends and you drank a little beer. You went to church, maybe you did a little fishing, or went to the dog track. It was a hard life but a good life.

Unbeknownst to one particular suburban family in "Jax," after the sixties, things would never be the same. Within the suburbs of Jacksonville was an area that came to be known as Shanty Town. Among the less fortunate living in the area was a solid base of hardworking blue-collar families. Among these was the family of Lacy Van-Zant. Lacy was born in 1915 in Nassau

Octogenarian Lacy Van-Zant with youngest son Johnny, 2000.

County, Florida, in a town called Evergreen, to logger George Van-Zant, Jr. and his wife Florence. One of eleven children, Lacy's name was a derivative of his grandmother's use of "lazy baby," given to him by his father. Lacy married his second wife, Marion Hicks, in 1947, after an earlier marriage and divorce, and in addition to Lacy's daughter Betty JoAnn by his first wife, the couple had five children of their own. Lacy held a variety of jobs, eventually settling on a career in trucking. He worked steadily and set a good example for his children as a hard worker and dedicated family man. A little fishing, a little hanging out with friends, a little beer. . . .

It would be Lacy and Marion's first child together who would change their life. Born weighting just a little over five pounds, Ronald Wayne Van-Zant entered the world on January 15, 1948, at St. Vincent's Hospital in Jacksonville. Ronnie was the second of Lacy's six children, which included Betty JoAnn, Darlene, Marlene, Donnie, and Johnny. Ronnie was a happy baby and the apple of his parents' eyes. Ronnie entered first grade at Hyde Park Elementary School at the age of six. By the time Ronnie was in second grade, the family had moved to Woodcrest Road on the west side of Jacksonville, to a house where Lacy still lives today.

Ronnie VanZant, as he would later spell it, was a fairly precocious child, always inventive and extremely curious. Interested in math and history in school, he dove headfirst into the things that he enjoyed during his leisure time: baseball, fishing, singing, and friends. He was too young for the beer. Whatever it was that Ronnie devoted his time to, he had a driving need to be the best. He felt the limitations of his somewhat grandiose aspirations but knew from the get-go that if he put his mind to something, he would eventually find few limitations. According to his family, Ronnie felt destined to somehow dig his way out of the barrenness of his lower-middle-class neighborhood in the Shanty Town community. "It was rough," Ronnie told reporter Scott Cohen. "Particularly where I grew up. It was like the ghetto, black and white, and there was a lot of street fighting and a lot of adventure. It was a rough area of town, the Shanty Town." Ronnie wasn't quite sure how his escape might come about, but he never had any doubts that it would.

Ronnie loved to fish and would spend quite a bit of time with his line in the water. He was a good fisherman, approaching the sport with as headstrong a desire to succeed as he did everything else. Ronnie was often seen headed down to nearby Cedar Creek to go fishing either with his tight circle of friends or by himself. Ronnie would often return to fishing as a means of leaving behind the troublesome distractions of the outside world. Ronnie loved to fish and think about things. The two pastimes went well together.

Ronnie also possessed a darkly mischievous side and enjoyed spearheading pranks with other kids in the neighborhood. Future friend and bandmate Leon Wilkeson was told one such story by Ronnie's childhood friend, Gene Odom. "There was a gang that stole bicycles from them for years," Leon recalled. "I mean, they were so slick, Gene said, that they'd steal a radio and the music would still be playing. Well, him and Ronnie caught a bobcat, put him in a suitcase, set him out on the road for this gang to pick up."

Teenaged Ronnie VanZant, dressed up and ready to go . . . everywhere, circa 1962.

In addition to taking on the kids of Shanty Town, Ronnie loved to sing. Lacy remembers him singing at the top of his lungs in the bathtub. It wasn't the squeaky voice of a developing adolescent but rather a lusty, heartfelt delivery. From an early age Ronnie had a knack for imitating singers he heard on his parents' radio or picking up a tune here and there from around the neighborhood. Ronnie especially liked country music. He had been exposed to it early and heard quite a bit of it during those times when he accompanied his father on some of his Atlantic Seaboard runs in the eighteen-wheeler.

"He loved country music," remembers his younger brother Donnie. "Merle Haggard was his favorite country artist. We actually grew up around that. That's what my mother and father listened to. We listened to Merle Haggard and Mel Tillis . . . Roy Acuff and all of them. That's what we grew up around. We were big Elvis Presley fans too."

There were times when Ronnie's soulful renditions got him into trouble. One time his mother had to go down to Ramona Elementary School to counsel young Ronnie against singing "Beer Drinkin' Daddy" and "Ricochet Romance" in the classroom. Ronnie may have gotten a whupping, but he couldn't help himself. Ronnie was never one to let anything get in the way of a good song.

As his teenage years progressed, Ronnie became less known for his singing and more infamous for his short temper and bullying personality. "Ronnie was a very aggressive person," says Robert E. Lee High School classmate Charlie Faubion. "Ronnie had a violent part of him that was very real. Ronnie was a mean, aggressive-type person. He would never take anything from any stranger or any person. If you crossed him, he would take care of you. That's the way he was in high school. He actually went out of his way to seek out confrontation. In high school, he was a bad person."

Ronnie was the first to recognize the badass components of his character. Although he knew fighting and mouthing off didn't endear him to a certain element of his day-to-day society, he did little to change his approach. He'd simply acknowledge his shortcomings and shrug. "I'm a boy only a mom could love," he'd often say.

When he was fourteen, Ronnie heard through the grapevine that a group of his fellow students at Lakeshore Junior High were putting together a band. They named their venture "Us" and held auditions for a singer. Ronnie didn't believe in pulling any punches. He appeared at the auditions and told the band they need look no further—he was their new singer. Ronnie had a well-earned reputation as a no-nonsense man of the fist. When he made his declaration, the band quickly huddled and decided that he was in. Ronnie VanZant would be Us' new vocalist.

Ronnie kept busy during his mid-teen years. In addition to going to school and singing with Us, Ronnie also started his first after-school job. He managed to land a position bagging groceries at the local grocery store. Ronnie also met Virginia-born Nadine Incoe while he was in high school and the two soon became more than friends. According to Lacy, Nadine was one hundred percent behind her boyfriend's ambition to perform as a singer.

Ronnie liked singing in the band and felt that it was something he could do well. Heck, singers in bands made good money. If he was as good as he thought he was, maybe he could make money too. That beat bagging groceries. By the time he started thinking of singing professionally, Ronnie declared himself a serious fan of the melodic rock ballads sung by Free's Paul Rodgers. "Ronnie idolized the man," Leon Wilkeson would later say. While others were turning to guitars and drums, Ronnie began to feel strongly that he might have something unique and dynamic to offer as a vocalist. Ronnie saw little difference in the deliveries and drive of Paul Rodgers and Ronnie VanZant. If serious music lovers appreciated Rodgers, why wouldn't they appreciate VanZant?

"What he liked about [Rodgers] so much was just that singing ability," says Donnie Van Zant. "He loved the group Free to begin with, the way their music was to begin with. I think Skynyrd got some of the influences from that, 'cause they had a bluesy sort of feel to 'em."

"There's a history that Ronnie's favorite singer was Paul Rodgers," says Charlie Faubion. "I think he learned to like him later on. To me, his early idol as a singer was probably Mick Jagger."

"I don't think [Ronnie] was influenced by Paul's singing," says Ronnie's widow, Judy VanZant Jenness. "He never really tried to put that into his voice. He thought Paul Rodgers was one of the best singers in the world. He truly thought Paul had a great voice. I think mostly the Free sound that I could hear [from Skynyrd] would be in the guitars. The drive that Free and Bad Company had in their songs. The heavy bass and the guitar. That's really where that Free thing came in. But [Ronnie] really thought Paul Rodgers had an incredible voice, which he does.

Ronnie VanZant at home with his music, circa 1965.

I wouldn't say the Stones were one of [his] top groups. When I first met the guys in the band, they were listening to groups like Creedence Clearwater Revival, Illinois Speed Press, Cream, stuff like that. [But] Ronnie didn't move near as much as Mick does."

Regardless of whom he was influenced by the most, Ronnie started to think about fronting his own band. He had a plan. He would surround himself with the best musicians he could find and through hard work, something that Ronnie was very familiar with through family ties and Southern roots, that band would have every reason in the world to succeed.

It is likely that Ronnie was so driven mostly because of his association with his father. Lacy Van-Zant had a strong influence on Ronnie throughout his life. Ronnie and Lacy had a very deep but complex relationship. While Lacy was extraordinarily supportive of Ronnie and his musical career, Ronnie gave the impression that he felt that he could never live up to Lacy's expectations, whatever they were. Ronnie would often point out that while all of his other siblings graduated, which made their father quite proud, he was a high school dropout. Yet it is doubtful that Lacy ever made Ronnie feel bad about not finishing school. Lacy was quite satisfied with his son's success in other areas.

Ronnie seemed as proud of his father as Lacy seemed proud of his son. He even sported a tattoo with his father's name on his arm. Lacy was certainly an inspirational example for Ronnie of the power of applied hard work. Yet Ronnie would say that he felt that he was letting his father down because he couldn't be the things that Lacy was—whatever they might be. He felt that Lacy wanted him to be more like him, yet in many ways he wasn't. Because of his later success in music, Ronnie VanZant was not, in his adult years, truly, by definition, blue-collar. Yet in so many ways Ronnie *was* like his father: hardworking, tough, and outspoken. People knew where they stood with Lacy Van-Zant and they certainly knew how Ronnie felt about them. Perhaps it is that age-old problem among fathers and sons. The son doesn't feel he lives up to the expectations of his father, while at the same time he becomes a mirror image of him. Yet anyone who knew both VanZants could clearly see that Ronnie's ambition was based firmly in his roots. And his ambition was to be a world famous rock-and-roll singer.

"At Lee High School I ran around with all these guys, that are now I guess sort of the icons of the Southern Rock music business" says Faubion. "If you were a musician, you kind of knew each other, 'cause of your age association. You knew where to go and you knew where to meet people in the music business. I happened to be in a math class in the eleventh grade and there was a guy sitting across the aisle from me . . . his name was Ronnie VanZant. I had just gotten in a band and we were called The Chosen Few. The band that I was in was playing a lot of music similar to The Rolling Stones. Ronnie kind of wanted to emulate the lead singer in our band and kind of saw himself as another Mick Jagger."

Everybody knew there was only one Mick Jagger in the world of rock-and-roll. But there had yet to be someone like Ronnie VanZant. Ronnie was ready to do whatever it took to fill the position.

2

One Percent

As much as Ronnie VanZant aspired to make professional music, this dream wasn't his first. He loved playing baseball and, as with most of the activities he undertook, he was pretty good at it. While growing up, he often dreamed of a career in major-league baseball. Sandlot and organized baseball games were major attractions to the boys in Jacksonville. Ronnie played American Legion baseball as a center fielder with a team called the Green Pigs, sponsored by the nearby Green Pig Restaurant. Ronnie managed one year to earn the highest batting average in the league. He loved the sport and played as often as his school and work schedules would allow.

One day during a Green Pigs' baseball game in the summer of 1964, Ronnie's line drive bounced off the head of an adolescent named Bob Burns. Burns was one of the neighborhood kids who also played baseball, with a team called The Bugs. He had been watching the game, in the company of his twelve-year-old friend, Gary Rossington. Rossington loved baseball too, and played for the Lakeshore Rebels. The ball hit Burns so hard that it knocked him unconscious.

Bob Burns having at the drums.

Ronnie felt terrible about the accident and ended up befriending both Burns and Rossington.

Over the course of a few weeks the new friends discovered that they all shared a serious interest in music. Even though Rossington and Burns were younger, all three of the boys enjoyed the same type of music—basically, rock-and-roll. Ronnie discovered that bands such as Free, The Stones, and Cream, among others, were popular with Bob and Gary too. The two younger boys liked their rock-and-roll so much that they had already considered putting a band together. Burns took up the

Enter Gary Rossington with one of his favorite guitars.

drums and Rossington had learned to play the guitar. Ronnie was interested in becoming better acquainted with the twelve-year-olds. Maybe they could be involved in his dream.

Gary Rossington was born in Jacksonville on December 4, 1951. Rossington's father died when he was ten and he knew well the struggles of a single-parent household. Gary was raised by his mother Berniece, for whom he would later name his Les Paul Sunburst guitar. Rossington, like Ronnie, had at first been drawn to baseball as a possible career. His ambition was a bit more specific than Ronnie VanZant's: Gary wanted to play second base for the New York Yankees. Although he continued to enjoy playing baseball, his dream would change too. After seeing The Rolling Stones on television Gary thought maybe a career in music would be more attainable. It was then that he and Bob Burns decided to form their band.

Rossington and Burns were at first both interested in playing the drums, but soon realized that a band with two drummers and no guitar players wasn't going to work. Gary decided to switch to guitar and saved his money to purchase a Sears Silvertone. Gary's older sister Carol was dating a local musician named Lloyd Phillips. Phillips was known around town as a very good, and fast, guitar player. Phillips was happy to show Gary how to play his new instrument and gave him guitar lessons while he waited for Rossington's sister to get ready for their dates. Gary Rossington was a quick study.

The band that Burns and Rossington dreamed about was ready to become a reality. Bob was now on drums, Gary had decided on guitar, and a third friend, Larry Jungstrom, was recruited to play bass. The band was called "You, Me and Him." Although he had yet to get anything substantial happening, Gary Rossington had already begun his rock-and-roll indoctrination by the time he met Ronnie VanZant.

Now that their common interest had been identified, Ronnie, Gary, and Bob decided to expand Burns, Rossington, and Jungstrom's little trio. It was a year of powerhouse bands and the only trio that had made an indelible mark was the English band Cream. The young musicians weren't foolish enough to pattern themselves after so strong an entity. They realized that they would have a better chance of attracting attention if they added a second guitar player. The name Allen Collins had been mentioned as a possible contender. Albeit young, Collins had the reputation of being quite the player. The kids in the neighborhood had been talking about his quick fingers and elaborate chording. After a consensus, and without even hearing him play, Ronnie decided to find the kid and see if he had any interest in joining them.

Larkin Allen Collins, Jr. was born July 19, 1952, at St. Luke's Hospital in Jacksonville, Florida. Allen's parents, Eva and Larkin, divorced when he was a small boy. He grew up in the Cedar Hills section of Jacksonville. Allen was nobody's fool. He quickly determined that his frustration with first a turbulent household and then a divided one needed some kind of outlet. Allen's mind seemed in perpetual motion and he decided to vent his energy by learning everything he could about racecars and speed. Allen spent many summer nights at the Jacksonville Raceway, enthralled by the loud noise and the colorful, and sometimes dangerous, competitions.

Allen's interests eventually grew to include rock-and-roll music. When a friend received a guitar for his birthday, Allen was intrigued by the instrument. Working two jobs, at a cigar store by day and Woolworth's at night, Eva Strunk saved her money and surprised her son Allen with a guitar of his own: a Sears Silvertone. Allen had little clue how to play the instrument until his stepmother, Leila Collins, taught him the basics, chord by chord. Leila played mostly country

Allen Collins—"Mr. Perpetual Motion."

and western, but Allen didn't mind the genre as long as he was learning to play. Leila taught Allen four notes at one sitting and the teenager was quickly on his way to mastering the intricacies of the guitar. Soon Allen had his own little band, which he called The Mods.

While Allen seems to have had support from the female members of his family, there is controversy among those who knew him as to whether or not his father took much interest in his guitar playing. "He was never there for Allen," says future bandmate Artimus Pyle, addressing the elder Collins' feelings about his son having a career in music. "It was Allen's mother that supported Allen and bought him an amp and let him practice. His father didn't come along until the big paychecks started coming in." It *was* Allen's father, however, who bought him an amplifier, after the young man went to live with his mother.

By the time Allen met VanZant, Rossington, and Burns, he already knew that what he wanted out of life was to be a rock star. Allen loved playing the guitar and he played incessantly, learning all that he could in preparation for the fulfillment of his dream. His mother fully supported his ambition and Allen had the opportunity to practice his guitar while she worked evening hours at Woolworth's. It was apparent to all who heard him play that Allen had an innate talent. Allen's future bandmate Leon Wilkeson would say later that Allen's contributions to music were "incredible. I think if Eric Clapton were to be sitting in the audience watching him, Clapton'd be a little nervous."

Allen Collins' guitar playing impressed most of those who heard it. "[Allen] is one of the greatest guitar players I've ever had the pleasure of knowing and playing with," says former Outlaws guitarist and future Skynyrd Hughie Thomasson. "He was a dear friend of mine. We hung out a lot together. He played a Fender guitar quite often that I loved, 'cause I play a Fender. He also plays his Gibson quite a bit but for some reason when he played the Fender that's what I liked about him the most. Allen playing his Fender guitar and his energy on stage is just unbelievable."

There had been quite a bit of talk around Jacksonville music circles regarding Allen Collins' abilities, and what Ronnie VanZant heard through the grapevine sounded good. A little advance buzz never hurt anybody. With Burns and Rossington accompanying VanZant, the search was on to locate the guitar prodigy.

Eventually, after asking around for clues as to where Collins might be found, the determined trio spotted him on a Jacksonville street. Ronnie called to him, but Allen ditched his bike and took off running. He had heard a lot of negative things about VanZant's character and figured he'd done something for which VanZant was intent on beating the shit out of him. No fool he, Collins decided that if he were to remove himself from VanZant's vicinity as quickly as possible, he might be able to avoid a fight. He wasn't quick enough. After chasing him for a few minutes, Ronnie and Gary caught up. They explained that they wanted nothing more than to ask him to be in their band. Allen was no doubt greatly relieved and agreed to listen to their plans.

"Gary and Allen were just young boys and they idolized Duane Allman," says Charlie Faubion. "You could hear [it] in their early music—it's all just Duane Allman. Duane Allman developed the Southern Rock guitar style and they just fashioned themselves after Duane Allman. 'Cause I think Duane was probably the most influential Southern Rock musician, and a lot of the sound you hear was a spin-off of his type sound—bottleneck playing and things like that."

The boys decided that Larry Jungstrom should remain the bass player for Ronnie, Gary, and Bob's new effort, along with the addition of the outstanding guitar of Allen Collins. "[Ronnie] had met a couple of guys, Allen Collins and Gary Rossington, who were fourteen years old at the time [actually they were even younger]," remembers Charlie Faubion. "He kind of wanted to build his band around these two guys who were very young, but who were somewhat talented guitar players. He saw that as the nucleus of his band."

Covering songs by The Stones and Them, as well as learning the traditional garage band anthem, "Louie, Louie," the new band started to pull it all together by the summer of 1964. Since they were just starting out and money was scarce, both the guitarists, as well as singer VanZant, plugged into Allen Collins' small Super Reverb amp. After some quick garage rehearsals, the band of five was able to secure some gigs at various local parties.

The quintet would play under a variety of names, including My Backyard, The Noble Five, Conqueror Worm, Wildcats, The Pretty Ones, and Sons of Satan. Eventually, Ronnie would dub the band The One Percent. "Only one percent of people who try to play music for a living succeed," he told classmate Charlie Faubion, "and I plan to be in that one percent."

Gary Rossington recalled that the name was decided on after seeing a Hell's Angels movie in Gainesville, Florida, in 1968. The bikers had tattoos that said one percent, because, according to

The One Percent/Lynyrd Skynyrd, 1970. Seated, left to right: Larry Jungstrom, Ronnie VanZant, Bob Burns, Gary Rossington. Standing: Allen Collins.

one of the characters in the movie, one percent of the world is a biker. Rossington says that name identified the band with bikers and made them think they were coming off as badass outlaws.

The band's first paid gig came in the fall of 1964 when they were known as The Noble Five. The boys had been practicing at Allen Collins' house, finishing their sessions shortly after 9:00 PM when Allen's mother would return from work. Ronnie was now working part time at his brother-in-law's auto parts store. He was all ears when talk around the store turned to the company's annual Christmas party. The party was to be held at a barbecue restaurant and the company didn't have a lot of money to spend on entertainment. The restaurant had a small dance floor, and an inexpensive band would be perfect. Ronnie offered his band's services. The Noble Five was hired to play the party for $10.00, total. The band played their seven-song repertoire over and over. Nobody seemed to care. The band was acceptable and the music was loud. The party was a success.

One of the band's favorite hangouts on the nights they weren't playing their own music was

Gary Rossington, outlaw rocker.

the Comic Book Club. "Downtown Jacksonville was wild," remembers Grinderswitch guitarist Dru Lombar. "[The Comic Book Club] was a dumpy place . . . downtown. It was the place right next to Kee's Chili Parlor. That's where everybody hung out. You could play original music, and make a little money. You could work there during the week. They ran early in the night and then they had an after-hours [club] too. So it'd be running from like 9:00 PM to 5:00 AM with two different bands. It wasn't like you played a set and somebody [else] played a set. You played four sets. It was Art Eisen's Comic Book Club. There were these real fat, greasy Italian-looking guys running it. With guns and things. They would advance you some money, but you had to pay it back *real* quick. They did have a booking agency that'd book into like topless bars in Daytona and stuff. They had a little underworld thing going there. But we didn't care . . . we just wanted to play. They moved it out in the 1970s, out towards the beach. Comic Book II. Bill Driscoll bought the place and it became Driscoll's. Then it went down, you know? He got busted and that was that."

"The Comic Book Club was very, very cool," says Judy VanZant Jenness. "I used to go in there. That's the first place I ever saw Duane and Gregg [Allman]. I was in there one night and they just came in. I thought they were the coolest things I'd ever seen. They just got back from California. They looked different than anybody in Jacksonville. Clubs were different back then. People went in to enjoy the music. I don't think they even [sold] alcohol there. It was a teen club. Then at 1:00 or 2:00 AM, it turned into a bottle club, and it would shut down as a teen club, reopen, and people would come in. You pay a cover, you bring your own whiskey or whatever, and buy the chasers from them. Going to a club then was totally different than now. I think people go to clubs now to drink and meet other people, but back then it was just to hang out and listen to the music. Cool music, too. I saw a lot of cool bands at the Comic Book Club."

"The owner of [the Comic Book Club], Art Eisen, kind of saw rock music as a niche that he wanted to fill with his club, that no other club in Jacksonville had," recalls Charlie Faubion. "So he allowed some of these rock bands to come in, which were not typical club bands of that time, and that was what he wanted to present to Jacksonville. It was a club where you could hear some of the latest rock musicians, so he became somewhat of a legend at that time, amongst all of us musicians, as a guy who would let you play in his club, and you could make money and everything. The club was kind of unique because it was located right where the Southern Bell tower is, in the heart of downtown Jacksonville. He'd bring in bands from out of town—not just local bands. Eventually Gary, Allen, and Ronnie's band became good enough and tight enough to where they felt like they wanted to play in a club like that. They got the audition and they got to start playing there."

The Comic Book Club provided both a paying venue and a rehearsal space to up-and-coming bands. Having changed their name to The One Percent, the band made good use of Eisen's generosity. "There was an upstairs to the club which was just a vacant floor," recalls

Faubion. "A lot of the bands would take their equipment up there and they'd start rehearsing. During the week, they'd go down there when the club was closed and play and rehearse in the upstairs, which Art would let them do for free. Then you'd have your house band who would play downstairs on the main floor at night. You'd always have a band rotating. I remember many times when my band would play on the main floor and then The One Percent would be rehearsing during the day. Then we'd finish up our week at the club, they would go downstairs and play on the main floor, we'd put our stuff upstairs and rehearse. Art Eisen just let bands do that 'cause rehearsing [space] was a hard thing to find. He really was allowing bands to have opportunities that they never would have had otherwise. It got bands out of the garage, and gave them a place to play."

The One Percent would often stay until the club closed, immersing themselves in the music. "Allen Collins had a paper route," Johnny Van-Zant remembers. "My dad worked for the *Florida Times-Union* too, as a branch manager and a paper delivery guy. [Allen] would come from the Comic Book Club and fall asleep in front of the branch, in his car with all his papers. We'd be done throwing our paper route and come back and Allen would still be lying there asleep. So we'd have to help him throw his."

Not only did the boys enjoy the time they spent at the Comic Book Club but they also learned something about rock music. The talent who played there was estimable and Ronnie, Gary, Allen, and their friends paid close attention to both the content of the music and the presentation. Sometimes The One Percent was given the opportunity to play and the boys had the opportunity to demonstrate what they had learned from other, more successful acts. At the same time, their presentation of cover songs was uniquely their own. They would play songs by the Yardbirds, Beatles, Stones, Creedence Clearwater Revival, Illinois Speed Press, Blues Magoos, Eric Clapton, Jeff Beck, the Animals, and Cream. Sometimes the line between The One Percent material and that of others became blurred. Because of their taste in covers, the band was known for playing psychedelic rock. Since most people in Jacksonville were into Top 40 music the band found it hard to get certain gigs and were happy to have the resources of the Comic Book Club at their disposal.

With Duane and Gregg Allman at the front, Hourglass was a talented and popular band. Hourglass keyboardist Paul Hornsby remembers an incident that clearly defines the character of Ronnie VanZant. Ronnie feared no one, even when it was someone he deeply respected. "We played the Comic Book Club," remembers Hornsby. "It was a team-type thing and it was great . . . just like The Beatles had come to town when we came there. So, we're playing in this little club and we're sitting in the dressing room, tuning up, waiting to go on. There's an opening band. I heard something very familiar being played and I stuck my head out the door. And there was the opening band playing one of the songs from our album that we had just finished. We were supposedly out to promote this album—that was our excuse for being back East. And they went from one song and then they played nearly every song off our new album. They played it better than the few songs that we actually played off the album. I mean, they did it as good or better than we played it. So, we came on . . . what are *we* going to do, hey, how are we going to follow this band? It was [The One Percent]. I reminded Ronnie of that later on. He just looked real embarrassed [and] he said, 'Man, I gotta tell you, man, we *worshipped* you guys in those days," Ronnie may have worshipped Hourglass, but not enough to restrain him from stealing their act. Bob Burns remembers Duane and Gregg coming up to the band at the end of their set and telling them they were too good to be doing cover material. The brothers Allman suggested that The One Percent write their own material, practice like hell, and see what they had.

Free and Bad Company had always been favorites of Ronnie and Gary. They loved the heavy guitar and the snarling, sensual vocals of Paul Rodgers. Gary and Ronnie started to write songs together reflecting that influence, as well as another of Ronnie's favorites, Merle Haggard.

One of the other bands The One Percent enjoyed and studied was The Revel Ons. Although the band was based in south Georgia, the better gigs were in Jacksonville. One of the Revel Ons was Rodney Mills, who would later engineer a couple of Skynyrd albums. "A lot of them from Skynyrd used to come see the band I was in, when they were real young, before they were actually playing that much," recalls Mills. "I didn't know this until much later on . . . several years after I had worked with Lynyrd Skynyrd when they found out I was in that band. . . . 'Well, Rodney, we used to come stand in front of the stage and watch you guys every time y'all came to town.'"

"They did a lot of Illinois Speed Press," remembers Dru Lombar. "They did a lot of stuff like 'Walk in My Shadow.' We were talking about it the other day, wished we had someone record it. And then their own stuff. They were a good band, you know? Old Ronnie . . . they called him Wicker. That was his nickname. He whipped them into shape, man. He'd get 'em over there and rehearse 'em for hours, and if they messed up he'd just whip their butts. He was tough. He was a taskmaster."

"They were practically forced by Ronnie to rehearse daily, hour after hour rehearsing," recalled Charlie Faubion. "I used to go and listen to some of their earlier stuff. They played Yardbirds, The Rolling Stones, Jeff Beck, that kind of stuff. They seemed to like The Yardbirds a lot. They played Free later on."

Judy VanZant Jenness, on the other hand, believes that the boys in the band were just as into the rehearsing as Ronnie. "I think they just really wanted to play," says Judy. "So they would get together and they would rehearse. It was the thing they did. You don't find bands that want to do that anymore. They would rehearse for hours and hours and hours. They would write songs and they would play. They just enjoyed being together and playing. I don't think it was like crack the whip, let's go out and torture ourselves, and rehearse for eight hours. It wasn't like that. It was just they couldn't wait to get out there to rehearse, to play. So if they weren't playing, they were rehearsing."

When it came to their original material, some people thought that Ronnie was too much of a perfectionist in his approach to the music and ultimately hurt the potential of the band to some degree. The One Percent and later Skynyrd straddled a fine line between structured rock and individualistic guitar playing. "Skynyrd was not one note spontaneous," says former Marshall Tucker Band guitarist George McCorkle. "Not one note. As I remember, [future drummer] Artimus Pyle told me later that he had to do the same crashes and the same rolls at the same time every night, or Ronnie got upset about it."

"There was no improvisation in Lynyrd Skynyrd," said future Skynyrd guitarist Ed King. "I could add things [to the music] if I needed or wanted to, but Gary and Allen never did. Things were worked out in advance and stayed pretty much the same."

Whether they were playing the raunchy rock standbys or the beginnings of their own unique repertoire, The One Percent played every recreation center and small club in North Florida that would have them, as well as the Comic Book Club. "When you're from the South, you learn to work your ass off," said Ronnie. "And we did. It was hellacious. Hellacious . . . and the best years of our lives."

High school had not been easy for Ronnie VanZant. It wasn't the academics, because Ronnie was very intelligent. The South in the sixties had very strict restrictions and school administrations were adamant about not allowing distractions that diverted attention away from the main purpose of being in school: to study and learn. Ronnie interpreted these rules as a personal affront and used them as an excuse to devote more time to what he saw as his real priority—playing music. He quit high school and decided to face the future in a different way than that which had been expected of him.

Ronnie now began working full time at the auto parts store of his half-sister Betty JoAnn's husband. Evidently he felt like his life was stabilizing a little and starting to make sense as he married Nadine on January 2, 1966. Later that year, daughter Tammy Michelle was born. Ronnie VanZant was now a salesman, a husband, a father, and . . . a musician.

The band may not have been as polished as some but they were developing an enthusiastic following. "I grew up with them guys," says Dru Lombar. "They're from the other side of town, man. They're west side boys, man, they are Southern rednecks. That's all there is to it, you know? I think that was part of their charm."

As the band increased its popularity, Ronnie seemed even further driven to succeed. His vocals were not smooth, nor even particularly melodious, but listeners were drawn to the emotional sincerity and gritty, down-home delivery that Ronnie offered. The guitars were shaping up and hinting at formidability as well. Allen Collins astonished people with his talent. He was still a teenager yet he played with the soul of someone much older. Gary Rossington was developing a signature sound himself. "A lot of people compare [Gary] to Mick Ralphs or Paul Kossoff of early Free," says Skynyrd keyboardist Billy Powell. "He listened to [them] a lot and he kind of got that laid-back picking style. He established his own identity with that."

The real Leonard Skinner (right) with fan Brian Nash at the Rock and Roll Hall of Fame
premiere of *Freebird . . . The Movie.*

Ronnie was not the only one in the band who had trouble with school authorities. Not only did Ronnie, Bob, and Gary show their disrespect of the old-school thinking regarding uniformity, but they also flaunted their disobedience whenever the opportunity arose. They refused to bow to the Robert E. Lee High School edict of not allowing exceptionally lengthy hair on its male students. The boys had been warned repeatedly by gym coach Leonard Skinner to cut their long hair or face the consequences. They initially responded to this challenge by slicking down their hair with Vaseline, but that didn't solve the problem. Coach Skinner had little patience for their consistent refusal to comply with his demands and felt his hand was forced to suspend the boys from school on more than one occasion. Gary Rossington said that regardless of what they did to hide their long hair, all was revealed when the boys participated in the mandatory post-gym showers. According to a history of the band from the Freebird Foundation, Rossington claimed that after being sent to the principal's office twenty or thirty times and being suspended for two weeks, he told Skinner, "Fuck you, I'm gone," and quit school.

Allen Collins had the same problem while attending Jacksonville's Nathan Bedford Forrest High School. Allen's father had been called with a request to take Allen to a barber, to get the boy a "real" haircut. Allen and his father had apparently not been getting on well with one another and this new wrinkle added a great deal of disharmony to their relationship.

Gary and Allen, like Ronnie before them, felt that the constant hassle wasn't worth the effort. They were rock-and-rollers and intended to earn their living in music. They felt that their long hair was not only their right but was essential to their livelihood.

Ronnie and Gary's test of wills with Coach Skinner had been the subject of much after-school conversation. Everyone waited to see who would win. There was a certain aura of victory when the boys finally left school and Leonard Skinner behind them. By quitting school, the boys became the stuff of urban legend.

It was not uncommon for Ronnie to introduce the band as something other than The One Percent. He enjoyed having fun with the audience. One night in 1970, the band played a show at Jacksonville's Forrest Inn. "It was this cool little place," recalls Judy VanZant Jenness. "It was actually over on the west side. I don't know what it was originally, but they'd have music inside and out."

"[It] was right down the road from my parents' house," remembers Johnny Van-Zant. "You could actually go down there on Sundays, see people play and stuff. That's where I seen the Allmans. It was a bottle club, so it was pretty wild. The land's still there but the building is gone. Nobody's never built on that land. Every time I pass by there going to my parents' house it's kind of like, wow, wonder how come nobody's ever done anything. It's kind of like part of history just went away."

Ronnie was amused by Gary Rossington's decision to follow his lead and quit school because of his constant harassment from Coach Skinner, and that night at the Inn jokingly introduced the band as Leonard Skinner. The audience thought the joke hilarious and roared their approval. The others in the band had begun teasing Rossington that Skinner was out to get him and now was uncontrollably irate because the band made fun of his name. As the members of The One Percent thought about it, renaming the band after their nemesis seemed appropriate to represent what the band was willing to sacrifice to play their music. Changing some vowels to dress up the name and not open themselves to any lawsuits, The One Percent became known from that point on as Lynyrd Skynyrd. (A poster from an early show in Jacksonville with Eric Burdon and War shows the original spelling of the band's name to be Lynard Skynard.)

3

On to Muscle Shoals

IN 1970, about the time their hometown heroes, The Allman Brothers Band, played the Fillmore East in New York, the boys in Lynyrd Skynyrd were realizing that *their* band needed to expand its base beyond Jacksonville and north Florida. They would continue to play Jacksonville clubs, teen recreation centers, such as the one in the Good Shepard Church, and the occasional local school, such as Forrest High. "During the peak of their popularity, I was a teenager at N.B. Forrest High in Jacksonville," says fan Carla Harrington. "Lynyrd Skynyrd were 'our boys.' Not only were they from Jax, but they were from the west side and weren't ashamed to admit it. The west side of Jax has always been the poor side of town. Living out there we didn't have much to brag about, so having them associated with our part of town, and to some degree our school, was an inspiration."

Ronnie, Gary, Allen, Larry (LJ), and Bob had been working hard to expand their repertoire and become more proficient on their instruments. Although they had established the ritual of after-school and night rehearsals in Bob Burns' family carport, the continuous complaints from the Burns' neighbors had forced the band to look elsewhere for rehearsal space. It seemed every night the cops would show up and tell them to shut the music down. Ronnie's backyard and Allen's living room weren't working out so well either. The band needed a place where neighbors and cops would not be an issue. Everyone in the band canvassed their friends to see if anyone might know of a vacant house they might rent. They were soon told about a ninety-nine-acre isolated farm just outside of Jacksonville in a town called Russell, near Black Creek, where a little shack on the property proved perfect for their purposes. The band paid sixty-five dollars a month for its use. Because of its extreme temperatures, mostly hot, the band's new rehearsal hall was named "Hell House."

"I never knew it as called 'Hell House,'" says Charlie Faubion. "I just called it the farm. I spent a lot of time out there when they were in town. They would rehearse for a while, then we'd [all] play baseball for awhile, then [they'd] rehearse, then play baseball. They had their own separate set of equipment out there at the house just to rehearse."

One night someone came up the creek, broke into the house, and stole a couple of amplifiers. The band couldn't afford to lose any equipment, so it was decided that they would alternate spending the night in the house. It wasn't too difficult an assignment. The band began rehearsal about 8:30 in the morning and played until sundown. By the time supper had been eaten, it was almost time for bed.

As the boys drove themselves hard, the stress on the individual personalities began to make itself apparent. Lynyrd Skynyrd was equivalent to strong dispositions. While Allen and Larry were fairly passive, Gary and Bob had tempers. And, of course, Ronnie's explosive personality was at the forefront. The steady and forced togetherness in such small quarters certainly didn't help matters. Occasionally there were blow-ups, both on- and offstage. The dark side of rock-and-roll was already beginning to rear its ugly head.

Even in their refuge in the woods, the band members were not immune to their occasional violent outbursts. "I remember one time taking this friend of mine who was a musician out there," remembers Faubion. "I'd always tell him about Skynyrd. He says, 'Do you think I could meet these guys?' I said 'Sure, I'll take you out there one time.' I remember we were outside and we'd been playing baseball. They'd already had some pretty heavy rehearsals. Ronnie said, 'Hey, I want you to hear this song we're working on.' He says, 'Hey you guys, I want you to play this song for Charlie.' So they all wandered back inside and they were all kind of dragging. I remember [Ronnie] told Bob [Burns], 'Play this song.' [The rest of the band] was dragging but they said, 'O.K., we'll try it one more time and see if it still sounds the same.' But Bob said, 'I don't want to play that song.' [Ronnie] says, 'Play the song.' [Bob] says, 'I ain't gonna play it.' They

Lynyrd Skynyrd at the infamous "Hell House," circa 1974–1975.
Standing, left to right: Billy Powell, Ronnie VanZant (note gun in waistband), Gary Rossington, friend/guitarist Jeff Carlisi.
Seated, left to right: Allen Collins, Leon Wilkeson, Artimus Pyle.

Lynyrd Skynyrd rehearsing at Hell House, circa 1975–1976.
Left to right: Allen Collins, Ronnie VanZant, Gary Rossington, Artimus Pyle, Leon Wilkeson's back.

were kind of getting into this verbal argument. All the [other] guys were ready to play. I thought, Ronnie has really not changed. He's really still the badass that he's always been. Bob was standing up behind the drums. There was something like boxes stacked and I remember Ronnie grabbed this gun that was sitting up there and walked over and stuck the gun up to Bob's head. He says, 'You play the motherfucking song or I'm gonna blow your brains all over this room.' This was just a rehearsal."

Rehearsing was a worthwhile pastime but eventually it came time to put those long months of practicing to a test. Lacy Van-Zant says that in the summer of 1969 he gave the band $130, filled the tank of their Chevy station wagon with gas, and told them to "hit the road with their music." Hit the road they did. Lynyrd Skynyrd played a few dates in Savannah, then southern South Carolina, and made their way further up into northwest Georgia.

One week during the spring of 1970 they played Mercer University. Tales told, they enjoyed the challenge of traveling, living in temporary Spartan quarters, and meeting fellow musicians along the way. "That spring I hosted the guys at Mercer University in Macon, Georgia," remembers Mercer alumnus Rob Scherini. "Everyone and their equipment was in one van then. They [said they] had been to Alaska and brought back some wild tales and something called Alaskan Thunder Fuck that we rolled. One of the guys had just learned to play the kitchen spoons and thought it was so cool. They called Ronnie a nickname back then. It was 'Wicker.' Ronnie really didn't like them calling him that, but they kept kidding him with it. Allen and I jammed a few hours after midnight, with him doing lead to my Gordon Lightfoot and Paul Simon picking style."

The band was thrilled when they secured dates to play both Gaslight Square and Peppe's A-Go-Go—two clubs in St. Louis, Missouri. They all piled into their van to make the long trek. Because the younger boys were underage, a local judge had to be contacted to grant them permission to play. Just as they pulled into their driveway on the way back from the gigs the van quit, having died a slow, painful death.

The gigs had been well received by the public and the boys were inspired to believe that they had what it took to be successful. By 1968, they decided that that they should familiarize themselves with a recording studio, if hit records were to be in their future. Shade Tree Records had been founded in Jacksonville the previous year by engineers Jim Sutton and Tom Markham. When Skynyrd walked into the studio one day to introduce their band, the two men were intrigued. A promise was made to have Shade Tree's owners come see the band at their next Comic Book Club appearance. Sutton and Markham were impressed and immediately offered the band a five-year contract.

The band recorded two of their original songs: "Michelle" and "Need All My Friends." Both songs were penned by Collins and VanZant. Although "Michelle" could just as easily be sung to a lover, Ronnie wrote the song with his daughter Tammy Michelle in mind. It is a poignant song, full of emotion. "Need All My Friends" is also autobiographical. It explains that while singing the blues for a living is important to the singer, he needs his friends to talk with and remind him of what is important in life. The songs were released as a monorail 45-rpm single on the Shade Tree label. The young entrepreneurs did their best to market their product, sending out 300 promotional copies to radio stations all over the country. Yet even follow-up calls evidently produced no airplay and the record tanked.

The following year Markham and Sutton recorded Skynyrd playing "No One Can Take Your Place" and "If I'm Wrong" on 8-track. These two songs added Gary Rossington to the composing team of Collins and VanZant. "No One Can Take Your Place" is a shit-kicking country loved-her/lost-her ballad, very much reminiscent of Gram Parsons singing "Hickory Wind." It clearly reflects Ronnie VanZant's admiration for the music of Parsons and Merle Haggard and demonstrates that Ronnie could sing this type of music with the best of the Nashville or Bakersfield country outlaws. "If I'm Wrong" displays a searing guitar intro and solo and is very much in the vein of Free or Bad Company, with a Paul Rodgers delivery from Ronnie. Again the execs at Shade Tree were left hitless. Part of the problem may have been the mixed genres of the record, as the songs could be defined as country blues. Although country blues would be a type of music that the band would develop and master as they matured, it was a relatively unknown style on popular radio, and radio stations probably were wary of how their audiences might respond.

By the summer of 1969, the band was experiencing adventures away from their home base of Jacksonville, the sound was getting tighter, and the "boys" were growing up. Allen Collins had met a girl named Kathy Johns and had decided he was ready for marriage. A wedding date in June 1970 was set and Allen's friends and bandmates were asked to participate in the wedding as ushers. There was only one snag. Kathy was worried about how her father would respond to the long hair of Allen and his friends. Kathy and her mother decided that in order to better preserve the couple's wedding pictures for posterity, the young men should wear wigs. At least they were fairly good wigs. In the wedding photos it merely looks as if Allen and his groomsmen were having a bad hair day.

The reception for the newly married couple was planned to be an exceptional event. Since the groom was a member of a happening band, it wasn't unreasonable to ask that band to perform. Allen had an idea. He had written a song with Ronnie VanZant and thought it would be perfect to debut it on this very special occasion. Allen had written the music and Ronnie the lyrics. The song had a powerful potential but the tempo seemed all wrong. Then Allen's guitar hit its groove. The song was "Freebird," and Allen and his friends played it with panache, albeit subdued panache, considering the circumstances. The "Freebird," that was played that day was a little different from the "Freebird" that would later rock the airwaves. Nevertheless it was performed in public for the first time and a rock-and-roll classic was born.

The first public playing of "Freebird" remains controversial, however. The band's friend, former .38 Special guitarist Jeff Carlisi, says that he believes the band played "Freebird" in public for the first time on a PBS-Jacksonville telethon which was held at the Jacksonville Art Museum in 1969. Skynyrd had been put on the bill through their connection with Shade Tree. The Art Museum was across the street from the studio. After Sutton and Markham heard how tremendously "Freebird" was received by those at the telethon, they decided to record the song.

Charlie Faubion remembers "Freebird" being performed at the Jacksonville National Guard Armory when Skynyrd played with Ted Nugent in 1970. "That's the first time I remember hearing 'Freebird,'" Faubion says. "I think that was actually the first night they actually played that to a live crowd." Regardless of where it was first performed and to whom, whoever was fortunate enough to hear it recognized "Freebird's" potential. The song, and now the band, raised expectant eyebrows.

It would later be said that "Freebird" was written about Duane Allman. But this was not the case, according to Leon Wilkeson. "There was a lot of confusion. 'Freebird' was originally *dedi-*

cated to Duane Allman. He was the first person that Ronnie ever dedicated that song to." When Ronnie sang of the "Freebird," he was either referring to himself or to the fictional self in the song. The anthem would later come to symbolize the freebird in *all* the song's listeners.

Charles Charlesworth would later write in *Melody Maker* magazine, "This particular number reminds me rather of Zeppelin's 'Stairway to Heaven' in the way it rises from a dramatically punctuated introduction into a classic power ending with all instruments fighting to gain an inch."

Tom Markham and Jim Sutton were greatly disappointed that they had been unable to break Lynyrd Skynyrd. The band was disappointed too and asked to be released from their contract in 1970, two years early. Markham and Sutton agreed and wished them well.

Later that year Lynyrd Skynyrd came to the attention of Alan Walden, the brother of Phil Walden, the founder of Capricorn Records. Alan had heard the band and thought they were promising enough to warrant his management attention. "I remember [the band] playing in Macon," says Judy VanZant Jenness. "So he probably had seen them [there]. Took all their publishing. 'Well, we'll make you a star but you gotta give me all your publishing.' That relationship didn't last too long."

But for the time being, Walden had some ideas on how he might break this band of unruly rockers. Many good things were coming out of Muscle Shoals, Alabama. Long the home of some excellent R&B recordings, and with a reputation for the very best of sidemen, the fairly new Muscle Shoals Sound Studio in Sheffield, Alabama, seemed to Walden an excellent place for the young band from Jacksonville to cut a demo. The studio had been founded by engineers Barry Beckett, Jimmy Johnson, Roger Hawkins, and David Hood, along with a financial loan and support from Atlantic Records president Jerry Wexler. Previous to Skynyrd's involvement with the studio, the studio produced records by The Rolling Stones, Leon Russell, and Cher.

Beckett and Johnson were not uninterested in producing some demo tracks for Walden's Florida band, but they didn't have the time to really listen to the band. They sent the band to their Sheffield cohorts Quinvy Studios, owned and operated by Quin Ivy. Lynyrd Skynyrd recorded six to eight live songs, without using multiple takes and tracks. Johnson was impressed with what he heard but the band only had enough money to pay for studio time to record a few songs. Johnson encouraged the boys to continue developing their sound, write some more songs, and return to the studio when they could afford to record an entire album of material. Johnson made a deal with Alan Walden to produce an album. Muscle Shoals would recoup the cost of the recording only if the resulting record were sold to a record label. Producer-engineer Tim Smith, who was also managed by Alan Walden, would coproduce.

Recording at Muscle Shoals became a priority. Together the boys borrowed money from family and friends in order to take Johnson up on his offer. They already had the material. And they certainly had the ambition. Skynyrd, as they referred to themselves, returned to Alabama to complete their album demo in January 1971.

Multi-faceted guitarist Rickey Medlocke, 2000.

The band was impressed with the studio's reputation and anxious to avail themselves of its expertise. Ronnie VanZant was ready to be made into a star. There was a small snag, however. Bob Burns decided that he wanted to return to school so he decided to quit the band. Ronnie and the others were sorry to see him go, but they didn't let his departure deter them. Ronnie quickly decided to take his Jacksonville friend Rickey Medlocke to Alabama to help with the percussion.

Rickey Medlocke was a friend of the band's during high school. "I think we met during our high school years and stuff like that," recalls Medlocke. "I remembered hearing about a group around Jacksonville . . . they changed their name from several different things and finally to The One Percent. We came across each other going in and out of the Comic Book Club. I can remember talking to Ronnie and Gary and Allen and it was the strangest thing. We just seemed to all kind of hit it off really well. One night I remember at the Comic Book Club they were playing and there was always a light show kind of thing at the Comic Book Club, like back in the sixties, you know? With all the psychedelic lighting and all that kind of stuff. They didn't have a light guy and I ran lights for them for two nights. That was kind of my first in-the-band gig."

Ronnie VanZant had liked what he heard from Medlocke's guitar when Rickey was playing with his group Blackfoot. He knew Rickey was a well-rounded musician. Blackfoot was another Jacksonville band that had met with initial success after being taken under the wing of some New York City music business executives. The band had relocated to the northeast, as that seemed to be where the action was.

The timing was right for Medlocke to become involved with Skynyrd. "I was up in New Jersey," Medlocke remembers. "We'd had management problems with this manager of ours . . . I just wanted to bail because I didn't want to be in the middle of all that stuff anymore. I called Allen Collins. I said, 'Allen, this is Rickey Medlocke.' He says, 'Hey, man, what are you doing?' I says, 'Well, I'll tell you what. I'm up in New Jersey right now and I'm looking for a gig. I'll drive a truck, load equipment, schlep, do whatever, set up the stage . . . .' He was like, 'Do you still play drums?' I'm thinking to myself, God, I haven't played drums in awhile [but] I said, 'Yeah!' He says, 'Well, here is the number. You need to call Ronnie.' So I called up Ronnie and he said, 'What are you doing, man?' I says, 'Well, I'm needing a gig, you know. I just called Allen and I told him I'd do anything like load equipment, or set up equipment, or drive the truck, or whatever.' He goes, 'You still hammer around on the drums a little bit?' I said, 'Heck, yeah, man.' He goes, 'Well, I'll tell you what, we need a drummer. We're getting ready to go into Muscle Shoals to cut some material and stuff for a record.' And I says, 'Man, I'll be there.' There was an extra set of drums around this house [in New Jersey] where we practiced and rehearsed and I says, 'God, man. I'll brush up on some licks and get myself together.' Three days later, I flew down to Jacksonville, they picked me up, we went by and dropped my bags off, and went straight to the rehearsal house and started practicing right then."

Rickey Medlocke, like many Southern musicians, had an intricate personal history that enabled him to write and experience music in a distinctive way. Rhythm and blues was nothing new to him. "I was raised by my mother's parents . . . actually my grandparents . . . they legally adopted me when I was like three months old," Medlocke explains. "So they really became my mother and father. My dad, Shorty Medlocke, was a musician all his life, entertainer all his life. He grew up on a sharecropping farm in Georgia, northwest Georgia, from the time he was, I don't know, he could walk. He listened to a lot of the black music that was played around him, because the other family that was on the sharecropping farm across the road from them was a black family. So between the family that he grew up across the road from and his own family, which was a big family, they got together at the end of the week and they would have meals together and play together, basically were like a family together. So I grew up listening to a lot of Mississippi Delta blues, old blues, bluegrass stuff, and that's basically where my roots are. When I was a kid I listened to [what] my dad would play, these old .78 records of Mississippi John Hurt and Huddie Ledbetter, which is basically Leadbelly, and Robert Johnson, and all these old black players. That's what my head got filled with, plus bluegrass music."

Medlocke was also exposed to the entertaining profession early on. "My dad had a lot of bands," he says. "He was a master at the five-string banjo, and actually was a master at a lot of instruments, period. He played—oh my gosh—he played banjo, guitar, dobro, harmonica, the upright bass. He played the fiddle, I mean, he played them all. He was in and out of Nashville all the time, was on a TV show out of Jacksonville, a local TV show called "The Toby Dowdy Show." When I was three years old, I took up playing banjo and joined him on that show. It was a father and son kind of thing, with me being really small, and I guess it was kind of a novelty thing—this little kid playing banjo on a country music show. I took up playing guitar when I was like five. And I played right 'til I was eight years old—the show lasted for five years."

Medlocke had started to seriously consider the guitar his life's work, but Lynyrd Skynyrd needed a drummer. "Being a kid," Medlocke muses, "I wanted to be just like [my father] so I ended up playing banjo and guitar and drums and a little bit of piano, and stuff like that. But I always really kind of ended up sticking to the one instrument, as far as the guitar goes. Although I did have these seizures where I went into being a drummer. That was my alternate personality. And, you know? I ended up playing with Skynyrd for about three years on drums."

Rickey Medlocke, like musicians before and after him, had begun his career in a garage. "I played in bands from the time I was about ten all the way up through my teenage years," recalls Medlocke. "When I was like fourteen, I was in a band called Hot Water Blues Band. I had a group before that called the Rocking Aces, which Jack [Spires] and Greg [Walker] were a part of when we were small kids. I played in a band called the Candied Apple, Sunday Funnies, geez, there were just a lot of bands."

Finally, with Greg Walker and Charlie Hargrett, Medlocke formed a band called Fresh Garbage. His association with Fresh Garbage would enable Rickey Medlocke to meet the up-and-coming band, The One Percent, while he was in high school. "At the same time, there was this band called The One Percent, which would later become Lynyrd Skynyrd," remembers Medlocke. "They always played around Jacksonville, you know, the Comic Book Club and the Forest Inn, and stuff like that. Well, we all used to play this same club together, the Comic Book Club, in downtown Jacksonville. From 8:00 to 12:00 PM it was a teen club, and then it would shut down for two hours, and then from 2:00 to 6:00 AM it was a bottle club. We hung in there and played through the summer. In fact, in 1969 when they landed the first man on the moon, we were playing the Comic Book Club that night, and took a break and watched it happen."

Fresh Garbage, with the addition of Jakson Spires, would become the band Blackfoot. While Blackfoot would later become immensely popular worldwide, the band had a slow start. Because of early interband turmoil, Rickey Medlocke grew dissatisfied and decided to leave. "What had happened is that I left Blackfoot and joined Lynyrd Skynyrd," Medlocke says. "[I] was playing with Lynyrd Skynyrd and got to know Jimmy Johnson and David Hood at Muscle Shoals, because Lynyrd Skynyrd went in to cut their first album. But after everything happened with the tragedy and stuff, MCA would later put it out and call it *Skynyrd's First . . . and Last.* The material that I recorded with them came out on that record, plus I had done a lot of other recordings with Skynyrd at the time. I had cut 'Freebird' with them and 'Simple Man' and a lot of stuff that they would later on rerecord for their first [released] album." While Rickey Medlocke would eventually return to Blackfoot, he was an appreciated member of the Lynyrd Skynyrd team for the time being.

After returning from Muscle Shoals, the first thing Skynyrd realized was that in order to get noticed they would have to broaden their base even more, so they started to play additional gigs outside of Jacksonville. Walden, with his connections, helped get bookings in various parts of Florida and Georgia. Soon they were playing in bars, small clubs, and high schools all over the South.

"We had this big box truck that we used to haul our equipment in," remembers Rickey Medlocke. "We rode in the very back of it and we'd stack equipment up towards the front. Then we'd put mattresses towards the back and lay on the mattresses. I remember one night we were leaving to go to Nashville to play a club called the Briar Patch. We were all in the back of the truck. The two roadies were up front driving the truck. We were all in the back and Ronnie and I were looking down the highway. We had the door open a little bit, looking down Interstate Ten as we were leaving Jacksonville. I looked over at Ronnie and I said, 'Man, there's nothing like this is there?' He goes, 'You know what, Rickey? One of these days we aren't going to have to worry about none of this bullshit. We'll have it made in the shade.' My old man had told Ronnie and all of 'em, 'One of these days, guys, you keep working hard like this, you'll have it made in the shade.' And they wrote that song ['Made in the Shade'] and dedicated that song to my father. I can remember times like that . . . they're priceless to me. I can't even put a price on those kinds of things, you know?"

Ronnie VanZant had a clear vision of what he hoped his band to be, and in his mind, it was time for a personnel change. "[Prior to the Alabama session, Ronnie] certainly wasn't achieving any kind of success," recalls Charlie Faubion. "He was just kind of a hanger-on who really wanted to make it. He just seemed to have more motivation than the rest of us. He had more dedication. I remember him telling me one night, he says, 'You know, I think I'm going to have to get rid of Larry'—Larry Jungstrom, the bass player. I said, 'No, that guy's been with you forever.' He said, 'Yeah' and I said 'Why?' He said, 'Well, I don't think he fits our image—you know, we're trying to project a certain image and I don't think he's got the image that we're looking for.'"

"I'm not really sure how that happened, to tell the truth," says Billy Powell. "[Larry] wasn't getting along with Ronnie and Gary and Allen. Just something to do with laziness and missing practices." Blackfoot's Greg T. Walker would be called in to play bass for the Alabama sessions.

Lynyrd Skynyrd paid their own way to Sheffield and checked into Blue's Truck Stop Motel, the least expensive in town. They were set to lay down their tracks in the late afternoon and at night and eat peanut butter sandwiches during the day. They played small clubs in the area and cashed in Coke bottles to provide for expenses. The band worked in the studio for several months. The sessions were long—mostly sixteen-hour days. Jimmy Johnson taught Skynyrd how to operate in a studio and the band enjoyed working with both Johnson and Tim Smith. The producers, engineers, and session musicians at Muscle Shoals Studio had been nicknamed the Swampers by songwriter Leon Russell. The studio was located in a fairly rural area of the southern United States—thus the term Swampers—but the production team at Muscle Shoals was up-to-date and innovative. Lynyrd Skynyrd would never forget them.

The tracks the band laid down were unique, in light of the signature sound they would produce in the future. Rickey Medlocke brought some Blackfoot-like songs to the table such as "The Seasons" and "White Dove," for which he also provided the lead vocal. Another Medlocke song included was "Ain't Too Proud to Pray," and Ronnie VanZant's "Preacher's Daughter" was based on Medlocke's "Keep On Runnin'."

The band also decided to rerecord some of the songs they had put down with Shade Tree. "Michelle" and "Need All My Friends" were reworked. "Wino" and "You Run Around" showed great promise from the guitars of Rossington and Collins. Medlocke provided the vocal on "You Run Around." Two other original songs, a real bluesy number titled "Bad Boy Blues" and the Cream-sounding "Hide Your Face," were also recorded. Some of the most interesting work, however, was the earliest recorded versions of VanZant, Collins, and Rossington-penned songs that what would later become Skynyrd classics, such as the defiant "I Ain't the One," the melancholy "One More Time," and the poignant "Coming Home."

The song that stood head and shoulders above the rest was "Freebird." "The very first version we [did] in Muscle Shoals, Alabama," says Billy Powell. "There's no slide in the song. It's just piano with vocals. The slide has got to be there—I never did like that version. The piano part's real pretty but that slide's gotta be there always." Yet Ronnie VanZant's vocal is probably the best he had to offer the song. The guitars of Collins and Rossington greatly impressed the producers.

Even though the band was young and inexperienced, they took their studio time seriously. They wanted to learn everything they could about the recording process. "One of the biggest memories that stands out in my head is standing in the studio when Ronnie was singing vocals for that thing," recalls Rickey Medlocke. "Ronnie would look over at me. Jimmy sent me out there because [Ronnie] was having a hard time with some different songs. He would say, 'Am I sharp? Am I flat? Am I sharp? Am I flat?' And I'd go, 'Ronnie, you're dead on, man. It's great.'"

The band was satisfied that they had produced a good representation of their music. Walden decided to shop the finished product around, hoping a record label would see the band's potential. Capricorn in Macon, Georgia, expressed some initial interest but two factors came into play. Phil Walden had a tight roster of acts and was more interested in developing his current roster than he was in breaking another musically immature band. Also, ever the businessman, Ronnie didn't feel he wanted his band to be signed to a Southern label that was devoting most of its time to promoting the South's largest act, The Allman Brothers Band. Skynyrd respected the Brothers. Ronnie VanZant would later quote Gregg Allman as giving him the advice, "You get out of it exactly what you put into it." But Lynyrd Skynyrd wanted to sign with a label that would make them a priority and they didn't think Capricorn was in a position to do that. They decided to continue to look.

Walden talked to Jimmy Johnson about the lack of label interest in the band, and they hoped to solve the problem by recording an additional six tracks in the fall of 1972. Lynyrd Skynyrd was asked to return to Muscle Shoals. By this time, Rickey Medlocke and Greg Walker had rejoined Blackfoot and Bob Burns had decided that he did, after all, want to play drums for Skynyrd. "After several years had passed, it got to me," says Medlocke. "I really couldn't see myself sitting behind a set of drums for my whole career. My dad, Shorty, after he'd been around the guys and got to know them and stuff, says, 'You know, I want you to understand, if you're going to leave these guys, I want you to understand there's something special about 'em. Especially Ronnie and Gary and Allen. There's something really special. I think these guys are going to make it. Just understand [that] if you leave, and they do, you gotta live with that. Now that's a decision you're going to have to think about. It's not the actual leaving, but can you live with the fact that you left and then all of a sudden they have success and stuff.' [But] I'd already made up my mind [that] I'll just do the best and try it on my own."

It seemed now that Larry Jungstrom was definitely out and Ronnie decided to include another Jacksonville friend, Leon Wilkeson, on bass guitar. Wilkeson was thrilled to be asked to go to Alabama. He knew how important the return session could be. Ronnie also knew that if the session went well and the music caught on with some professional entity, the band could be on its way.

"I said [to Ronnie], '[Who] are you going to replace [Larry] with?'" says Charlie Faubion. "By this time my band had broken up and I was just jamming. One of the guys I was jamming with was Leon Wilkeson, who was a bass player at that time. He went by the name of 'Thumper.' I never knew him as Leon, no one ever called him Leon, we just called him Thumper."

Leon was born April 2, 1952, and like most of his contemporaries, was a Paul McCartney and Beatles fan. After listening intently to McCartney's music, Leon decided that playing bass guitar was something he could learn to do well. Wilkeson's parents purchased a guitar for their son.

"I was in the school band," remembered Leon. "I dropped out and got an electric guitar. I didn't know I was a bass player. I had me a Sears Silvertone guitar with the amp built into the case, a compact deal. Sears happened to have one readily available, handy for me at the time."

One day fourteen-year-old Leon was approached by his next-door neighbor, Betty JoAnn Morris. Leon didn't know at the time that she was Ronnie VanZant's sister. Betty JoAnn asked the teenager if he would be interested in giving guitar lessons to one of her sons. She also told Leon that her brother Donnie needed a bass player for his band, The Collegiates. That sounded good to Leon. He knew if he was going to get anywhere in music it would most likely be through working with a band.

"So I auditioned," said Wilkeson. "My first bass guitar audition, on a six-string guitar. It was to acquire the position of bassist for this band called The Collegiates, which was Donnie Van Zant's first band, my first band. Junior high. We'd play every other weekend at a community teen club center and we made $2.50 apiece on the weekend. So, it was enough of a taste for me to pursue it further."

The association didn't last long, however. Leon began spending most of his free time rehearsing with the band and his grades dropped significantly. His father made him leave the band and devote more time to his studies.

Evidently Leon's grades came back up, because Wilkeson began to play with other garage-type bands. "I played in about a kajillion garage bands," he laughed. Leon decided that he wanted to stay focused on the bass guitar and see if he could make a career out of playing it. He soaked up everything he could learn about the instrument. He listened to a variety of bass players.

"It started out with Paul McCartney," he recalled. "I learned McCartney bass riffs off of Beatles records. And the British invasion was happening. Chas Chandler, the Animals, bass parts [from] 'We Gotta Get Out of This Place.' All those classic songs like that, with classic bass parts to it. Jefferson Airplane's [Jack] Casady was a big hero to me. John Paul Jones of Zeppelin was a big inspiration to me. Lead guitar-style bassists . . . free-form bass. I didn't want to just be a thumper. I wanted to be a player. Berry Oakley was pretty much an inspiration to me. I never got to play with him but I went and watched him. I was a big, big bass player watcher. I went and just really researched anybody that had the balls to stand on the stage and pluck one of them things. Not to steal licks, but just to learn. So I'm basically self-taught. Actually, Ronnie [VanZant] was the one that really helped me to focus my career and learn how to be a true bass guitarist."

At the time Ronnie was having his discussion with Charlie Faubion about wanting to replace Larry Jungstrom, Leon Wilkeson was ready to make a change as well. Larry Jungstrom was an excellent bass player and would later find massive success with .38 Special. But when Ronnie got something in his head that might strengthen his band, he acted on it.

"[Ronnie] said, 'I really want Thumper in the band,'" says Charlie Faubion. "He talked to him and of course [Leon] decided to go with 'em. Then I remember going out to my car, parked in front of the Comic Book Club. Larry Jungstrom came up to my passenger side, and leaning in the window, says, 'Can you believe it, man? They fired me, Skynyrd's fired me!' At that particular time in his life, I'm sure it was a devastating thing to him, 'cause they were just starting to gel as a band and all of a sudden he's out. But I think looking back on that experience today, he wouldn't have it any other way because he has been, financially, much more successful than he would've ever been with Skynyrd. He could've been in that plane and been a tragedy also."

"[Ronnie] loved The Rolling Stones," continues Faubion. "He loved that bad-boy image that the Stones projected. I'm not sure that he liked the way their music sounded, but he did have that Southern touch he wanted to put to it as far as the words. The lyrics of the songs had to be something he could really relate to. But as far as the overall sound of the band, the style of the band, he wanted them to be kind of raunchy, with lots of guitar playing, and projecting a bad-boy type image. Larry did not fit the image. Larry was just a high school buddy that had been a high school buddy for a long time. Leon, if you clean him up and everything, he's a good-looking guy. [Ronnie] just felt that Leon would fit with the image of Gary and Allen at that time. He wanted kind of good-looking, attractive guys that would have an appeal. Leon fit the image. Ronnie was always thinking success."

Leon had continued to work with a variety of bands and at one point spent most of his time playing with a group called the King James Version that included fellow Jacksonvillian Dru Lombar (later of Grinderswitch fame). He liked playing with Lombar, but wasn't too keen on the band.

"It was a learning experience, I guess," he said. "But actually, working with Dru Lombar always was a pleasurable experience. I was in the King James Version working in central Florida, playing bars, five sets a night. Really in the bullpen, getting in good shape, working out in the musical gym, so to speak."

Then Leon heard that Larry Jungstom was leaving Skynyrd. "I got word that Larry Jungstrom had been fired," he remembered. "So I zipped up to Jacksonville with my bass guitar in tow. I located where they were practicing and they offered to let me jam."

Ronnie invited Wilkeson to play some songs so that they all might hear what he could bring to the band. "They already had a bass player from Blackfoot worked in somewhat," remembered Wilkeson. "Rickey Medlocke was the drummer at the time. Shortly after that Rickey and Greg Walker, the bass player, quit [Skynyrd] to go return to Blackfoot. So it was just Ronnie and Gary and Allen. So they called the original drummer, Bob Burns, and asked him to come back."

One night after meeting with Skynyrd, Wilkeson went to listen to Donnie Van Zant and Skynyrd roadie Billy Powell rehearse their band Alice Marr upstairs at the Comic Book Club. "I don't know why, but for some reason, I made sure that my parents knew if anybody was looking for me that evening where I'd be at." Wilkeson's intuition paid off. While at the club, Wilkeson had three visitors. "In walks Mick Jagger, Keith Richards, and Brian Jones from Lynyrd Skynyrd," Leon laughed. "Everybody's wondering what in the hell are they doing here? Allen

"Bassist Extraordinaire," Leon Wilkeson.

Collins came up and said, 'Leon, we're fixing to take a ride around the block. Why don't you come ride with us?' And my heart's in my throat, you know, 'cause I know, hey, they're not asking me to go for a ride to smoke a cigarette, you know. There's something up here. So anyway, I'm in the back seat. Allen is driving, Ronnie's in the passenger side, Gary's sitting next to me in the back. Ronnie says, 'Well, you probably heard we lost a drummer and a bass player. Rickey and Greg have gone back to Blackfoot. But anyway, a while back when you came and jammed,

Gary was pretty impressed with you and he suggested that we consider asking you if you'd be interested in filling the position of bass.' I went, 'God, yeah, thanks for thinking of me. When do we start rehearsing, about five minutes?' And he's going, 'Yeah, O.K., that's great. We're real happy that you accepted our offer.'"

Ronnie's offer didn't come without some ground rules. "'One thing I gotta tell you about playing with this band,' Ronnie said," Wilkeson recalled. "'I'll put it to you in terms of sports and baseball. You know when a professional ballplayer steps up to the plate, he's got several choices. He can bunt, he can try to hit a single, or a double, or a triple. The basic requirement of everybody that plays in this band is, every time you step up to the plate, you gotta put it out of the park. Every time. Gotta be a home run.'"

Leon was happy to be in the band. "They were just hip, man," he said. "They were the real deal. Their originality . . . their desire to be themselves . . . . Everybody else was playing 'Hey, hey, we're the Monkees' and all that commercial bullshit. They were playing Jimi Hendrix, Blues McGoos, acid rock . . . inspired by The Allman Joys and the Hourglass, Duane Allman, and Gregg, particularly."

Leon Wilkeson started attending rehearsals and enjoyed playing with the band very much. He liked the creative process and felt that his expertise as a bass player was growing by leaps and bounds. Wilkeson was professionally gratified to record with the band in Muscle Shoals. He felt he was in for the long run with the band of gypsies known as Lynyrd Skynyrd.

Gary Rossington had now been playing guitar with some other very good players and was getting better and better. "He's very original," says Hughie Thomasson. "His way of playing and the way he puts his songs together, the way he defines his slide guitar, which is great guitar playing—slide guitar playing. He's got signatures all over, up and down . . . everything he plays just about is a signature. You know it's Gary Rossington playing when you hear it and that to me says a lot about somebody."

Ronnie, Gary, and Allen had started to devote a lot of time to writing their own songs by this time. Ronnie was absolutely certain that he was onto something unique with Lynyrd Skynyrd and he encouraged the others to devote every waking hour to creating new music, sweetening their popular initial compositions, and developing their stage act.

"Ronnie ran Skynyrd like Stalin ran Russia," said Leon Wilkeson. "Very, very disciplined. He was a genius. He was kind of like a football coach, or a sports coach, in a way. He just basically put it that everybody's part has to fit like a puzzle piece. There's only one part, and if it's not the right part, you don't complete the [puzzle]. He was the master. The mastermind—he was a genius. If Ronnie said, 'Jump' you said, 'How high?' He had a heart as big as all outdoors. He'd give you the shirt off his back and the last place you wanted to be was on his bad side. But it always paid off. It takes a full crew to sell a show, but he was the guiding light, so to speak."

Ronnie, on the other hand, felt the need for inspiration from the band. "I think I'm a very demanding lead singer," he said to Lisa Robinson in an interview for *Hit Parade*. "I need to be pushed hard and they're a hard-pushing band. Sometimes they'll push me too hard with tempos or whatever, and that can be hard on the throat . . . ."

The second Muscle Shoals sessions went as well as, if not better than, the first. This time the Skynyrd-penned material was exceedingly strong. The self-descriptive "Simple Man"; "Down South Jukin'," a celebration of night life; Ronnie's bar encounter "Gimme Three Steps"; "Was I Right or Wrong," which questioned VanZant's musical involvement; "Things Goin' On"; and "Trust" all represented well the music of Lynyrd Skynyrd.

Gary Rossington later implied that "Things Goin' On" was a political statement. The song was about government spending and the fact that people weren't aware of, let alone supported, the final destination of their tax dollars. If the song was written to be a statement, it was one of the very few Skynyrd songs in this vein.

To test the waters, a single titled "I've Been Your Fool," which had been recorded in Sheffield, was released to generate some interest in both the minds of the public and the music industry. "I wrote it and I had a harmony part," said Leon Wilkeson. The tape generated no airplay and nothing came of this initial venture. None of the record companies that Walden approached wanted to hear songs that exceeded three minutes, and those by Lynyrd Skynyrd most often did.

As fine as the recordings were, again there was little or no interest from any of the major labels. There had been a mix-up with one of the tapes having been sent out rewound backwards and it is possible that this was part of the problem. But it seemed clear to the band that their time had not yet arrived. The demo tapes were shelved for the time being.

The band continued their public appearances. "They played a lot of clubs around the South," says Charlie Faubion. "They really paid their dues." Not all the gigs were pleasant experiences, but they were gigs, after all. "The bars were really tough," Gary Rossington later told *Sounds* magazine. "One night we saw a guy get his head blown off. But we didn't mind playing them 'cause we didn't know nothin' different. Hell, if three people clapped you'd feel so great you'd tear the place down."

Ronnie VanZant decided that although his music was currently his focal point, there was also time for his personal life. He wasn't happy that his marriage to Nadine had failed after so short a time, and he longed for some type of romantic involvement. He began dating a Waycross, Georgia, girl named Judy Seymour who had been introduced to him through Gary Rossington and Skynyrd's roadie Dean Kilpatrick. "I had a house with Dean on Riverside Drive [which they also shared with Mary Hayworth, one of Judy's best friends] and The Allman Brothers were right down the street," remembers Judy. "We were actually roommates, friends only. Our house was called the 'Green House' and their house was called the 'Gray House.' That's where Duane and his girlfriend and Berry Oakley and Linda lived. And I think Butch

Trucks and his wife. Gregg was back and forth when he would come into town. So, they were kind of like in the same neighborhood and all." Judy had earlier lived with Dean and his friend Bonnie at the Cedar Shores apartments in Jacksonville. Judy and Dean were happy to have more room with which to entertain their music-loving friends.

"When I met Ronnie I wasn't a hippie," laughs Judy. "He was a hippie. I was born in Athens [Georgia]. My father was going to the university. We moved around quite a bit in Georgia. I lived in Waycross, Georgia, when I graduated. And I moved to Jacksonville. Just didn't want to go to college. I just moved to Jacksonville."

Ronnie had been continuing to work days at his brother-in-law's auto parts store at the time when Gary introduced him to Judy. "Dean met Gary at a place called the Comic Book Club, down on West Forsyth Street," recalls Judy. "They were playing down there as The One Percent and Dean would go down there and hang out. Dean was a real flashy dude, always hanging around. He met Gary and then he introduced me to Gary and then I met Ronnie, and Allen, and the rest of the guys."

Ronnie and Judy dated for some time and eventually moved in together. Before bassist Larry Jungstrom left the band, his parents had moved to Miami, and LJ had stayed behind. Since the house was fairly big, LJ had invited Ronnie and Judy, Bob Burns, and friend and Skynyrd roadie Chuck Flowers to share the house with him.

Judy understood Ronnie's ambition and supported his dreams for Lynyrd Skynyrd whole-heartedly. "I always said that if you're going to be involved with a musician, you might as well know right from the get-go that that's the most important thing in their life," says Judy. "You have to accept that, and if you can't, then you need to get out, because you can't take it away from them. It would kill them."

Judy and Ronnie decided to get married, regardless of any financial struggle Ronnie's ambition might create. "I cared a lot about Ronnie," Judy says. "When I first met him he was working a job in the daytime and that was in the days when long hair wasn't cool. He'd have to put this wig on every day to go to work to sell auto parts. Then he'd come home at night and they would rehearse. The other guys were still in school, or too young to have to work at stuff like that. It was real frustrating to him so I just said, 'I'll work, you quit, you concentrate on the music.' I accepted it from the beginning, this is what he wants to do. I worked and he concentrated on the music. We struggled for awhile but it worked out fine." Judy and Ronnie were married on November 18, 1972.

Dean Kilpatrick was more than just a Skynyrd roadie and Ronnie-Judy matchmaker. Dean had met Ronnie at the auto-parts store. He had watched the band develop with keen interest since hearing them play at Jacksonville's Comic Book Club. Born on May 30, 1949, Dean loved good rock-and-roll, although his ambition to play bass guitar in public never developed. He especially liked English blues and noticed the similarity of Ronnie and his friends' music. Dean quickly

Artist Dean Kilpatrick in Venice, Italy, 1968.

became friends with the band. The band enjoyed hanging with Dean, as he was extremely intelligent and could be counted on to talk about something other than just Skynyrd's music. After Judy became involved with Ronnie, Dean and Ronnie soon developed an important friendship.

Although Dean earned his living in a variety of ways, he was first and foremost an artist. Dean was constantly drawing and those in the Jacksonville club scene enjoyed the pictures Dean drew of the bands and their friends. If he couldn't find any paper, he would draw on whatever surfaces were available. During a Skynyrd recording session rehearsal years later, Dean drew caricatures of the band on the wall of the Jacksonville studio. (These drawings would later be used for the album centerfold of Skynyrd's *Gold and Platinum* album.)

Art wasn't just a casual hobby with Dean. As a young man, Dean had boldly introduced himself to Salvador Dali in a New York restaurant. At age seventeen, he spent several months working in a monastery in Florence, Italy, restoring flood-damaged works of art as part of Jackie Kennedy's Committee for the Restoration of Italian Art.

Dean was known as a pretty stylish dresser and Gary and Allen, in particular, were always

asking him for pointers with their stage clothing. Dean had purchased some trendy velvet
jackets while he was in Europe and the
Jacksonville locals were quick to note that
Kilpatrick had style. "Dean wore very dramatic clothes. He especially liked long capes. He
would stride through airports or stores or
whatever with the cape flailing behind him.
He made quite an impression, especially with
the girls, with his good looks, beautiful hair,
and tall, thin body. Sometimes he looked like a
Jesuit priest or a shepherd leading his flock
through airports with the band," laughs his
mother, Harriet Kilpatrick.

Dean's flair often extended beyond his
clothes. He indeed had a creative bent. "Dean
had the heart and soul of an artist," says Mrs.
Kilpatrick. "He wanted everything beautiful
and in harmony around him. Mrs. Rossington
said he once walked through her house and
said, 'Those drapes have GOT to go!'"

With his tall stature and Celtic good
looks, Dean was a magnet for the opposite sex.
A little jealousy would sometimes erupt within
the band, as Dean always had women hanging
around him. However, the band soon realized
that they could work their friend's magnetism
to their advantage. Skynyrd was delighted
when Dean decided to sign on as a full-time
roadie for the band after they returned from
the first Muscle Shoals session. He was a welcome addition to the Skynyrd family.

"Dean Kilpatrick is part of Lynyrd
Skynyrd history because he goes back to day
one," says Judy VanZant Jenness. "Chuck
Flowers goes back to day one. Chuck Flowers
and Dean. Chuck Flowers was one of the orig-

A pre-show Dean Kilpatrick.

inal roadies for the band. He was like Dean. In the early 1970s, they didn't have these sophisti-cated roadies. They had a couple of guys who did everything. Unloaded equipment, tuned the guitars, strung the guitars, ran to the store to get beer. I mean they did everything."

Everything was certainly a word Lynyrd Skynyrd understood. And now they believed that they were ready for it. It was time for Ronnie, Gary, Bob, Allen, and Leon to push for a major breakthrough in the music industry. They had worked hard and knew they were good. Now they had to convince the professionals that they were a new, exciting musical entity. They were ready. They only needed to find someone in a position to do something substantial for them. They wanted an opportunity to demonstrate what they could do, and they wanted it now.

4

Mister Yankee Slicker

YOUNG MEN SUCH AS Dean Kilpatrick were viewed by Ronnie as assets to his musical venture. Ronnie often told friends that "Dean will be with us to the end." Anyone who cared about Ronnie and his music was important to him. Ronnie had come from a hardworking, dedicated family, and to show his commitment to his new family he had to work even harder if he was going to advance his career. By 1973, Ronnie was a full-time musician, and his dream to make Lynyrd Skynyrd a household name was no longer just a fantasy.

The other guys had jobs too and it became increasingly difficult to find time to work, rehearse, and perform. "The music is all we're into, it's all we know," Ronnie later told rock journalist Lisa Robinson. "If it wasn't for that we'd have to pick cotton. For about seven years, we played clubs and some of the guys delivered flowers in flower trucks and I worked at an auto place. Finally, we just said fuck it, we want to play music or die."

The boys in Skynyrd knew that if they were going to get any notice at all they would have to play Atlanta and play there often. There were three major clubs that offered opportunities to new talent: Funochios, Richard's, and the Mad Hatter. It was at these clubs that the music industry reviewed acts and awarded contracts to southeastern bands. Skynyrd was finally booked into Richard's and soon were performing there on a regular basis. The audience at Richard's responded enthusiastically to Skynyrd's loud and rowdy music. "Alan [Walden] was their manager, so I would assume that he probably got them that gig," says Judy VanZant Jenness. "The Paragon Agency booked them, a guy named Carey Rhodes, who was with ICM. [There were] all these people around, so they probably got the gig for them. They played Atlanta quite a bit."

News of the band's appeal spread quickly and Lynyrd Skynyrd was able to land a gig at Atlanta's premier club, Funochios, early in 1973. Super-session man and producer Al Kooper often visited the club looking for new talent. Kooper had recently formed his Sounds of the South label as an Atlanta-based alternative and competitor to Phil Walden's successful Macon-based Capricorn Records. The small label would be subsidized by the extensive Los Angeles-based entity MCA Records.

Kooper had a keen ear and years of experience playing with the top names in music. Kooper was one of the founding members of Blood, Sweat and Tears and of the Blues Project. He played organ on several Bob Dylan albums, including *Highway 61 Revisited, Blonde on Blonde*, and *New Morning*. It is Kooper's memorable organ intro that opens Dylan's classic "Like a Rolling Stone." Kooper's musical career includes associations with The Rolling Stones, Jimi Hendrix, the Tubes, Nils Lofgren, Mike Bloomfield, and Stephen Stills. Al Kooper knew music and he knew it well.

Kooper felt there was an exciting sound developing in the South. "I moved there because of the club scene," Kooper remembers. "I sent roadies to pack up my apartment [up North] and stayed in Atlanta. There were a lot of bands that didn't get to be heard that were really good. Moses Jones, Hydra, Eric Quincey Tate . . . but there were only so many pieces of the pie. If Capricorn didn't buy into you, there was nowhere to go."

When local bands heard about Kooper's interest in presenting their music, they were excited. This was a unique time in rock music and not all of the experiences were positive. There seemed to be a lot of new very talented bands but landing a spot on the roster of a big record label was difficult, if not impossible.

"Everybody called it corporate rock," remembers Rickey Medlocke, "because big corporations had taken over radio stations and the focus was on making the big money. So to make the big money, the bands had to turn out the hit records. As long as the focus was on the hits, they would make the bands bigger and bigger and bigger. As soon as one of those bands stumbled and didn't have a hit, they were over with. It became not building the career [but rather] let's build the career of the record company and the radio stations. Let's use these guys to make us. The idea of being a musician first and a rock star second became totally screwed up. All of a sudden it's like, I want to be a rock star and how am I being a rock star? I learn how to play the guitar and I learn how to play the drums and I'm going to get in a band and I'm gonna make it. Go to California, live in L.A., do the L.A. scene, and buddy, I'll have it made. We didn't give a damn about being rock stars. We loved playing music and wanted to make a living out of playing music. All of a sudden, as it happened, we were very blessed and very fortunate to write hit songs that became classic tunes, that were catapulted into that stardom thing."

There seemed definitely to be a place for a smaller, artist-friendly label. Kooper would fill a void that would allow rising musicians not only a voice but a career. "In our day when a label [like Sounds of the South] signed you, they signed you to build a career," said Medlocke. "In other words, this band looks like they're gonna have a great future. Let's sign 'em, put it into them, and build a career."

Although initially Kooper thought Ronnie VanZant was an offensive frontman, he was mesmerized by him. The more he listened to Skynyrd during one of their Funochios sessions, the more he liked what he heard. He listened carefully to the band every night for six nights. "This was the time of Genesis, Emerson, Lake and Palmer, King Crimson," Kooper recalls. "These were thought and skill bands, but they sometimes lacked heart and soul. I remember thinking, if someone came along with a great rock-and-roll band right then, they'd clean up. Lynyrd Skynyrd was a panacea to the problem."

By the fourth night, Kooper was sitting in with the group. Ronnie later said that when Al Kooper introduced himself to the band, they were awestruck. They had never actually met a real rock star. They were delighted to have him join them onstage. By the fifth night, Kooper had decided that Lynyrd Skynyrd had a sound worth producing and recording, and seriously considered signing Lynyrd Skynyrd as his first Sounds of the South act.

Kooper negotiated with Alan Walden for over two months. One night Ronnie called Kooper to tell him that the band's van had been broken into and their equipment was stolen. VanZant said the band was up a creek if they couldn't replace the equipment in order to fulfill their gigs and that they needed $5,000 to do it. Kooper didn't hesitate. He sent Skynyrd the money. Ronnie told him he had just bought himself a band for $5,000. "Mr. Yankee Slicker" was in. (Although he never considered himself to actually be a Yankee slicker, Kooper was amused when the band called him one.)

Kooper foresaw big things for Lynyrd Skynyrd, but he wasn't particularly enamored of their name. He felt that such a strange moniker could be detrimental to the marketing of the band. The band was adamant: Lynyrd Skynyrd it would stay. Kooper accepted their decision, and began to think of ways he could work with the name to get the most mileage.

Buddy Buie, a renowned Georgia-based producer, had opened a small, yet state-of-the-art, recording studio in the Atlanta suburb of Doraville, which he called Studio One. Al Kooper made plans to get Skynyrd into the studio to put down some tracks and see what might develop. "Skynyrd was years ahead of their time," says Kooper. "They were twenty-year-olds playing like thirty-year-olds. I'm not interested in producing anybody I can't learn from."

"Lynyrd Skynyrd came to Studio One through Al Kooper," remembers Buddy Buie. "Al

Kooper and I had the same manager. A guy by the name of Jeff Franklin. Jeff managed me at the time and he was making record deals for me. Then I started doing my own thing with the [Atlanta] Rhythm Section and Jeff called one day and said that Al Kooper loves your studio and wants to make a deal. So we ended up making a deal where Al cut in the daytime and I cut at night. And then we just closed it down to the public. Skynyrd was the first project in there. They were a bunch of Jacksonville punks, too. Whoooo. A good story is the Rhythm Section recorded all night and they were upstairs asleep at the studio. Skynyrd came in and just started raising all kinds of hell. Ronnie [Hammond] ran down the stairs and yelled, 'Shut up, you bunch of rednecks!' And they all came running up the stairs. Ronnie had to lock the door to keep them from coming in . . . ." The folks in Doraville were just starting to learn what the folks in Jacksonville already knew. "They were all pretty wild back then," laughs Judy VanZant Jenness.

"Al moved to Atlanta from New York and started a record company," remembers engineer Rodney Mills. "Skynyrd was one of the first bands he signed. Al came down here and he kind of picked Studio One as the studio where he wanted to record all the artists he was signing and working with, so he brought Lynyrd Skynyrd to the studio to do their first album. I think I was working on an Atlanta Rhythm Section album, so the other engineer in the studio did most of the work on the very first Skynyrd album. I did do a little bit of recording on the first album with Skynyrd but not an awful lot. I got to know them there and then they came back [for their *Street Survivors* album]."

"When they met Al, they were really starstruck," says Judy VanZant Jenness. "He's the legend in the business. Just to have him interested would make anybody feel good."

Amidst the excitement of meeting Al Kooper and discovering that he was interested in the band, Leon Wilkeson began to have cold feet. Leon had enjoyed traveling the road perfecting Skynyrd's music, but as the time drew near to record an album, he started to have serious doubts about whether or not he wanted to make rock-and-roll his career. "I just thought I was too young," Leon recalls. "I didn't have to have my face shoved into the asphalt to appreciate how hard the world is. I just had haunting premonitions about becoming famous, you know, having my mug on a cardboard album cover. I didn't feel I was ready for it yet."

Other things were bothering the young musician. "Rickey [briefly] returned to the band when we had double drums," remembered Wilkeson. "He decided to leave and left town. I ended up choosing to resign from the band as well. My parents were supporting me. When I was in King James Version my father went in debt over his head providing [the band] with equipment. I was like paying them monthly, paying them back. When I joined Skynyrd, I wasn't making any money. When we went out and played gigs, the reason we weren't being paid was because Ronnie was investing all the money in our equipment truck, our equipment. All the money had to go right back into the band, so to speak. So I wasn't making any money and I guess that I assumed that, 'Yeah, I'll go back to King James Version and make money.' Which was a terrible,

terrible choice to make. But that was when Al Kooper approached [Skynyrd]. Their first big break, record deal with MCA and all. Maybe I felt that I just didn't have what it took to cut what Skynyrd needed to take that big of a project, that giant a step in their musical careers. So I went to work for [a company called] Farm Best Dairy Products."

The band was surprised by Wilkeson's decision, but there was no arguing with the discouraged young man. Al Kooper had to do some quick regrouping. He was ready to record Lynyrd Skynyrd and now they didn't have a bass player. Ronnie VanZant felt that they were on the verge of a breakthrough and knew that whomever he recruited to take Wilkeson's place had better be top-notch. The band knew lots of guitar players, but Ronnie was inclined to go with someone who was not only an excellent player, but who had played professionally and knew what was involved in breaking a band.

Ronnie's thoughts turned to a guitar player the band had met years before, when they opened for the Strawberry Alarm Clock. The Alarm Clock's songwriter and guitarist Ed King had been greatly impressed with Lynyrd Skynyrd when the band opened for him. He told Ronnie that if the band ever needed a guitar player or bass player to give him a call. Call Ronnie did. Much to the band's delight, when he was approached to join Lynyrd Skynyrd, King accepted. Al Kooper was pleased with their choice. "Ed was the icing on the cake," Kooper remembers. "He knocked out the whole back door."

Ironically, as VanZant and his friends celebrated their "Southerness" through their approach to music, Ed King had been born not in the South but in southern California. Born on September 14, 1949, in Glendale, California, King grew up in the small San Fernando Valley towns of Panorama City and Glendale. Regardless of where he had been born, King knew how to rock hard, Southern style. His first guitar was a Stella acoustic, which was difficult to play. That didn't stop Ed from learning all he could about the instrument. His early influences were Duane Eddy and the other guitarists associated with the surf music of the early 1960s. As he became more exposed to a variety of professional guitarists, Ed started to listen to Pete Townshend and Duane Allman.

"Duane Allman was an amazing guitar player and a huge influence on me," says King. "I saw him play on October 9, 1971, at the Santa Monica Civic and October 12 at The Whiskey. He was dead two weeks later. I couldn't believe it."

In 1967, Ed found himself heavily involved with a band named the Strawberry Alarm Clock that he had formed with his friend, keyboard player Mark Weitz. Fledgling songwriters Weitz and King wrote the music for a song they titled "Incense and Peppermint." "Mark Weitz wrote most all of it," says Ed King. "I wrote the bridge." The lyrics were supplied by the record company. Weitz and King's credit did not appear on the finished product, which became a national hit record, at one time reaching #1 on the Billboard Singles chart. King was obviously not pleased with the encroachment of the record label on his art and his enthusiasm for the band abated.

Guitar virtuoso Ed King, circa 1973.

The band went bankrupt in 1968.

In 1971, King and Weitz heard that a bogus Alarm Clock was touring Florida. Annoyed that someone else should again be profiting from their creative efforts, they decided that the "real" Strawberry Alarm Clock should hit the road and put the pretenders out of business. It was on this tour of college dates that a band named Lynyrd Skynyrd opened for them.

When Ronnie VanZant later sought to fill Lynyrd Skynyrd's bass position, he would remember those dates and how impressed he was with Ed King's guitar playing. King's effectiveness as a guitar player would impress most of those who encountered his playing. "Actually, out of every guitar player that's ever been in this band, I think Ed was the best," keyboardist Billy Powell would later say. "He could play classical, I guess, if he wanted to. He's grouchy on the outside, [but] he had a heart of gold on the inside."

King was happy to be with the band. He appreciated their unique appeal and felt that they definitely had a future. "They were a rock-and-roll band with a country singer," says King. Relocating to Florida from California, King was asked to stay in a duplex on Rayford Street which served as home to Ronnie, Judy, and Bob Burns.

Al Kooper was satisfied with Skynyrd's addition of King and was excited about the band's guitar line-up. Kooper felt Allen Collins' playing was Claptonesque and that Gary Rossington had a certain Ry Cooder–Paul Kossoff sound. King reminded him of James Burton.

"Ed King's another great player," says Hughie Thomasson. "I used to love watching Gary [Rossington] play with Ed in the band, 'cause I thought he got one of the best guitar sounds that I ever heard. He played a Fender guitar." Instrumentally, Lynyrd Skynyrd was coming together.

Kooper would be available to contribute mellotron, organ, and mandolin. Bob Burns was once again the principal drummer and was doing a good job. Although Rickey Medlocke's drumming had briefly been available to Skynyrd again, he decided to move on to other musical ventures, again taking up the Blackfoot reins.

The music of Lynyrd Skynyrd was a reflection of the social atmosphere that surrounded the band. Perfecting their music was of the utmost priority and the band spent most of their waking hours together. They were all becoming the best of friends and were much like a family of brothers. Three other guys who were there from the beginning of Skynyrd's career would prove themselves invaluable to the band.

Dean Kilpatrick had become one of Skynyrd's best friends and a most trusted family member. He was happy to assist the band both on and off the road. He had the utmost confidence that Lynyrd Skynyrd was going to hit, and hit big. "Dean was there from the beginning," said Leon Wilkeson. "He came from the classier side of town, Ortega. He was nothing but A-1 class, first class," he laughed. "And he come in handy, because a lot of people mistook him for Allen."

"Dean was as dedicated a guy as you can imagine," says Ed King. "He was somebody you could always talk to." Dean easily fit into the band's family as a loyal and trusted brother.

Kevin Elson was also a member of Skynyrd's early crew. He had met the band early in their existence while playing organ in a venture with Donnie Van Zant and Jeff Carlisi. Elson had been invited to contribute his organ to the Muscle Shoals sessions. He had an incredible ear for sound and was able to assist the band in several ways both on and off the road. Elson soon became the band's sound man, roadie, and brother.

Another friend of brother Donnie Van Zant's, Billy Powell, had signed on as a roadie. Powell pitched in and lugged amps, wired mikes, carried equipment, and did whatever else needed to be done. His first gig working for Lynyrd Skynyrd would be a temporary job when the band opened for Mountain at Wolfson Baseball Park, the day after Allen Collins' wedding in 1970. When local band Sweathog canceled, Skynyrd stepped in. He was appreciated as a roadie, but Billy's position in the band was soon to change.

Billy Powell was born June 3, 1952, in Corpus Christi, Texas. Powell's father Donald died of Hodgkin's disease in 1958, while stationed in Italy as a lieutenant commander in the Navy. The family decided to move to Jacksonville, where Billy's mother Marie took a civilian job at the Naval Air Station to help support her three children.

Billy had been picking out notes on the piano since he was a toddler. "I took piano lessons when I was six," says Powell. "At first I hated taking lessons. I could pick out music by ear—little things like 'Mary Had a Little Lamb' and all that. My mom saw that I might have a talent and so when I was six years old, she bought me a piano. [This was] shortly after my father died when we moved to Jacksonville. I didn't like it but she made me practice good and take my lessons and all that because I said that I wanted to do it, at first. It got a little strenuous there for a while and then all of a sudden the Beatles came out. I don't know what it was but it was just something that clicked saying, 'hey, maybe I can end up making a living doing this.' I started diving into it, headfirst. My first dream was to be in a rock-and-roll band when I was a teenager. I used to go to concerts all the time and watch bands play, and I'd always dream what it would be like to be up there instead of be out here [in the audience]. Just to be up there playing to the audience."

Music was a great comfort to Powell during the three years he spent in Sanford Academy, a military boarding school in Florida. Things didn't go well for Billy in the institutional setting, but before he was expelled from the academy in his third year, music teacher Madeleine Brown had the opportunity to give the young man advanced piano lessons.

Billy then enrolled in Jacksonville's Bishop Kenney High School. Throughout high school, Billy took lessons from four different piano teachers. He learned enough to know that he wanted to pursue study of the piano further. He decided after graduation to pursue a degree in music theory at Jacksonville Community College.

"I majored in music in college for a year and a half—just going to junior college," says Powell. "That's where it got real strict. [I] had to learn the scales and all kind of fingering and stuff. That's what's so important about being a good piano player is fingering, doing the right

Billy Powell at the keyboards.

fingering. Once you learn the right fingering, you can do anything. A lot of players are self-taught and just like play rhythm with both hands, you know they're real good with rhythms and stuff, but when it comes to real fast note solos, it's a lot more difficult. But I just started really getting into it. Then [I] started coming up and being creative. I could read music real good, and I started writing my own stuff on staff paper."

While he was able to play the intricate compositions of the music masters, it was still the music of the Beatles that gave Billy the spark to believe that he might be able to make a living through his piano playing. He didn't quite know how to reach that goal, but he knew involving himself in the local music scene would be a good start.

"I was kind of chums [with a band] called Sweet Rooster," says Powell. "Donnie Van Zant sang for them, Don Barnes [played] guitar, Bill Pelkey [was] on drums, and Kevin Elson was the keyboardist. I met Kevin Elson and he just knew I played piano somehow. I got to be good buddies with him and we hung out and did everything together. We were thinking about getting [together] a keyboard band with two keyboard players. He played the organ and I played the piano."

Through mutual friend Roy Simpson, Billy met another young man named Leon Wilkeson. "The very first band I was really in was the band with Leon," says Powell. "I played Silvertone six-string guitar 'cause Leon did, and I envied him so much I was jealous. So I got my mom to get me one. We both got in a band with a guy that played keyboards. He couldn't afford a whole drum set so he used his floor tom as a bass drum too, the way he rigged it up. We didn't have a name. We played one party. We were going to play for $5.00. The only song we knew was "Little Black Egg." So we played it over and over. They said, 'Hey, play us something else or you're not gonna get paid.' We didn't know anything else, so we kind of faked it like one of the amplifiers blew up so we could leave. So they didn't have to pay us. Then the band broke up and that was it."

Kevin Elson had introduced Billy Powell to the members of Lynyrd Skynyrd. Elson liked Powell and knew he was anxious to learn more about the music business. Elson thought it would be a good idea to bring Powell on full time as a third crew member.

"He hired me as one of the roadies for Skynyrd," says Powell. "I was a roadie for a year with the guys, believe it or not. I was wiring their amplifiers and stuff like that. I set up the amplifiers and wired them and everything, Kevin Elson worked the sound, and Dean Kilpatrick got the women and the drugs. Dean was a crazy guy. He was outgoing . . . a real outgoing guy. But if it wasn't for Kevin Elson I would've never known Skynyrd." Even though both he and Ronnie were young and fairly inexperienced, Billy knew he could learn a great deal about music from Ronnie VanZant.

 One night after playing a prom late in 1970 at The Bolles School in Jacksonville, Elson mentioned to Ronnie, Allen, and Gary that they might be interested in listening to some keyboard playing that Billy had worked up to fit into "Freebird." "I had an original version on the piano with 'Freebird' that I wrote and never played for anybody really," says Powell. "There was an old beat-up upright piano on the stage. When the prom was over, I sat down and played my version of 'Freebird' and they just all three dropped their jaws. Ronnie went, 'Wow, you play piano like that and didn't tell us?' I said, 'I never dreamed you'd ever want a piano player in the band, 'cause you've been so long without one.' Then that's when Ronnie said, 'Would you like to join the band as keyboardist?' Then my jaw fell to the floor. That was like an instant dream come true. Just like that, I was in the band."

It's hard to imagine "Freebird" played any way other than the version we have come to know, but Powell says there were some real changes made to the structure of the song. "There's just a piano version," says Powell. "I just picked out the melody by ear and listened to the song and then just put a piano part to it, which wound up being the beginning of the song now. It's like a solo piano part at the very beginning where there used to be guitar coming in at the very beginning. Guitar and then slide guitar came in, where it's now piano, then the instruments [came] in, and then the slide guitar [came] in."

Playing music professionally was a far cry from what Billy felt his alternative career might be. "If it wasn't for Kevin Elson, I might be in the Navy," he says. "Because my father died in active duty, I was automatically discharged from any service. But before I found that out, I was going to join the Navy instead of being drafted. That was going to be my career. I was going to try to be a pilot. I passed everything, passed all the physicals and everything. I told the truth when they [asked] if I had ever smoked pot and done LSD. I said yes. So they had to send out a character report on me. It'd take about two more weeks [to get the O.K.]. Just two or three days after that Congress passed the law that any son or sons of deceased veterans that died in active duty was discharged. If I'd lied and said, 'No, I've never done this,' I'd have been in the Navy and never met any of those guys. Maybe that'd been the better thing to do, 'cause I could've been at least a pilot. I love flying still, to this day I love it. I flew the airplane that crashed. Not on takeoff and landing, just flying it when I was already up there in the air. I think it's just in my blood from my dad."

Although impressed with Powell's musical abilities, Ronnie had a problem with Billy's style of playing the piano. Powell had played some with Alice Marr, while he was a roadie for Skynyrd, but the actual gigs of that band were few and far between. He really had little experience playing in a rock band.

"I was in there [Alice Marr] for about nine months," says Powell. "We rehearsed for nine months. We kept getting kicked out of different practice houses, because of the noise. After nine months, we played two concerts. One was at the beach coliseum, which was a real crappy one. [We] didn't have hardly any equipment or anything. The other one was at a bar called the Castaways. The stage was behind the bar. It was big enough for like two people, and there's five people in the group. That one was hilarious, 'cause we got fired from the job 'cause we wouldn't turn our volume down. We had to leave. When we tallied up how much they owed us, they determined that instead of them owing us anything we owed them money for drinking all their beer. That [band] didn't go anywhere, but that's when I was a roadie for Skynyrd. I quit them when I got the offer for Skynyrd. They went on and they kept rehearsing and they became .38 Special."

Ronnie remarked that while he knew Billy had good potential, Ronnie felt he was too technical. "I liked technical bands back then," Powell remembers. "Emerson, Lake and Palmer . . . to me they play with feel and technicality. Ronnie couldn't stand them. 'Bunch of damn educated fools,' [he'd] say. He called *me* [an] educated fool. We'd be riding down the road in a van and Yes would be on one station, and Merle Haggard on the other. I would want to listen to Yes and Ronnie would want to listen to Merle Haggard. I can give you one guess as to which one we wound up with."

Powell himself says that he was a very technical pianist and he had to learn from the other band members how to actually *feel* the music. He listened to Billy Joel, Nicky Hopkins, Elton John, Nigel Olson, Bobby Whitlock, and any other recorded musician he felt could help him learn to play rock-and-roll piano.

Powell would leave it to his new association with Lynyrd Skynyrd to help him develop even further. "Once I joined Skynyrd, I [relied on] those guys to teach me the difference between feel, technicality, and boogie-woogie," he says. "That's when I knew this was my calling, to make my living playing the piano. So instead of being so technical and precise and 'Mr. Perfect,' I finally started learning a little bit about feel, original[ity], and stuff like that. Now that's where I got the speed from in some of my solos. I can just do a real good solo with one hand, it's that easy for me. Rock-and-roll's real easy to play. I can still play classical music pretty good too. I think I'm the only one in the band that can read music."

Billy Powell looked forward to the challenge of interweaving his piano with the guitars. "With three of 'em, there's always something happening with guitar and it's really hard to find all the little entry spots to fill in the spaces in between," Billy laughs. "I had to play in between the lines and I think that established the band not only as a guitar army, but [me] as a real good keyboard player."

While subscribing to the Lynyrd Skynyrd sound—jam-packed and guttural—Powell was free to pursue his own unique keyboard sound. "Ronnie always said, 'You guys just play your instruments, think of music, and I'll do the business,'" recalls Billy. "And that's the way it was. We knew we could trust him. We knew we could count on him, and we knew he had the head for it, and he did. He was father, founder, and leader of Lynyrd Skynyrd."

By the spring of 1973, Al Kooper was ready to take Lynyrd Skynyrd into the studio. They were all certain that they finally had the material and the line-up that could create the magic they wanted to create. With Kooper's recording expertise, Lynyrd Skynyrd was poised to take on the world.

5

Pronounced

RONNIE VANZANT was now satisfied with the line-up of the band and felt that Lynyrd Skynyrd was, at last, in a position to record a ready-to-release album. The first album would feature Ronnie VanZant on vocals, Gary Rossington and Allen Collins on guitar, Ed King on bass, Bob Burns on drums, and Billy Powell on keyboards. The record would be something that would really represent the band's distinctive sound. Skynyrd entered Studio One to put down the individual tracks that would culminate in their August 1973 debut album, *Lynyrd Skynyrd (Pronounced 'Leh-'nerd 'Sky-'nerd)*. A couple of the band members would later say that the pronunciation depicted in the title was incorrect inasmuch as *they* pronounced the name of the band "*Lynn*–erd." But that was later. At this point there was an album to record, regardless of what either it or the band was called. The band was excited but nervous. This was the moment for which they had been waiting, and they were ready to rock.

Ronnie in the studio (far right), emotionally supported by brother Donnie,
soundman Kevin Elson, and (standing) friend Jeff Carlisi.

Although Jimmy Johnson had cut tracks with the band, Al Kooper would serve as the band's first record producer. His vast experience allowed him to instruct the members of Skynyrd throughout the sessions in the creative use of the studio without any ill will. The band knew that there was a lot that they didn't know about making their sound come across on tape. Kooper was there to lead the inexperienced members of Lynyrd Skynyrd through the intricate steps of selecting songs, enhancing arrangements, and getting them recorded. Kooper had worked with the best: Dylan, Hendrix, The Stones, Mike Bloomfield, and other superstars. "Al had a vision," says Ed King. "He knew how the band should be presented and how it should be recorded."

Because Kooper was very opinionated, as was Ronnie VanZant, there were periodic clashes between Kooper and the band, but the results were well worth any temporary animosity. Kooper would maintain that because of his experiences he had definite opinions on what would work and what wouldn't. Yet Kooper's ideas were suggestions, not demands. Ronnie and the others were always free to do as they chose. "Ronnie said to the others, 'Maybe once in twenty times Kooper will have a good idea,'" remembers Kooper, "but I will suffer the other nineteen times because the twentieth time will be something to make us sound better."

Ronnie was, of course, considerably less experienced, but he knew what he wanted from his band. He and Kooper would sometimes disagree, and the scenes that followed were not pretty. Here were two vitriolic, sensitive musicians. It was not only their approach to music that may have caused a problem, but a shared nature. "Ronnie butted heads with everybody," according to his wife Judy. "Ronnie would make comments about Blood, Sweat, and Lynyrd Skynyrd." This was especially true when it came to what he felt was best for Lynyrd Skynyrd. Yet VanZant could and would learn a great deal about recorded sound from the talented Kooper. Any arguments they may have had resulted in a better musical presentation of the band.

Ronnie was known as quite the taskmaster when it came to rehearsing his band, and he respected the fact that Kooper was the same when it came to recording. "He can get moody at times," said Ronnie, referring to Kooper, "but when he gets moody with us, we get moody with him. And there's seven of us. We don't put nothin' on record unless we like it too." Most times Kooper liked it just fine. He knew good music when he heard it. Sometimes he disagreed. Ed King remembers Kooper was less than enthusiastic about Skynyrd including the song "Simple Man" on that first album. Kooper particularly enjoyed "Was I Right or Wrong" and the sneering "Mr. Banker" and wanted to be certain to include those songs on the album. The band loved "Simple Man" and insisted that a place on the record be found for it. They were firm in their conviction and decided it would be recorded and placed on the album whether or not Kooper approved.

"Basically, Ronnie led Kooper over to his Bentley, opened the door, and told him to get in," Ed King recalls. "After shutting the door, Ronnie stuck his head in through the window and said, 'When we're done cutting it, we'll call you.'"

Al Kooper doesn't remember it that way. He says that one night when he thought the session was over he left for home. The band remained and sweet-talked the engineer into letting them record the basic track for "Simple Man." Kooper says it wasn't that he had anything against the song, he just preferred other songs when it came time to select what was going to be included. When it came time to complete the song, Kooper actually provided the organ. King agrees that Kooper loved the song after it was completed, and was glad that it was included. Kooper's choices were not forgotten. "Mr. Banker" later served as a 45 B-side and "Was I Right or Wrong" was released after the airplane crash.

"Simple Man" meant a lot to the band because they felt it personified their collective personality. "We are just simple, common people who are not trying to be big actors," said Allen Collins. "We're trying to get people off, just trying to be good. That song is about us."

The in-studio differences of opinion were loud and frequent but that was part of the creative process. Ronnie supported Kooper's views the majority of the time and had no hesitation when he was later asked if Kooper would continue to be involved with the band's music. "If it was left up to us, and we're sure it will be," said Ronnie, "Al Kooper will be doing it again."

The guitarists of Lynyrd Skynyrd favored a variety of instruments. Throughout the recording

"Simple Man" Ronnie VanZant.

Gary used his Les Paul and Allen mostly played his Gibson Firebird. From time to time Gary would use a Gibson SG and Allen would alternate between his Firebird, a Gibson Explorer, a Fender Stratocaster, and a Telecaster. King favored a Stratocaster as well, but also employed a variety of other guitars, depending on the mood he wanted to invoke. He was proficient and could make good use of a Pensa-Suhr, Gibson SG, or Paul Reed Smith. Leon Wilkeson has used a variety of bass guitars including a Fender Jazz, Fender Telecaster Bass, and 1965 Gibson Thunderbird. Most of the band used Peavey amplifiers. They now considered themselves a professional unit.

The band continued to rehearse while recording the album. "Ronnie ruled the band with an iron hand," recalls Ed King. "We'd go to that little house and work from nine o'clock in the morning to late at night. I'd look forward to what we were going to do—what we were going to write."

The songs included on *Pronounced* were excellent and would set the standard for the band's future recordings. Most of the songs stemmed from real-life experiences and were delivered, vocally and instrumentally, with conviction and sensitivity. If the songs had not occurred in life as they were related musically, there were bits and pieces of many experiences entwined throughout. Reality and literary license were indistinguishable. Most times Ronnie would write the lyrics to songs that were musically composed by Allen, Gary, and Ed. Sometimes the lyrics would come first, other times words were provided for the music. The musicians of Skynyrd were without egos when it came to creating songs. If someone had an idea, the others jumped in to build something noteworthy and memorable.

"Gimme Three Steps" was one such tale. Ronnie and his friends had been in the W. T. West Tavern in Jacksonville one day when the incident played out much the way it is related in the song. Ronnie had been dancing the Monkey with a girl on the dance floor when her boyfriend objected. It seems the couple had been arguing and the girl looked to VanZant to make her friend jealous. When the jilted lover pulled a gun, Ronnie asked that he please be allowed to leave. He didn't want anything to do with the girl. As he started walking out the door, the acerbic singer mentioned that if he was going to be shot, he would be shot in the elbows or the ass because he was *out of there*. The song was written after the guys piled into their car and took off. The "Jug" mentioned in the song actually does exist. It was the Little Brown Jug at the corner of Acosta and Edison streets in Jacksonville.

"Simple Man" harkened back to Ronnie's roots and upbringing. The lyrics mention advice from "mama"—likely Ronnie's own mama. It wasn't hard to imagine his mother saying those very words to him. Being a "simple kind of man" was a tenet of living that Ronnie embraced. "It kind of says it all, doesn't it?" mused Leon Wilkeson.

"It just seems like there's more truth in the lyrics of Southern music," says Billy Powell. "That's one of the things that made Skynyrd famous. Real-life stories, like 'Three Steps' and [later] 'That Smell.' To me the lyrics [are] more down to earth, and they're more genuine than a lot of Yankee music."

Collins, Rossington, and King created music that perfectly suited VanZant's lyrics. Each guitar solo was worked out in advance of its recording. Kooper loved that—it gave him a lot of room to arrange their unique sound on tape.

Other standouts are "Tuesday's Gone," a lilting love-lost melody containing better-than-average VanZant vocals and an impressive guitar intro; the driving "Mississippi Kid"; and the strong guitar pace of the tongue-in-cheek "I Ain't the One." While a common thread is the real-life experiences, a variety of presentations were used. Some songs are pretty ballads, others raunchy boogie-woogie. There is a definite rock-and-roll feel, but some of the songs are deeply rooted in country and blues.

The musical pièce de résistance was the anthem that would become the hallmark of Skynyrd's live appearances for the next thirty years. Allen Collins' soaring tribute to independence utilized everything that was available to him within his guitar forum. "Freebird" was almost a classic from the first time it was heard at Allen's wedding. Collins' playing of the song on the album was spectacular.

"Certainly Allen's legacy is the guitar solo in 'Freebird,'" says guitarist Jeff Carlisi. "[He] will always be remembered for that. It'll live forever. It's a classic, but it went way deeper than that. It was the spirit and the passion that he had every time he picked up a guitar. He became that guitar."

Al Kooper mixed the album three times until it met with his satisfaction. When the band heard the final mix, they were delighted. Through Kooper's Sounds of the South, the record was to be distributed by mega-label MCA Records. Skynyrd was excited to have the support of such an established and far-reaching operation behind them.

Ronnie would later say that, in his opinion, the first album was the best. He liked the song selection and the variety. After all, there had been years to prepare for it. The band felt good about the record. They were anxious to unleash it on the public and see what would happen.

Kooper thought up an innovative ad campaign, which MCA subsidized. Six weeks before the release of the album in August 1973, the words "Who Is Lynyrd Skynyrd?" along with the Kooper-designed skull and crossbones logo, appeared in the music trade journals and significant alternative press. The inspiration behind the design of the logo was "the brawling and general attitude of the band," according to Al Kooper. Each week the size of the ad grew and a little more information about the band was revealed. The week of *Pronounced*'s release, a two-page ad appeared. The buzz was tremendous. *Pronounced* was the album most added to rock radio play lists within ten days. After two weeks, Lynyrd Skynyrd was getting significant airplay.

"I remember when their first album came out," says Charlie Faubion. "Ronnie asked me to come over to his house—he was living in an apartment. I went over there and he said, 'You know, we've known each other a long time and we're just starting to get successful.' We talked about the early days. I had the album and he said 'Let me sign your album for you.' I said, 'Great!' I remember he signed it, 'In memory of the good ole days, Ronnie.'"

The public face of Lynyrd Skynyrd: publicity photo, 1973. Standing, left to right: Bob Burns, Allen Collins, Ronnie VanZant, Billy Powell, Ed King, Gary Rossington. Seated: Leon Wilkeson.

Because Lynyrd Skynyrd was a new band, the reviews weren't abundant, but those who noticed them were favorably inclined. *Sounds* magazine called the record "a raw blend of blues, hillbilly country, and British boogie packed with typically Southern flavor: moaning slide guitar, country pickin' mandolin, aggressive guitars, driving rhythm section in straight 4/4, and dry, thirst-parched vocals. VanZant's lyrics completed the geographical picture with tales of disapproving daddies, guns, trains, rides, ghettos, the Lord, and getting high on dope and booze."

The album cover would be the first in a line of Lynyrd Skynyrd covers that would underwhelm. The photo showed the band members sitting or slumped against a downtown Jacksonville wall, appearing humorless and somewhat hostile. Ronnie VanZant would later say, "I read somewhere that we had the worst album covers ever made. Shit, that's just that we don't give a fuck."

Skynyrd knew that in order to get their record played on the radio and pave the way for their future recordings, they were going to have to hit the road hard. Touring in promotion of *Pronounced* offered the boys many surprise receptions, almost all of them positive. They found that the anthem "Freebird" was an immediate monster hit with their new audience. "The first time I heard 'Freebird' I knew that kids would want to hit their heads against the wall," recalls Al Kooper. "Freebird" received major FM radio play when it was released as a single in 1974. It eventually climbed to #19 on the Billboard Singles chart.

Skynyrd played a variety of clubs, certainly at least one step up from what they had played before their debut album. Alan Walden and Paragon Booking Agency found that venues were more interested in their band now that they had an album out. Ed King later recounted to *Circus* magazine what that first album tour was like. "Man, we used to play this area out," he said, referring to Greenville, South Carolina. "We played here when we were nothin'. We used to cram all of us into this little Toyota and drive to Charlotte to play this little club called the Cellar."

They played with other up-and-coming local acts, such as The Atlanta Rhythm Section, their old buddies from Studio One. "We used to see them all the time," says Billy Powell. "Playing the same clubs we played, back in Atlanta, years and years before we made it. If The Atlanta Rhythm Section and Skynyrd [were] playing, boy, everybody flocked to those shows."

Unfortunately, everybody flocking to those shows was not always a good thing. The partying got pretty intense when the band played Atlanta at Georgia Tech that year. "You can't come to Atlanta without something bad happening," Ronnie told Tom Dupree of *Rolling Stone*. "There are a million people backstage. And you know most of 'em." The something bad that happened to Ronnie that night resulted in a tremendous hangover the next day. Yet there was no denying the pride the band felt when the show was well received by the Atlanta crowd. The crowd roared when VanZant punctuated the sentiment of "Simple Man."

Although the executives at Los Angeles-based MCA had little in common with the redneck band from the South, they were professionals. They almost immediately sensed that Lynyrd Skynyrd—unpolished, brutal, and raw—was something exceptional. The limited reports they heard back from the road reinforced what they had hoped the band would accomplish. Lynyrd Skynyrd was a hit with the rock-and-rollers who were buying tickets and albums.

The Marshall Tucker Band had released their first Capricorn album, *The Marshall Tucker Band,* at about the same time. Backed by the searing guitar of Toy Caldwell as well as a flute, among other instruments, the Tucker boys were a unique blend of country and rock-and-roll.

Hitting the road, 1973. Standing, left to right: Ed King, Gary Rossington, Ronnie VanZant, Leon Wilkeson, Allen Collins, soundman Kevin Elson, Bob Burns. Seated, left to right: Billy Powell, manager Alan Walden, Dean Kilpatrick.

They well knew that in order for the band to establish a record-buying following, they had to have their exceptional sound sampled in concert by as many people as they could pull in. Once the word got out as to how unusual and proficient Tucker was, the crowds flocked to their shows. Opening for them occasionally was definitely in Skynyrd's favor. "We played a lot with them [over the years]," recalled Leon Wilkeson. "Seemed like Marshall Tucker and Skynyrd were kind of in a rivalry sort of thing. Both our first albums were kind of happening at the [same] time and it seemed like there was a little bit of a competitive thing going. Who's going to be more famous, Marshall Tucker or Skynyrd? They seemed to have a little bit more of a country tendency, it felt, to my liking."

The music press was quick to label music by the Allmans, Skynyrd, and Marshall Tucker "Southern Rock." "It's just a tag that they gave bands back in the 1970s and 1980s that were from the South," says Johnny Van-Zant. "It was kind of fitting, but I think all it really is is rock-and-roll. Hell, it would be called country these days, a lot of it. I was talking to Deanna Carter yesterday . . . she's in the studio here where we're at. She goes, 'I don't know how come the Southern thing isn't happening. All it is, is country music.' I kind of figure we were all raised on country music. Maybe it was just a tag for guys who had an edge who kind of played country music. But hey, I don't care as long as they call me."

The term "Southern Rock" started popping up regularly in reference to Lynyrd Skynyrd and the other bands from the South. "In the early 1970s, right after The Allman Brothers had a couple of albums and then The Marshall Tucker Band and Lynyrd Skynyrd started taking off . . . actually, at the same time," remembers producer Paul Hornsby. "With the strength of those three bands, all of a sudden, we'd read reviews in the trades and so forth and I started hearing 'Southern Rock.' I guess it had something to do initially with those three bands to begin with, whatever it is that they do."

"That's when [Skynyrd] became famous, was at that same period of time," says Judy VanZant Jenness. "So that's where they kind of fit into the Southern Rock thing. But they were a universal band. They could play anywhere, with anybody."

"Southern Rock sounds like a promotional label," said Leon Wilkeson. "And we don't care to be labeled that, actually. We'd like to consider ourselves a band from anywhere. We just happened to have originated in a southern location. We always considered The Allman Brothers were the ones that broke the ice, that provided the inspiration for everybody else to be the Southern sound, or whatever. I call it the Macon Syndrome. The Allman Brothers are kind of successful in that [they] showed us that it would work and it was worth pursuing, putting your neck on the chopping block for. [Skynyrd] is just a little ole band from the South. Like ZZ Top, that little old band from Texas? We're just a little old band from Jacksonville."

Rickey Medlocke believes that the sound categorized as Southern Rock at this time was not only different from what was being played, but also had long-term stamina. "We tried to form our own sound," explains guitarist Medlocke. "We tried to be really different from everybody else. And I think basically, just because we were rock bands that happened to be from the South, it was labeled Southern Rock. I guess there's good points and bad points to everything. I don't view it as really necessarily a bad thing. When Southern Rock was really hip, when *Urban Cowboy* was a hit movie, and the South was really going, when you had a lot of bands from the South, it was a very in thing to wear cowboy boots and to wear hats and be into Southern Rock. And as soon as that fad kind of became passé, then all of a sudden the Southern bands became passé. And I think it's a very unfair thing, because I think that the Southern bands had a lot of great music, as everybody can attest to now. And Lynyrd Skynyrd . . . probably their songs more than anybody, are played continuously on all kinds of radio stations. And you know, [Skynyrd has] basically fans as young as twelve and all the way up to fifty, and most of our audience that we see nowadays is in the age [range] of eighteen to thirty-five. That's what we're seeing at almost all of our shows. Seventy percent of the audience is that. So there's gotta be something said for the Southern bands that can hang in there that long, and have those kind of classic hits that people want to hear continuously."

That assessment dovetails with the way Ronnie VanZant felt about the term. "I just think he considered himself as a rock band," says Johnny Van-Zant. "It was a tag. Any kind of rebel doesn't like a tag. Except for the rebel tag."

Yet as closely identified as Skynyrd was with Southern Rock music, there still seemed to be a gap between Skynyrd and the others who were associated with that term. Skynyrd was labeled as Southern Rock, but didn't exactly fit the mold. "[Skynyrd] was tight with a few bands but they weren't in the circle like the Brothers, Tucker, Charlie Daniels, Grinderswitch, Wet Willie," explains Dru Lombar. "They weren't in that circle 'cause they were just a different way. I mean the Macon thing [was] more secure and the other thing was less secure. I don't know if Skynyrd ever believed that they were [important to the other Southern Rock participants] or felt comfortable with it, or secure with it. The Allman Brothers were secure [with it], man. [Skynyrd] just had to fight their way out of Jacksonville, you know?"

Ronnie lay awake nights thinking about all aspects of the band. The thought of Lynyrd Skynyrd rarely left his mind in those days. He was pleased with the recording they had produced, but during rehearsals he was bothered by one thing.

Ed King was living with Ronnie and Judy as the time drew close to take Skynyrd on the road and debut their album. After rehearsal one night, VanZant went to King and put his arm around him. "He told me, 'You're the worst bass player,'" remembers Ed. King acknowledged that bass guitar wasn't his primary instrument. Ed suggested that he be moved to guitar and Leon Wilkeson be asked back into the band. "Leon is my favorite guitar player," claims Ed. "He's a great player." Ronnie liked the reception he received from King. It was obviously what he had in mind. Now all Ronnie had to do was approach Wilkeson with the idea of rejoining the band.

During the recording of *Pronounced,* Ronnie had suggested that King learn Wilkeson's bass parts for "Simple Man." Ed was happy to oblige. Leon had continued to keep in touch with both the boys in the band and Skynyrd's music. Wilkeson, independent of the band's needs and intentions, had already decided that he wanted to continue to be a part of Lynyrd Skynyrd.

"I did approach Billy and I told him if there was any possibility that Ronnie might consider putting me back in the band that I was gung-ho ready for it," said Wilkeson. "So I guess Billy Powell passed the word on." Bob Burns and Billy Powell appeared on Leon's doorstep one day to tell Wilkeson that Ronnie was out fishing and wanted to talk to him. Wilkeson was curious about what VanZant might want to say to him. He found Ronnie down at the dock.

As Ronnie fished, he indicated that there might be room in the band for Leon. "Ronnie says, 'Well, we just cut our first album,'" remembered Wilkeson. "I said, 'Yeah, man, congratulations, look forward to hearing it, wish you the best of success on your album . . . .' He said, 'Leon, you know Ed played the bass, did all the bass parts, and he also did some guitar overdubs. He really would rather play guitar than bass, and we haven't got a whole lot of time 'cause we gotta promote the album.' Ronnie was basically just telling me that the sound he preferred required three guitars, instead of just Al and Gary. And that Ed would rather be a guitarist. So I was the most eligible candidate for bass guitar because I already have been preestablished with the band."

Wilkeson wasn't all that happy with his current employment. "[I was] working with a bunch of long-haired potheads at Farm Best Dairy, getting sick of ice cream," Leon laughed. "I worked in the tank. You know, putting ice cream products on a rack and a guy on a forklift would come over and pick them up. I was working in a giant refrigerator. Thirty degrees below zero. I had to wear an Eskimo suit. But that's a whole 'nother movie right there. But you know, it was like a childhood fantasy come true in a way. I mean, all the ice cream I could eat."

Regardless of the perks, Leon knew his career wasn't in ice cream, but rather in music. "I'll never forget having to sneak off to go see Led Zeppelin," he laughed. "I had to have a friend call in and claim my father was suffering from a stroke. I *had* to go see 'Houses of the Holy.'"

Leon didn't have to think about his answer before he quickly accepted Ronnie VanZant's offer. "I said, 'O.K., when do we start rehearsing . . . five minutes?'" Wilkeson laughed. Ronnie nodded his head and handed Wilkeson his fishing pole. "He says, 'Cast the line over there by them lily pads floating on the water,'" Leon chuckled. "So I very, very scientifically, carefully obeyed his command. He says, 'I guarantee you're going to catch a fish in like less than a minute.' So I caught a fish. I'm holding up a fish, looking at Ronnie, going 'I consider that a good omen.' He said, 'I do too . . . see you at rehearsal tomorrow.'"

So Lynyrd Skynyrd, changing once again, continue to advance towards its ultimate goal of overwhelming success. The music was definitely coming together but the business end of things needed tweaking. After having brought Al Kooper aboard and having their album distributed by MCA, Ronnie felt that the band was starting to exceed the limited expertise Alan Walden could offer the band. Ronnie wanted the band to be perceived as "big time" and he felt that Walden was too regional. "I think he may have been inadequate as a manager of a band of our caliber," says Ed King. "But he knew it and was willing to be bought out."

Ronnie would meet Peter Rudge of Sir Productions, whose company managed tours for The Who and The Rolling Stones, and ask his view of Lynyrd Skynyrd. Rudge thought the band had great potential, but he didn't offer to represent them. He knew they had a manager and wasn't one to step on another manager's toes. As it became apparent that Rudge was a man with many connections in the music industry, Ronnie asked Rudge if he would consider taking on the band. Rudge said that while he wouldn't actively pursue the band, he would manage them if they made the overture to him. Not a problem. "We didn't have much of a problem with Walden, except Peter Rudge nudged himself into our inner circle and won Ronnie over," claims Ed King. "He seemed to be bet-

Manager Peter Rudge (left) with Dean Kilpatrick, August 1974.

ter equipped for the job. Walden got a real nice buyout, though."

Peter Rudge had a personality that evidently didn't charm everyone. While the original members of Lynyrd Skynyrd seemed excited about the possibility that a manager of Rudge's influence would represent them, future drummer Artimus Pyle later said that he felt there was another side to Rudge. "Peter Rudge was very manipulative, and kind of shady," says Pyle. Yet after Rudge came on board in August 1974, he was often just doing the job a manager is supposed to do.

Ronnie VanZant seemed very pleased with Rudge's business sense. "I put all my trust in Peter Rudge," he told Lisa Robinson. "When he says jump, I jump, because we were eating peanut butter and jelly until he got a hold of us and he really has developed our career. He is the Number One manager in the world . . . he's my man. I've said it before and I'll say it again, I have a Jesus in heaven and on earth, but in music I've got Peter Rudge."

Peter Rudge had become friendly with Lynyrd Skynyrd in an interesting way. In an extraordinarily beneficial career move aimed at providing the band with strong national exposure, Lynyrd Skynyrd was added as the support act on The Who's *Quadrophenia* tour. Al Kooper says that he brought Lynyrd Skynyrd to the attention of Pete Townshend and Peter Rudge (The Who's manager). The Who were looking for an act that was viewed as up-and-coming. Skynyrd would be perfect. The tour began in late November 1973. "We didn't know we were even on the tour until the day before it started," remembers Ed King. "We knew it was being worked on, but Pete hadn't given his approval yet. I'm sure some people were working on it but I wasn't packing for it until the day before."

Pronounced had been receiving airplay and over 100,000 copies of the album had been sold by the time the tour began. Being on the road to promote the album was important, but being part of a major rock event took record sales to a new level. "I sat in the fifth row watching Pete Townshend in 1971 before I was even with Lynyrd Skynyrd," Ed King remembers. It would be unbelievable to the guitarist that a band he was in would be opening for the superstar only two years later.

Al Kooper asked the band if they would mind if he personally mixed the sound on the tour. Kevin Elson and Dean Kilpatrick had no experience working in such large venues. Since Elson and Kilpatrick had no problem with that, neither did the band. Al Kooper, president of the record label, would be on hand at each concert to personally mix Lynyrd Skynyrd's major venue debut. Kooper remarked at the time, "Let's see Clive Davis go on the road and mix Barry Manilow!"

This was the moment for which Ronnie VanZant had been waiting. "That was big time," remembers Judy VanZant Jenness. "Making it. Playing with The Who. That was a crazy time for Skynyrd. I don't think it mattered to them, the bigger the better. It was like more of a challenge. They were never intimidated by anybody they played with."

"The tour opened in San Francisco at the Cow Palace in front of 18,600," Gary Rossington told *Sounds* magazine. "We walked out on stage and went, 'Ooohhh, God, what [are we] going to do?' Everything was played ten times too fast. We were awful, but by the time we got to the third night everything was just fine."

Ronnie VanZant was also affected by the size of the crowd. "Before The Who tour, the biggest crowd we ever played was maybe 1,200," he later said. "The first night at the Cow Palace we faced 18,000 people and we were shitting."

Having their music revealed to the raucous Who audience was perfect. Lynyrd Skynyrd could rock with the best of 'em and the band took advantage of this exceptional opportunity to demonstrate their raw and powerful three-guitar assault. The raunchy lead vocals of the impudent VanZant introduced The Who's audience to a Southern musical aggression that could not be ignored. The Who, on the other hand, were in the midst of one of their Keith Moon-induced problem periods. They had trouble keeping their eccentric drummer off heavy drugs and into the music.

"We were prime," says Billy Powell. "We were one hundred percent that [first] night and every night, as far as that tour. [But] The Who wasn't. Back then the role I played was just [as] a real ambitious young musician that was ready to make it big. The whole band was doing that. No band has really scared us, except maybe The Who, in that very first twelve-city tour." The audience may have come to the show to see The Who, but the opening act from Florida seized their attention and commanded them to listen.

"Everybody else was scared shitless for us," Ed King told *Circus* magazine. "The record company was a little leery. They took us to a Who gig with Mylon LeFevre fronting and he was just booed off the stage. He got eaten up. Nope, we had nothin' to lose. We were just amazed to be there. We stayed real loose and played as good as we knew how. It helped us because we didn't bomb. Hell, if we had bombed no one woulda ever heard of us again."

Ronnie VanZant was certainly a different kind of frontman. His intense yet languid presen-

Lynyrd Sknyrd, circa 1973–1974. Left to right: Allen Collins, Ronnie VanZant, Gary Rossington.

tation of the various styles of Lynyrd Skynyrd music was not something rock audiences had previously experienced. His aggressive, barefooted performance demonstrated that while he was there to do business, he approached that business with a certain nonchalance. His working-man image seemed out of sync with his hippie's bare feet, but to Ronnie there was no inconsistency. That was just the way he liked to deliver his songs. Ronnie said several times in interviews that the reason he performed barefoot was because he liked to feel the heat of the stage. His brother, .38 Special's Donnie Van Zant, indicates that going barefoot was a long-standing habit. "He liked being barefoot," laughs Donnie. "He hated shoes. So when you seen him on the stage barefooted, he loved that but it wasn't none of this act stuff. My mother couldn't ever get him to wear shoes."

Ronnie's widow Judy has given the question thought and seems to have the bottom line on the matter. "He had a pin in his ankle, for a football injury at school," Judy says. "That's what kept him out of the draft, actually. I think wearing weird kinds of shoes probably irritated that. When I first met him, he would wear a white loafer type shoe, low cut. He was just comfortable without his shoes. I think he probably did it a few times and it kind of became one of those things like the gambler hat [that he always wore onstage and had made especially for him at Texas Hatters in Bud, Texas]. Then people started asking [him] so then [he] had to come up with excuses and he probably said, 'Well, I like to feel the heat, you know?', That's a great thing to say."

Maybe the bare feet were planned or maybe they weren't. Regardless, Ronnie had created a gimmick for himself and it always received notice. As with many of the things Ronnie did, his barefooted performance seemed to influence others. "Someone was telling me this new guitar whiz Johnny Lang wears no shoes now," says Judy. "He said that's why. [He said] 'the guy in Lynyrd Skynyrd said he liked to feel the heat of the stage, so that's the way I do it.' So that's cool."

The crowds erupted when Skynyrd launched into their ferocious, no-holds-barred music. The brutal musical aggression encouraged the audience to participate in the show by working themselves into a frenzy that clearly defined their reaction to the band's assault on their senses. Gender was not an issue with the audiences: males and females alike cheered, whistled, and stomped their approval. If they knew the lyrics, and more than a few did already, they sang along. If they were unfamiliar with each individual song, they were content to boogie in their seats and in the aisles. For the hour or so Skynyrd was on that stage, everyone in the audience was a rebel.

Skynyrd's undiluted musical assault, coupled with the audience's anticipation of another outrageous Who performance, occasionally created offstage chaos. The crowds drawn to these concerts were already inclined to be rowdy and certainly were not content to sit in their seats and passively watch The Who destroy the stage. It was commonplace for the audience to surge forward to get closer to the stage. Security guards were kept busy pushing back fans and trying to protect, sometimes with little result, those on stage from being assaulted by their devoted congregation.

That first night at the Cow Palace in San Francisco, The Who had a slow start. "That first gig we did, Keith Moon, the drummer, passed out on the first song," says Billy Powell. "He was doing so many drugs. They rushed him to the hospital. For thirty minutes the audience sat there waiting for something to happen. He finally came back and got back on the drums. They started playing the same song, the first song. He passed out again. He took all the drums with him. That's when he fell over them. And they took him off again." Eventually the band continued on with their set without Moon.

It didn't take long for Lynyrd Skynyrd to experience firsthand The Who's aggressive atmosphere. During the Cow Palace show, Billy Powell fell victim to an assault by both a security guard and the show's promoter. Powell had been in a hurry to get himself down in front of the stage during The Who's set so that he would be able to see the excitement up close. In his rush, Powell had failed to reveal his stage pass.

"[Legendary concert promoter] Bill Graham and [The Who's] bouncers started throwing these people over this fence that was in front of the stage," says Powell. "All these people that didn't have backstage passes hung around their necks. There was this seven-foot tall black guy throwing them over this fence. I was standing there right next to the stage, watching this happen. Then this guy comes to me, and gets ready to throw me. I went down to my knees. I had a coat on. I said, 'Hold it . . . I'm in the Skynyrd band.' I was trying to get my backstage pass out of my coat pocket, I wasn't wearing it. We were kind of getting in a fight there and I was finally back on my feet still trying to get the thing out of my pocket."

Powell wasn't fast enough. "Bill Graham came running down the stage, down this ramp from the stage and punched me in the mouth," Billy remembers. "I mean with full momentum. Knocked me about ten feet. He knocked me silly. I was bleeding everywhere, and I was about to pass out. I showed [the pass] to him, and he finally realized that [it was] people that were playing for Skynyrd he just hit." Apparently, Graham didn't realize that the kid arguing with the security guard was actually a member of the opening act. "He apologized, swear to God, ten times, sent flowers, even after the tour he sent me flowers at home, apologizing. We became real good friends after that, laughed it off and all that."

"Billy Powell was like backstage," recalled Leon Wilkeson. "And Keith Moon crashed his cymbals a couple of times and then he fell into the drum kit. He got carried off the stage. Bill Graham was all freaked out. Pandemonium broke out and they were throwing people out. I'm standing out front watching and some long-haired guy is sitting there talking me to death. I'm going, 'O.K., can I listen to The Who please?' And he's going 'Man, what happened to the Flower Power, peace, and love? Look over there, even Bill Graham. Where's all this violence coming from? Altamont . . . Rolling Stones . . . .' And I look over and Bill Graham like dove into our keyboardist, Billy. What happened was a security guy was going to throw him out and Billy was looking for his pass. He squatted down on his knees and he looked for the pass. A black guy grabbed him by his hair to pull him up and manhandle him. So Billy comes off the floor, fist cocked, punches the black security guy. Bill Graham saw it and he dove and tackled [Billy]. I go running to Billy's aid and here comes Ronnie, Gary, and we're all up there. [We] got it straightened out [when] they found out he was a performer. Then when we played the 'Whiskey A Go Go' after that, Bill Graham sent him a five-foot tall basket of apology." It was an entertaining start to Skynyrd's first major tour. Soon it would be the band itself that would be causing the same pandemonium.

Skynyrd was elated to open for one of the biggest rock-and-roll bands in the world on a national tour, and they knew that what little exposure they were given on the tour needed to showcase the best they could offer. Skynyrd was only given eight inputs into The Who's mixing board. This didn't make for a crisp, discernible sound. Ronnie was a bit worried about how the music would come across. He needn't have been. Although the band was allotted only thirty minutes to play, Skynyrd eventually delivered a set that was above reproach. "It scared us at first on our first gigs," Ronnie remembered. "We were supporting The Who and our first night we were playing too fast, the tempos were all wrong. After awhile we got to know The Who. They had a great influence on us. They're the type of people who tell you what you're doing wrong. By the end of the tour we were playing good and still getting our asses kicked by The Who."

"It went around that Skynyrd was blowing The Who off [the stage]," says Billy Powell. "At the time maybe I thought, we're blowing the doors off . . . [But] we don't use the term, 'We're going to blow these guys off the stage.'"

The experience was a unique and welcome opportunity for a fledgling band, but being thrust into the rock-and-roll arena with so major a musical force created problems for the boys from Jacksonville. "We were terrified, and were told things like no band has opened for The Who that hasn't been booed off stage," recalled Leon Wilkeson. "That's when we commenced drinking. We decided to take the bar atmosphere on stage. Had a little portable bar up there and everybody was drinking then. Problem was, we never stopped."

Once the Skynyrd boys started drinking on tour they found it difficult to control. Even in the permissive rock-and-roll environment, the boys were drinking too much. They were overwhelmed to be appearing with a band they would have paid money to see only a few months before. They didn't handle their uneasiness as well as they would have liked. Things started to happen that would have mortified them under other circumstances. Ed King remembered Roger Daltry entering Skynyrd's dressing room one night at the precise moment a bottle of beer was being hurled across the room. "The beer went all over his famous leather vest," Ed recalls. "But he was O.K. about it."

The band continued to be exposed to people and musical acts that they were both awed by and excited to know. There was a date booked to play Willie Nelson's annual picnic in Tulsa, Oklahoma. "We were supposed to be picked up by this chartered plane in San Francisco," Judy VanZant Jenness remembers. "It was supposed to go to L.A. to pick up Waylon and Willie. Everybody was real excited, including the guys in the band. And when we got there, all we picked up was Hell's Angels that were their bodyguards at that time. [Waylon and Willie] weren't even on the plane and everybody in the band was just freaking out. Ronnie told everybody not to say a word. It was the first time I've ever seen them sit so quiet from L.A. to Tulsa, Oklahoma."

The twelve-city tour had been long and sometimes difficult but definitely a positive experience for Lynyrd Skynyrd. They had survived a major rock-and-roll national tour and were inspired now to make some new music. Their next album would be titled *Second Helping* and would once again be produced by Al Kooper. With Rudge and Kooper part of their organization, the boys felt in good professional hands. They knew the kind of music they wanted to put out and knew that Kooper and Rudge could help them make a major splash. "Look out America," they seemed to be saying, "here comes Skynyrd."

6

Second Album, Second Helping

IT WAS TIME to reenter the studio in February 1974. This time the music would be recorded using the sophisticated facility of the Record Plant in Los Angeles. Not only did the Record Plant provide a relaxing environment for a recording band, but it was certainly the most happening studio at the time. There were pinball machines, comfortable sofas, everything to drink, and all kinds of food. Everything you could want. *Everything.* The down-home boys of Lynyrd Skynyrd enjoyed running into the other popular musicians who frequented the Plant, such as the Eagles and Jackson Browne. Even John Lennon dropped into Skynyrd's studio. After Lennon made an appearance one day to say hello to Al Kooper, Ronnie claimed that the band was so awed by the superstar's presence that they couldn't play for an hour. Although some of the recording was transferred back to Atlanta, the boys enjoyed the prestige that recording at the Record Plant afforded them.

After Skynyrd heard Kooper's first mix of the album, they weren't entirely satisfied, and Kooper decided to return to the mixing console to make some changes. He decided to use the facilities of Record Plant's northern California studio. Ed King accompanied Kooper as a representative of the band. By the time the work was done, everyone was happy with the album. Ronnie, Ed, Gary, and Allen had written bits and pieces of various songs while on the road. "Ronnie exposed me to country music," says King. "He could really express himself. He taught me a lot." It was time to take the songs out of their suitcases and see what they had. Some songs needed a lot of work while others already had a good start and just needed polishing.

One of the songs they were tweaking stood out in Ronnie's mind. It was a flippant little number that Ed King cowrote with Ronnie called "Sweet Home Alabama." One day Ed had heard Gary Rossington noodling a little tune. He didn't give it much thought but the notes hadn't left his mind. Ed always keeps a guitar by his bed and one night a seemingly magical guitar solo permeated his sleep. "I woke up, wrote down the music, complete with all of the guitar parts, and then played it for Ronnie," Ed remembers. Ronnie put lyrics to the music and the band completed recording the song five days later. "Ronnie would take fifteen minutes to a half hour to write his songs. He had an incredible feel for what would work and knew what he wanted to say. He was a thinking man's writer," King believes. "Sometimes [all I had to do] was say, 'this is a song about a train.'"

The inspiration for the song's lyrics stemmed from Skynyrd's time at Muscle Shoals. "Lots of people cut [Alabama] down 'cause [of] people like Wallace and the rednecks," said Allen Collins. "But we did two albums there. We thought we were going to get killed 'cause of all our long hair. But the people are really nice, everybody's smiling, and the country is real pretty. So we wrote a song about it."

"They'd written 'Sweet Home Alabama' and started playing it," remembers Rodney Mills. "People were saying, you know, you guys need to record that song and get it out. So Al brought them in the studio and in one night's time, I think, we recorded everything on that song except for the background vocals. I engineered. We did the whole thing in one night's time, lead vocals and everything."

Mills was impressed by the way the recording came together so quickly. "All of us thought it was something pretty special," he recalls. "Ed had a lot to do with that. Ed was the cowriter of the song, plus Ed played most all the guitar parts on the song. Ed was a pretty spiritual guy. The main guitar solo on that was a first take all the way through by Ed. I can remember the amplifier he did it in. It was a Fender Twin, and he did the solo. I don't know how many people in the band were in the control room when he did the solo; everybody was just jumping up and down. They thought it was great. Al Kooper wanted him to do it again, and the whole band just kind of said, 'What are you talking about?' I think we may have recorded another solo, but I think we kept the very first one. I think that was the one that Al used on the record."

Kooper remarked that the solo was played in the key of G, but that the song was in the key of D. No change was made as the band liked Ed's original vision of the music. Kooper remembers it sounding a bit like John Coltrane in the middle of a country groove, but it grew on him. Ironically, future Skynyrd guitarist Steve Gaines couldn't play it as Ed did, and the version that is now performed in concert is played the way Al Kooper thought it should be played. It was Kooper's decision to leave on the record Ronnie saying "turn it up," as he requested more headphone volume. To this day that request is chanted by Skynyrd's audience when the song is performed in concert.

Bobby Keys provided a horn overlay and Kooper and the band thought the song could be enhanced by using female backup vocalists. The convivial vocals of Merry Clayton and Clydie King of the Sweet Inspirations were added to the track while Kooper was in L.A. on other business. Kooper surprised the band with the background vocals. Ronnie and the band liked the sound so much that they later added a trio of female singers they called the Honkettes for their live performances. While the band was initially resistant to Kooper adding horns to various tracks, horns were also later added to the touring ensemble. Kooper was pleased with the end result. Ronnie believed that the song was good and would make a welcome addition to the album.

"When I was recruited by Skynyrd," Leon Wilkeson mused, "the first song we recorded was 'Sweet Home Alabama.' When everybody went and bought *Second Helping*, then they went and bought the first [album]. They discovered 'Freebird' and the rest is history."

It was decided that the song "Don't Ask Me No Questions," an in-your-face VanZant statement on leisure time, would be the first single to be released. The record died a very quick death. Despite an industry ad campaign, the band wasn't well known enough to release anything other than an A single. The radio programmers had listened to Skynyrd's debut album. While the MCA promotion department was busy trying to get airplay for "Questions," the radio people were asking when "Alabama" was going to be available to them as a single. The market was ready and waiting. It was time for Lynyrd Skynyrd's first major single release: "Sweet Home Alabama."

The band was back on the road as soon as they finished recording and the album was released soon after. "Sweet Home Alabama" received significant notice when it was played in concert and when radio programmers pulled the track off the album to play for their listeners. Lynyrd Skynyrd had a hit on their hands. "Sweet Home Alabama" was pressed and released as a single.

"Alabama" became a monster hit when it was played in the South. "The single just sort of happened," said Ronnie VanZant. "But we're glad we did it. Al Kooper wanted another song at first, but this one just got out."

The presentation of the song in concert was accompanied by the unfurling of Skynyrd's traditional backdrop, a huge Confederate battle flag. The reaction of the audience was always the same: vigorous, fervent, and instantaneous. Neil Young's song "Southern Man" had offended many Southerners by seeming to accuse *all* people born in the South of being intolerant racists. Young's observations were obviously generalized and not accurate and Southerners were ecstatic when Skynyrd defended their honor by releasing "Sweet Home Alabama" with its direct references to Young's faux pas. The idea that the Southern man, or woman, didn't need Neil Young around to point out the problems of their society was overwhelmingly supported by Skynyrd fans.

"We thought Neil was shooting all the ducks in order to kill one or two," Ronnie told *Rolling Stone* regarding the creation of the answer song. The band felt that Young's lyrical content was representative of the shortsighted "Yankee" belief that all Southern men should be held accountable for the verbalizations and actions of a racist minority.

While the rebuttal was heartfelt, Skynyrd held Neil Young in high regard for his musical achievements and they weren't intending to start a feud of any kind. "Neil is amazing, wonderful . . . a superstar," said VanZant. "I showed the verse to Ed [King] and asked him what Neil might think. Ed said he'd dig it; he'd be laughing at it." Ed King says that the tune was not so much a direct attack on Young but just a good regional song.

The song was well received but immediately put a stigma on the band as rednecks. Whether true or not, it was not a tag they particularly liked. "['Alabama'] was put out as a last-minute thing," Ronnie told writer Susan Joseph. "It wasn't expected to do as good as it did. It was a joke song. It hit Top 10 and we've been paying for it ever since." Al Kooper added, "Hey, you have to be more careful when you write a song now. But I'll tell you something—Neil Young loved it. That's true, he told me so to my face."

Radio programmers in general liked "Alabama." The song charted at #8 on the Billboard Singles chart when it was quickly released to generate additional interest in the new album. "It's been paying the rent for twenty-seven years," says Ed King. Industry insiders began to sit up and take a second look at the band from the South. Lynyrd Skynyrd was starting to receive major notice, both inside the music business and from those who listened to music for entertainment.

Ironically, a lot of the attention was from Skynyrd's own hometown, which in the past had not made a big deal of Lynyrd Skynyrd. "[When] 'Sweet Home Alabama' became a hit *then* Jacksonville decided to claim us," Leon Wilkeson laughed. "We didn't get a whole lot of home-town support [before that]."

The album *Second Helping*, released in April 1974, offered thanks to Toby, Cockroach, Moochie, Punnel, Wolfman, Kooder, Mr. Feedback, and Gooshie. Fans would wonder who these oddly named characters were. The nicknames were just the Skynyrd boys having fun. Some of the nicknames are long forgotten, but it has been determined that Toby was Allen Collins, Cockroach was Gary Rossington, Moochie was Dean Kilpatrick, Punnel was Billy Powell, Wolfman was likely Bob Burns, Kooder was Al Kooper, Mr. Feedback was Kevin Elson, and Gooshie was roadie Joe Barnes. The name Wicker was reserved for Ronnie VanZant. Ed King says he used to know the origins of the nicknames but doesn't remember them now. As to Wicker, King says, "I think it was the name of a gay guy in a movie they all saw once." The

Woton and Odin mentioned in the credits were the sun gods involved in the pinball game "Fireball," which resided in the recording studio's playroom.

In the summer of 1974, soon after the release of "Alabama," Skynyrd hit the road supporting The Marshall Tucker Band. "The first time I ever met Ronnie was at a club down in Jacksonville," remembers Tucker's singer Doug Gray. "They come up through here [South Carolina] and did some shows with us. That was right at the very beginning. This was before their record was coming out. [Then] Ronnie and I was in this head shop in L.A. We were standing there and all of a sudden on the rock station their song played ['Sweet Home Alabama']. I said, 'Well, I guess that's it for y'all opening the show.' That's what happened at that point in time. Their stuff just took off."

The tour was not only successful, it was enjoyable. The band was having so much fun playing that their exuberance was returned ten-fold by their audiences. "My friend Gary and I arrived at the Memorial Auditorium [in Sacramento, California], just as Skynyrd, the bottom-billed band at a concert featuring Marshall Tucker and Elvin Bishop, were starting their set," remembers fan Rick Thomsen. "We opened the doors to the auditorium and were met with a sonic blast of "I Ain't the One." I remember it being so loud that it just knocked us over. I had seen a lot of concerts that were also very loud but the difference with Skynyrd was that it was crystal clear, not distorted like so many concerts were around that time. You could hear every individual note that the three guitarists were playing. Lynyrd Skynyrd ripped through all of their hits like 'Three Steps,' 'Breeze,' and 'Sweet Home Alabama' with fierce precision and authority. One highlight that I remember is when they played 'Crossroads' by Cream. Ronnie explained that they were big Cream fans and it showed in their enthusiastic version. Of course, Gary and I were completely blown away by 'Freebird.'" Johnny Van-Zant laughs at the thought of Skynyrd music being perceived as earsplitting. "It gets pretty loud," he says.

"Crossroads" was not only a tribute to the band Cream, but to guitarist Eric Clapton. While Clapton's style wasn't directly reflected in the playing of Skynyrd's three guitarists, his intensity was. It seemed there wasn't a guitar player around during that time period who wasn't in complete awe of the British musician. "We once collected Coke and soda bottles for weeks to save enough money to see this man," said Ronnie VanZant. "To us he is God."

"Crossroads" would be well received up alongside Clapton, when Skynyrd later opened for the revered guitarist in Memphis. It had been hoped that the English blues guitarist would be well supported by the Southern band and that Skynyrd would bring in people to see Clapton who might otherwise skip the concert. The promoters made a wise decision by having Skynyrd open and once again Skynyrd ate 'em up alive.

The boys were enjoying the tour. It wasn't all wine and roses, though. Ed King remembers just one of the incidents which occurred as the band traveled in close quarters: "We had just finished recording *Second Helping* in L.A. It was late February 1974. We rented an Econoline van and were driving through New Mexico on our way to Texas in the middle of the night. It was *cold* outside . . . and wasn't so warm inside either. Then someone woke up and asked, 'What's that smell?' (No, this isn't the inspiration for the song.) In two minutes the rest of us were awake and gagging. Our driver pulled off to the side of the road so that we could get rid of the pillowcase in which Leon had just taken a shit. Why'd he do it? 'I didn't want to stop the van and wake everybody up.'"

Meanwhile, back in the "real" world, having already realized that Lynyrd Skynyrd was a loose cannon from which anything could discharge, there were some in the rock press who were watchful of Skynyrd's new album *Second Helping. Rolling Stone* claimed that "the group is frequently compared to The Allman Brothers but it lacks that band's sophistication and professionalism. If a song doesn't feel right to the Brothers they work it out until it does. If it isn't right to Lynyrd Skynyrd they are more likely to crank up their amps and blast their way through the bottleneck. . . . *Second Helping* is distinguished from their debut album only by a certain mellowing out that indicates they may eventually acquire a level of savoir faire to realize their many capabilities."

Revered music critic Robert Cristgau thought *Second Helping* was a worthy follow-up to Skynyrd's first album. He wrote in his 1981 *Cristgau's Record Guide*: "Any suspicions that the substantial, tasteful band blew their best stuff on the first platter should fall in the wake of the first song ever to make Top Ten ('Sweet Home Alabama'), which will expose you to their infectious put-downs of rock businessmen, rock journalists, and heroin."

Some critics liked the album very much while others felt that it lacked the promise of *Pronounced.* Regardless of how *Second Helping* compared to anything that Skynyrd had done in the recent past, there was still a great deal of interest from the rock press as to what Skynyrd would do in the future, both on vinyl and in concert. The initial record-buying fans, however, seemed well pleased with the band's follow-up effort. *Second Helping* eventually charted at #12 on the Billboard Album Chart.

While the musical content wasn't as awe-inspiring as the first time out, there were a handful of important songs on the album. One of these was a soulful ballad titled "Curtis Lowe."

"Here's typical Ronnie's sense of humor," said Leon. "Curtis Lowe was a Black man. But look at the last name, Lowe. That's a Jewish name. That's Ronnie's sense of humor. Curtis Lowe was really Shorty Medlocke, [a guy named] Bob Warmer, and somebody else . . . three people, from what I understood. And a Black man that used to play around the neighborhood. Gene [Odom] told me that 'Curtis Lowe' was written about him and Ronnie collecting soda bottles to go to Carleton Warmer's midway [gatherings] to play dobro."

Others say that the name Curtis Lowe was Ed King's idea. It seems King thought it would be amusing to conjure up an old Black bluesman named after the Jewish theatre chain, Lowe's Theaters. The corner store mentioned in the song was based on Claude's Midway Grocery, which was on the corner of Lakeshore and Plymouth in Jacksonville.

Exactly who the song was based on is unclear. Several of those in the band support the following premise: "The song 'Curtis Lowe' was really based upon my dad," says Rickey Medlocke. "They didn't want to say actually Shorty Medlocke 'cause he'd probably get hassled by people. My father Shorty was probably the biggest, major influence on my life. Not only was he a parent, but he was my real buddy, a real best friend, and mentor. I looked up to him so much as far as a musician goes. As it would happen, the guys from Lynyrd Skynyrd, Ronnie and Gary and Allen, would come over to my house the first time I was in the band and sit with my dad and listen to him play Black music, the blues and stuff. Later on they dedicated a record and a song called 'Made in the Shade,' [which would be included later on [*Nuthin' Fancy*] and then 'Curtis Lowe.' So he was a big influence on myself and other people. To this day, he's still with me in spirit." Celebrated as the fictional Curtis Lowe, Shorty Medlocke's influence, not only on his son, but on Ronnie VanZant, was very evident.

"Workin' for MCA" was a sarcastic albeit direct tune that was written by Ronnie and Ed King for Skynyrd to present to the record label during a showcase at a Sounds of the South press party held at Richard's in Atlanta on July 29, 1973. Its impudent references, about making sure that the band was paid what it was due from the Yankee slickers, were just impertinent enough to get the attention of those in charge. The label execs loved it and decided that they were going to keep their eye on Lynyrd Skynyrd.

Ronnie very succinctly sent a message to his friends and fans about how he wanted to be treated when he was off the road in "Don't Ask Me No Questions." "When [Ronnie] was coming into town, he'd call me and tell me they were coming into town and he wanted to play baseball," remembers Charlie Faubion. "They loved baseball. What they enjoyed is what he wrote in one of his songs, about his business. 'Don't ask me about my business tonight.' When he came into town, he just wanted to get away from it all. He wanted to be around people that wouldn't interrogate him, like the song says. He wanted to share the success, but he didn't want somebody probing the success and trying to find out every little detail."

Although "Questions" had a tongue-in-cheek seriousness, Ronnie turned quite earnest with the self-descriptive "The Needle and the Spoon." VanZant obviously wanted to convey that while he was known to overindulge in liquid entertainment, he took little truck with heavy drug abuse. Then it was Southern boogie with the romping "Swamp Music," and songwriter-blues guitarist J J Cale's "Call Me the Breeze," a song that would be well received in concert. As usual, there was something on the album for all tastes.

MCA was so supportive of Kooper's efforts to break the band that the director of special projects, Dick Williams, and regional promotion man, Jon Scott, engineered a live Lynyrd Skynyrd showcase on WMC-FM out of Memphis. WMC's powerful signal sent the show out over most of the Southern states. The band played several songs from *Pronounced*, as well as "Sweet Home Alabama." Also included was a song Ronnie wrote with Leon Wilkeson, "Woman of Mine." The event was a bona fide hit. The boys were so delighted that they decided to visit Graceland and pay their respects to Elvis. They even wrote a song titled "Memphis."

The band was overwhelmed with the reception they received both on the radio and when they took the stage. The attention and glorification were not easy to adjust to. The boys were, however, comfortable with the knowledge that whatever success they experienced was based on their commitment to being themselves. Good, bad, or indifferent, what you saw was definitely what you were going to get. Lynyrd Skynyrd in no way was a manufactured band, like so many others in 1970s rock. Skynyrd played to their roots. They were proud to represent their homeland and the sincerity and integrity they believed it to possess. The songs they played represented commitment to ethical living and the honor found in a deep commitment to family. If there were references to drinking and rambunctious behavior, well, that was a part of the redneck's parcel as well. Lynyrd Skynyrd would never mislead the public, no matter how many records they might be able to sell. They were selling records successfully just by being themselves.

Sometimes the rowdiness portrayed in their songs was acted out in the band's personal lives as well. While playing the Louisville Convention Center on September 30, 1974, a scuffle broke out among their roadies. Tycobrahe Sound representatives accused the band of throwing microphones into the audience as well as kicking monitors and speakers offstage. It was related by the sound company that one of Tycobrahe's employees was attacked when he attempted to talk to Skynyrd's roadies about the situation. A fight ensued, with one of Skynyrd's roadies receiving a broken jaw. Skynyrd saw it differently. *They* said that the employee turned off the sound and attacked the roadies when he was asked to leave the stage.

Several stories were told by crew members of face-offs with roadies from other, non-Southern bands. Oftentimes the Skynyrd road crew felt, as did the band, that they had to prove themselves as professionals. Ironically, this sometimes manifested itself in short tempers and ready fists. On more than one occasion Skynyrd's roadies, often with the physical support of one or more members of the band, found themselves in a brouhaha.

Lynyrd Skynyrd's tour of the United States in support of *Second Helping* had been solidly sold out when additional dates were added in Europe in support of Queen, Humble Pie, and Golden Earring. The boys from Jacksonville couldn't believe that they were actually outside the United States, playing to international audiences. The first tour outside of the U.S. would be brief but Skynyrd intended to make their mark on all who came into contact with them. During their first visit to England, in late December 1974, the band played to a full house at London's Rainbow Club.

In England, Ronnie was compared to a barefooted Paul Kossoff, and he undoubtedly enjoyed the comparison to the Free guitarist. He worshipped Free. Such compliments did not fall on deaf ears. Ronnie prided himself on his songs and delivery and was anxious to make a name for himself. Yet when he talked to representatives of the British press he seemed exhausted

Immersed in the music: Allen Collins (left) and Ronnie VanZant.

and was most often interviewed drinking from a nearby bottle of whiskey. An appearance at the Oxford New Theatre had to be canceled when Ronnie's throat was just too sore for him to sing. The band didn't seem to notice the toll that the hard living was taking on their singer. They plugged away, playing louder and harder than ever.

A review from Skynyrd's stint at the Rainbow in December 1974 shows that the band felt no intimidation on British stages. *Sounds*' Pete Makowski wrote, "They plugged in and immediately tore into 'Workin' for MCA,' which has opened the set for all their British concerts. The guitars gelled immediately, swirling and twisting in unison, while VanZant spat out the vocal lines venomously. The group's strength lies in their tightness and songwriting expertise."

The tour proved to be an eventful one for Skynyrd. When they played Glasgow, the crowd seemed more interested in hearing more from Skynyrd than from headliner Golden Earring. "To the strains of 'Dixie' and dwarfed by a huge Confederate flag hanging over the stage, six-piece

Skynyrd ambled on looking like they'd just walked off the farm, natural as you like," wrote Billy Walker in *Sounds* magazine. "Vocalist Ronnie VanZant looked from the circle like a heavyweight Paul Kossoff, barefooted but ready to party."

The PA was faulty and the monitors failed to work at all, but nothing stopped the band from delivering the goods. Walker wrote, "VanZant kept on the move tracing a line from his front mic position back to keyboard man Billy Powell, while the twin leads of Allen and Gary sat the Apollo audience firmly on their arses—Skynyrd are here, LISTEN. . . . VanZant showed just how good a vocalist he is. Everyone suffered from the dead monitors, but the band's class compensated and the crowd appreciated it. One of the band's secrets is to get their audience up and keep them there—no lulls or dead spots. Skynyrd work from start to finish on high energy."

After Scotland, the band went on to play in front of a group of American GIs, among others, in Frankfurt, Germany. Something happened at this particular concert that made the boys somewhat homesick. "We carried our Confederate flag with us and played 'Dixie,'" said Ronnie. "As soon as the flag fell open, we saw a bunch of guys stand up and salute and we thought, 'Hell, they're for sure Rebs!'"

They had been scheduled for a return trip to London's Rainbow to open for Golden Earring, but when the promoter heard the band and saw what they could do he put them at the top of the bill. *Sounds* magazine easily saw the reasoning behind the switch: "Supporting ain't their style, they're too damn good for it." There's a certain edge that comes with opening for acts that aren't as dynamic. "We're all just underdogs," said Leon Wilkeson. "But we like it that way. I always root for the underdog."

The band liked the warmth of their new international fan base. "It was real fine," said Allen Collins. "It's very much like the South over there. The people seem much closer together, [they] care for each other much more than they do on the West Coast or in New York."

In mid-November they had been forced to cancel their appearance at the Oxford New Theatre due to Ronnie's minor throat infection. An additional show at London's Rainbow was booked in December, which they were again invited to headline due to the tremendous reception they had received opening for Golden Earring.

Charles Charlesworth wrote in *Melody Maker*, "It was a master plan that worked: everyone who went to the Rainbow on Thursday evening went home well satisfied." The rest of the month Skynyrd played Frankfurt and Hamburg opening for Queen; and Brussels, Breda, and Paris opening for Humble Pie.

Pete Makowski interviewed Ronnie VanZant for a profile in *Sounds* that November. He mentioned that VanZant looked disheveled and tired and pointed out to his readers that Ronnie drank quite a bit of whiskey over the course of the interview. When Makowski mentioned to VanZant that Al Kooper had told him that Skynyrd was the American answer to The Rolling Stones, Ronnie replied, "If we were a pimple on The Rolling Stones ass I'd be happy."

Ronnie's singular persona as a rebel country boy was established early on. Ronnie's bare feet and, ironically, the band's battle flag set an immediate congenial mood. Tattoos were prevalent with all members of the band. Ronnie had two: an eagle with wings spread over an American flag and a scroll with his father's name, Lacy. The boys wore their hair long, talked with drawls, and brought new definition to the word "redneck." They were proud of who they were and were especially proud of their music. The audiences ate it up.

While Skynyrd seemed to be having a great deal of fun onstage, there was a dark side that soon began to rear its ugly head. Back home in Jacksonville, Skynyrd's reputation for drinking and brawling had been grudgingly accepted. Yet now, their newfound success seemed to accelerate their bad behavior. The excesses they had enjoyed as wild young men in Jacksonville became more acute as they became rock stars on a rampage. They felt that they had to live up to their image as good ole boys who poured whiskey down their throats and counted the days before they could be involved in a lusty bar fight. Their raunchy ways may have been good press, but it soon became a personal problem for the boys in the band. They were frequently arrested for brawling and many times sported broken bones encased in a variety of casts and slings. Although Ronnie could be depended on when it came to the musical professionalism of the band, he picked fights at the drop of a hat when he had been drinking. "He was a ruffian, but what a great writer," says Dru Lombar. "Some great songs."

"When he got drunk," claims Billy Powell, "he was definitely in the Dr. Jekyll and Mr. Hyde syndrome. He knocked my teeth out twice . . . a four-piece bridge the first time." The cause of the fight was alleged to have been because Billy was "bugging" Ronnie. The second time that happened, Billy needed a six-piece bridge and decided Ronnie should pay for it. Ronnie laughed the incident off. "It got infected and my jaw swelled out like I had a big softball," says Billy. "I could barely talk. I went to his apartment . . . back then we all had apartments, no houses . . . and he opened the door. I knocked on his door real hard. He opened the door and I went, 'Wemlidl . . . motherfucker dldi dlld . . . you're gonna pay for the dentist bill.' He laughed his butt off. Filled out the check for whatever I told him and laughed the whole time. I just turned around and walked off. And he's going, 'I'm sorry Billy. Here's the check, man.' And he's laughing the whole dadgum time. He thought it was really funny. [But] when he was straight, he was just an all-around good guy. He was really a Southern gentleman. He really was, and that's what I hope everybody remembers him for."

Ronnie wasn't the only one in the band who drank. Not by any means. Gary Rossington told reporter Jim Esposito that the band used to drink six fifths of Chivas a night. "We used to drink 'em all," he said. "It was like water to us. Then we started getting the shakes and playing so bad we quit drinking. Now we just drink moderate and have a few to calm down." Skynyrd's idea of moderate was quite a bit different from everybody else's.

Ronnie wasn't the only one in the band who fought. He was probably the major catalyst but the others had their fair share of touchy moments too. They thought nothing of duking it out, no matter where they were, even on airplanes. Still, when all was said and done, Lynyrd Skynyrd was one big, if dysfunctional, family. "Yesterday we had a fight but we have a fight, and then it's over with," Ronnie told *Hit Parader* magazine. "I mean, we're all brothers, but it's a way to let off steam, and we love each other and there are no hard feelings about it."

The sudden, dramatic realization of the American dream seemed too much for the band to comprehend, let alone approach with a certain maturity they had yet to attain. They quickly descended headfirst into the world of rock-and-roll dissipation. The toll of the endless flood of groupies, too much champagne and Jack Daniels, and very little sleep soon had the members of the band constantly at odds with one another. Their fistfights became instant fodder for the rock press, especially since the bandaged hands, busted teeth, and broken noses and arms of virtuoso guitar and keyboard players were difficult to hide. Some of the people who worked with them thought that since the band was trying to do exactly what it should have been doing musically, the fights were frustration-fueled. Nonetheless, regular physical confrontation became standard rather than an aberration. "We made The Who look like church boys on Sunday," said Ronnie. "We done things only fools do."

The boys didn't waste any time purchasing custom cars and were even quicker running them into ditches and trees. Although Ronnie was into alcohol, most of the band members found drugs to be a welcome departure from the whiskey rampages, and indulged often. This was, after all, the era of cocaine, and Skynyrd partook frequently and in great quantities. "There's a wild bunch," laughs Dru Lombar. "They were the wild cards of Southern rock. They were getting in trouble a whole lot more than the rest of us were, you know. They were just guys from the west side. Not poor or poverty-stricken, but I mean they weren't rich or nothing. They never had anything and all of a sudden they had everything. And I think it was overwhelming to 'em and it made 'em crazy, that's what I think."

Following in the rock-and-roll tradition, their homes away from homes were not immune to the destruction. "We used to mangle hotel rooms," remembers Billy Powell. "Ronnie'd come in [to the hotel room] and take Jack Daniels and just pour it down the back of the TV. I remember one time the TV blew up and caught on fire, and we threw it out the window into the swimming pool."

Reporter Scott Cohen summed up the Skynyrd road experience nicely when he said that while the Holiday Inns loved Lynyrd Skynyrd because they threw a lot of money around, the Holiday Inns also hated them because of the damage they did. Ronnie described the band's relationships with hotels when he told Cohen, "We get really hyped up before we go on and when we do a show, sometimes we don't let all the steam off and when we come back we raise hell. The next day it begins all over again, from hotel to hotel. We're a bunch of hyperactive people gettin' on with it. If we didn't let it all off at the gig, we're gonna make the hotel a wreck. We usually wind up getting thrown out owin' money. In Atlanta we got to split up, one person registerin' here, another there. It's the only way."

Sometimes, however, the band felt that they were being singled out because of their reputation. Gary Rossington reported that once one of their roadies got into a physical altercation in the company of the crew from Bad Company. The next day's report mentioned Lynyrd Skynyrd but not Bad Company.

Yet despite all the inner turmoil, the band somehow was still able to put on a great show, and Skynyrd bowed to no one once they were on stage. "Even Eric Clapton didn't intimidate them," remembers Judy VanZant Jenness, referring to a night when Skynyrd opened for Clapton in Memphis. Skynyrd was on the road to play and believed zealously in their music. They knew that no band was better when it came to doing what they did. They felt that they had earned every bit of their success by simply playing their music. Allen Collins told *Creem* magazine, "We're trying to get people off, just trying to be good." They didn't feel that they had to apologize to anyone for any behavior in their personal lives.

Ronnie VanZant was an active participant in most of the offstage debauchery, yet he continued to nurture the band that was now his dream come true. "Ronnie was a great leader of a great band," says Outlaws guitarist Hughie Thomasson. "He took his music very seriously and made sure the rest of the band did too. He was a good teacher. We [fellow musicians] learned a lot of respect for the music and carry it to this day. If you're there for any other reason than playing music, then you're bogus. If you're there because of the money, or the superstar status, or any of that stuff, that meant nothing to Ronnie. It was about the music."

When he was sober, Ronnie tried to encourage the others to focus on the music when it was "focus-on-the-music" time. "All of the Skynyrd stuff that was done prior to his death, you hear Ronnie all over that stuff, writing it, singing it," says Charlie Daniels. "He was a ramrod in the band. And kind of a spark plug. He was just the personification of what Lynyrd Skynyrd was all about."

The band may have tasted success abroad but their hearts remained in their beloved South. "Now [Ronnie] used to call me the King of Dixie," laughs Charlie Daniels. "I was in, I think it was Utica, New York . . . it was my birthday. This is years and years ago. I was in the bar or a restaurant or something and somebody came in and said, 'You have a call from Europe.' I said, 'Who the heck is calling me . . . .' I went to the phone, and it was Ronnie. I thought he called to wish me a happy birthday. But I don't think he knew it was my birthday, maybe . . . I don't know. He said, 'How you doing?' I said, 'Fine.' He said, 'Charlie, I want to ask you something. You know that big Dixie flag that we carry on the stage with us?' I said, 'Yeah.' He said, 'Well, last night it fell on the floor and we took it out in the alley and burned it. Do you think it'd be all right if we went onstage without that flag? You're the King of Dixie, tell me.' And I said, 'Well, yeah, Ronnie. It's all right with me.'"

It is interesting to note that Ronnie and the rest of the band had such a high level of respect for the Confederate flag that they would burn it if it touched the ground. Their family and friends would say that the band used the Confederate flag because they were proud of their heritage. Ronnie's father Lacy believed that his son was devoted to the South. "He loved the fact that he was from Dixie," Lacy wrote. "Every song he wrote and lyric he sang told the story of growing up in the South. He spoke like a true rebel. The word 'door' was pronounced 'doah,' a 'floor' was pronounced 'floah,' the word 'more' was drawled out to sound like 'moah.' And the more fun poked at Ronnie about his Southern accent, the thicker the drawl rolled from his lips."

Gary Rossington said that the band decided to get a big flag to put behind them on the stage when they noticed the flags waved by their audience. They were from the South. No big deal. It wasn't meant as any kind of a political statement. According to Rossington, it was the band that decided to use the flag as a promotional tool.

Yet Ronnie told Nat Freedland of *Billboard*: "That was strictly an MCA gimmick to start us off with some identity label. It was useful at first but by now it's embarrassing—except over in Europe where they really like all that stuff because they think it's macho American." As with his later comments about George Wallace, VanZant seemed to be riding both sides of the fence when talking to the "serious" music press.

The image of racists and rednecks was not one Lynyrd Skynyrd was promoting. All of the band members claimed that they were not racists. Lynyrd Skynyrd would redefine the term "redneck"—at the time rednecks wore crew cuts and disapproved of "longhairs." Many of the fistfights the band participated in were sparked by rude comments about their hair from rednecks they met along the road. Of course there are many who would say that, crew cuts aside, the Southern redneck was simply a man who was a blue-collar worker, drove a pickup truck, watched football, went to church on Sundays, and loved his family. This definition wasn't far from the image that Lynyrd Skynyrd fostered. Even though the general definition of redneck, sans the racist views and crewcuts, fit the band, Ronnie felt that it was an image that the media had foisted on them. He complained that they were either treated like "children" or a "bunch of rowdy drunks." He said the band had been accused of being rednecks in disguise, having grown their hair long to cover up their inner essence.

Still, the boys of Lynyrd Skynyrd enjoyed many of the down-home rituals that they had grown up with. Birthdays were usually special events for those associated with the band. Stella Powell remembered one of Ronnie's birthday parties right after she and Billy started dating. As soon as the birthday cake was brought out, Allen Collins reached into its middle and smeared the birthday boy's face with cake and frosting. Ronnie responded by emptying a bottle of champagne on Billy's head. By the end of the party there was cake and champagne all over the room. Just another birthday celebration with Skynyrd. . . .

It wasn't unusual for Allen Collins to "start something." He could be counted on to be the life of any party. Allen was basically a kid at heart. He was known for his honesty and open attitude

Allen Collins, the party animal.

towards life. He loved experiencing new things, and with Skynyrd's new celebrity, he went for the gusto. Allen drank too much, partied too much, and was most often a ringleader when something crazy was going on. Allen Collins loved life and his recent ascent into a lifestyle where there was so much to experience with very little responsibility fit him like a glove. Allen was everybody's favorite party animal.

Skynyrd returned to the United States to play almost nonstop from February through late December 1974. They appeared in nearly every state, traveling by chartered bus. The itinerary was brutal. More than ever the band members got on each other's nerves as they all struggled to make the best of each appearance. The crew ceremoniously christened the outing "The Torture Tour." "That was probably the hardest tour we ever did," says Billy Powell. "Just going, going, going. It *was* a torture tour. We just never knew we were going to be working that hard. I don't think we've worked that hard since, either. That went on so long that we started getting at each others' throats, and we fought amongst each other. Nobody ever does that anymore, ever, but back then we sure did. It was just a grueling, grueling tour."

Not every show was a success. Ed King remembers some of the low points of the tour, especially one night when they opened for Black Sabbath. "It was at Nassau Coliseum," he told *Circus,* "and we weren't getting much of a reception. These people were there to hear Sabbath and couldn't get into our music at all. But all of a sudden the crowd goes wild. I thought, hell, we finally got 'em, they're really going crazy, and for some reason I turned around and saw this huge cross all lit up with the words Black Sabbath in fire. I really wanted to quit the show."

Leon Wilkeson wasn't intimidated. He was wearing a holster with a real gun on stage. When the hoopla started, he drew the gun and shot a blank over his head. The frenetic Ozzy freaks backed off.

Everyone was on edge and the constant infighting and the dementia of being on the road week after week caused Ed King and Bob Burns to have second thoughts about continuing with the tour. They finally decided that Lynyrd Skynyrd was going to have to go on without them.

Bob Burns was engaged at the time and his fiancée was pregnant with his child. The others claimed that he had started acting weird. There was a lot of pressure on the young man and it became increasingly difficult to put up with all of the bullshit that was happening within Lynyrd Skynyrd. Burns later claimed, "I just had to leave for my own sake. The touring, the recording, the constant motion was too much. I'm very proud of my contributions though, even today, when I listen to the radio and hear me, I can hardly believe it."

Although the parting would not be entirely amicable, the others had to understand. King and Burns felt they were fighting for their mental and physical health. To stay might cause them irreparable damage. Ronnie himself would voice support for the decision. "When a guy splits a band, people assume there were some heavy vibes," he told writer Andy McConnell. "There was nothing like that with Ed. He just couldn't take the road, whereas most of us thrive on it. We're on the road all the time and Ed just couldn't take it. We really miss him, especially in the studio where he'd always come up with something."

Ed says that it wasn't just a matter of being tired of the road. The tour had been grueling and *everybody* was exhausted. But there comes a final straw. Things came to a head on May 26. "About two weeks before I left," remembers Ed, "Ronnie came to me and said, 'You take charge for awhile. Cancel everything if you think it's right . . . I'm burnt out. We're all burnt out.' So . . . after seeing Gary and Allen moaning mid-tour (in Springfield, Illinois) about going home (with Allen in tears, I might add), I called the manager and said we needed to take some time off. Shortly thereafter, the manager, Rudge, flew out to meet with us. And days later in Phoenix, Ronnie was overheard at the bar saying that I had to go. And then a few days later in Pittsburgh, me and Ronnie got into a real heated argument in the limo on the way back to the hotel after the show. I had broken two strings during 'Freebird' that night because my guitar tech had been thrown in jail in Ann Arbor the night before *with* Ronnie, and both were late getting to the show in Pittsburgh that night. I had to play on old strings. The argument got so bad the limo driver pulled over and got out of the car for a while. That night I packed up and left. I had *had* it."

There have been varying reports about the animosity involved in the parting. Ronnie had told some reporters that there were no hard feelings but others said he was no fan of King's at that time. King himself says that Ronnie told Leon Wilkeson to tear apart King's Fender Jazz Bass at the end of 'Freebird' during one of the shows a few months after King left, after King let Wilkeson use the guitar. King said he was eventually asked back into the Skynyrd fold by Gary Rossington and Al Kooper, but an invite from Ronnie never came.

In the midst of all the internal turmoil, it was important to the band that the music continued to be above reproach. Skynyrd's devotion to their music made the demands on them even harder to bear. "It was typical management attitude," remembered Leon Wilkeson. "When you're hot, run 'em, run 'em like slaves, man. All the travel . . . I especially felt for Ronnie, the vocalist, you know? How he was able to stand that strain? I mean, you can't go to a music store and buy a new throat, you know what I mean?" Regardless, Ronnie was a professional and the thought of turning tail and running from the road probably never crossed his mind. "But it was worth it, I guess," laughed Leon.

Lynyrd Skynyrd had now become famous internationally as much for its offstage hedonistic lifestyle as for its strident, down-home raunchy rock-and-roll. All things considered, the tour was musically successful. *Record World* reviewed the band's New York City show at Avery Fisher Hall as a "power-packed, albeit short, set of some of the finest rock and blues to come across the Mason-Dixon line since The Allman Brothers took the big plunge and headed up to Yankee territory."

Skynyrd continued to proudly display their Southern roots regardless of where they played. Their music, born and bred in Dixie, had an international appeal. It was good rock-and-roll, plain and simple. In its April 25, 1975, issue, *Performance* magazine's Michael Point wrote, "Their rock and roll, with punchy, three-guitar licks and Ronnie VanZant's strong and surly vocals, makes Skynyrd probably the only Southern band capable of retaining the interest of say, a New Yorker strong on Bad Company."

Their logo served to spice up the bad-boy image even further. The banner used was the skull wearing a Stetson hat, a Confederate neckerchief, Harley glasses, and smoking a cigar. The logo was designed by George Osaki, a photographer and graphic artist, and would appear all over the place in conjunction with Skynyrd advertising and promotion.

In May, Ronnie told Andy McConnell of *Sounds* magazine that there had been some changes. He was off hard liquor and only drank wine. He told the reporter that he had bet $4,000 with various members of the band and crew that he wouldn't drink hard alcohol. It wasn't a problem for him to start drinking wine instead. He had no intention of paying off.

Judy and Ronnie had moved into an apartment complex on the Cedar River in suburban Jacksonville before the tour. Shortly after moving in, they were joined by Ed King, who took an apartment right below theirs. Soon Skynyrd roadie Craig Reed found himself living in the complex as well.

Even while they focused on expanding their audience to non-Southerners, the band could not distance themselves too far from their roots. In the spring of 1975, the members of Lynyrd Skynyrd were declared honorary lieutenant colonels in the Alabama state militia. The honor was bestowed by someone about whom they had sung in "Sweet Home Alabama": "In Birmingham they love the governor, boo, boo, boo"—Governor George Wallace. There was speculation that Skynyrd might do some kind of benefit for the controversial governor, and a brief public debate ensued. Did the members of Lynyrd Skynyrd actually share the same political views as Wallace? No one was quick to either confirm or deny that they were in agreement with Wallace's political views. Even the usually outspoken VanZant was vague about the issue. "We *say* 'boo, boo, boo,'" he told a reporter. He indicated to the same reporter that perhaps the boos were not sarcastic. "Of course I don't agree with everything the man says," Ronnie told the journalist. "I don't like what he says about colored people. Chances are he won't even want us. He doesn't have much use for longhairs, y'know. 'Course the real reason I'm doin' it is my daddy would whup me if I didn't. Aw shit, I don't know anything about politics anyway."

Ronnie tried to tell Yankee reporter Lisa Robinson how he really felt about the situation. "We received a plaque from Governor Wallace to become a Lieutenant Colonel in the state militia, which is a bullshit gimmick thing," Ronnie said. "My father supports Wallace but that don't mean I have to. I think he's a gentleman and has a lot of nerve. Balls. And I admire that. He's got a lot of guts to go back out there after what happened to him. Anyway, all these people have been saying that we're going to go out on a campaign for him, and that's a lie. We're not into politics, we don't have no education and Wallace don't know anything about rock-and-roll. We have very little in common, and besides that, I disagree with a lot of his views. I've heard him talk and wanted to ask him about his views on Blacks and why he has such poor education and such a low school rate there, such a low housing rate. I wouldn't say anything bad about him in Alabama, but I'm not from Alabama, we're from Florida. And we wrote 'Sweet Home Alabama' as a joke except for the last verse—about the Swampers who taught us how to play music. But it broke nationwide and we've sort of been branded with it. As far as the Confederate flag is concerned, we've been carrying that with us for a long time before we did anything, it's just part of us. We're from the South, but we're not bigots."

No benefits for Wallace materialized and so Skynyrd's stand on the issue remained obscure. One benefit that did happen that year was a festival in Gainesville, Florida, to raise funds for a young lady named Karen Robeson whose need for a kidney transplant had been brought to Skynyrd's attention. Skynyrd invited several other bands to participate, and the idea that Skynyrd had compassion and was interested in local outreach was well received.

In fact, in 1976, Lynyrd Skynyrd would receive the Outstanding Public Service award at the second annual Rock Music Awards. They were honored for their multiple benefits for those who were less fortunate, ill, or without funds, and for presidential candidate Jimmy Carter.

Ronnie VanZant wasn't short on charisma and showmanship on the tour. Lynyrd Skynyrd appeared at RFK Stadium in Washington, DC, in June of that year. It was an outdoor show and it rained during the band's performance. At one point Ronnie announced that he was going to sing a song to make the sun shine. While the band played "Sweet Home Alabama" the rain did indeed stop and the sun came out. It began to rain immediately after the song was finished.

With the success of their latest tour, Skynyrd's tenure as an opening act ended once and for all. Headliners balked at playing on the same bill. Skynyrd was simply too powerful a band to follow. As Billy Powell put it, "Who's gonna want to get up on stage after 'Freebird,' you know?"

"Freebird" Allen Collins.

"Freebird" continued to be a popular song and was released as a single in the last months of 1973 or January 1974. "When [Allen] did that solo, that became the number one solo in the world at that time," claims Powell. The band celebrated when the record reached Billboard's Top 20. The crowds called for the song to be played from the first notes of Skynyrd's set. "'Freebird' is Skynyrd's automatic encore, a tribute to the late Duane Allman and the late Berry Oakley," wrote celebrated rock critic Robert Cristgau. "It combines an assertively banal ramblin' man lyric with a non-virtuoso rave-up in which all three guitars soar in effortless kinetic interplay. A perfect example of techno-pastoral counter-culture transcendence. Its central image: male freebirds like Duane and Berry flying off on their motorcycles."

Skynyrd fans loved the gentle opening piano of "Freebird" and the heartfelt lyrics sung by Ronnie VanZant. By the time the frenzied guitars kicked in the audience would be on their feet, equally manic and totally involved. Not only was "Freebird" an opportunity for the guitarists to let off steam, but for the fans as well. It was almost impossible for anyone in the audience to not become involved in the presentation of Skynyrd's landmark anthem.

Some people understood the meaning and heartfelt presentation of the song, and others did not. The enchantment with "Freebird" was something Skynyrd could not have ignored even if they had wanted to. "'Freebird' is classic, up there with 'Stairway to Heaven,' and I still enjoy playing it," said Leon Wilkeson in 1999.

Despite their exhausting tours and hard living, VanZant, Rossington, and Collins continued to be prolific songwriters. VanZant's lyrical efforts broke out from writing about romance and partying and turned more introspective and socially conscious. His songwriting continued to develop and give voice to what was on his active mind. "If you really sit down and concentrate, and listen close to, lyrically, what the man had to say, you can get very acquainted with him," said Leon Wilkeson. "He spoke straight from the heart. He wrote about true life experience and real people and he would just change the names."

"[Ronnie] didn't play piano or guitar or anything," says Judy VanZant Jenness. "So he didn't sit down and do that part of it. But I think he knew where he was going with the song before he started putting the music to it. And he was way ahead of his time. He was writing about gun control and environmental issues and drugs, you know, all that stuff, years and years and years ago, before people even started talking about that kind of stuff. There were problems and so he wrote about 'em. People could relate to it and I guess that's why their music is as popular as it is today. Twenty years from now it will be just as popular."

Ronnie VanZant was a dedicated lyricist who motivated Allen Collins and Gary Rossington to set his words to some incredibly inspired music. The guitars, piano, and backbeat fiercely enveloped the words of each song. Each instrument was indispensable. Yet the Skynyrd sound was equal parts lyric and music. The partnership was working and the songs were coming fast and furious. Through the songs alone, Lynyrd Skynyrd was already making a legendary impact.

It seems a murky situation when it comes to the matter of Skynyrd's early publishing. Al Kooper apparently commented that while he saw no reason that Sounds of the South should own the band's work, MCA did, and likely asked for that as a contingency for the band signing with them. Kooper's initial deal with the band was that he would take ten of their fifteen percentage points until they became more famous than he. He said that situation changed after the second album. Ten months after an initial overture, MCA told Kooper they wanted to buy his points in the band. He sold them for $1,000,000. This way Lynyrd Skynyrd would be signed directly to MCA rather than to Kooper and Sounds of the South. Ronnie VanZant told Kooper that the million dollars was charged to Skynyrd's account and the band paid it. When Kooper was asked by the band to produce the third album, new points were negotiated.

MCA claims that the band asked that their contract be bought out by MCA in order to procure a greater royalty. To meet this end, one million dollars was advanced to the band by MCA to pay Kooper as a buyout and Skynyrd's future royalties would pay back that advance. So although the business entity of the band was undergoing changes and intricate financial adjustments, the boys in the band chose to be more involved with what they did best: making good music.

Rolling Stone reported on May 20, 1975, that Gary Rossington had broken the ring finger on his left hand when he slammed a door on it. As careless as this action might have been, Rossington was certainly proving to be injury-prone. Whether his broken fingers, hands, or other body parts were the results of accidents or fistfights is speculative. Gary liked to drink and Gary liked to do drugs. Gary defined the term whiskey rock-and-roller. It wasn't unusual to see the guitarist somehow attempting to overcome his latest injury. Whether or not it affected his guitar playing is also speculative. Ed King thought Rossington was occasionally capable of remarkable solos, such as in "Saturday Night Special" and "That Smell," but thought his playing inconsistent. Regardless, Rossington certainly didn't let this latest injury sideline him. He continued to rock as hard as ever.

After Skynyrd's performance at the Capital Centre in Washington, DC, on June 20 with Marshall Tucker and Elvin Bishop, the *Washington Post* reported that "when one guitarist gets tired or runs out of ideas, another is ready to carry on."

The Post reported that the gig was most successful. "It was obvious from last night's show that the Southern boogie sound has become the most popular style to emerge in the past year. More than 1,000 fans were turned away from the concert, and those who had tickets showed an excitement and adulation that hasn't been seen much lately. There's no doubt about it, Southern boogie is the hottest sound around."

Ronnie VanZant was a hard personality to read. To anyone who knew him it was an established fact that he loved his music. But from the onstage performance that he gave, it was difficult to tell if he enjoyed the live presentations. He certainly didn't feel the need to convince his audiences that he was there to party. His stoic approach to delivering the songs, which were the essence of his life, was not only casual, it was sometimes lethargic. Yet that was only the outward appearance. The words—the essential quality of the message he wanted to convey—were always genuine and from the heart. It seemed to be VanZant's desire to have the music speak for itself. He had never been a fan of large-scale rock-and-roll productions. He felt no need to put on a show, no need to prance and posture. Here was a guy, like any guy in the audience, singing about the things he loved. It was that simple. "I think he loved performing," says Judy VanZant Jenness. "He's just so laid-back. It was his life."

There were many incidents and accidents that weren't as innocent as Rossington's recent hand injury. Publicly, Skynyrd's fans were becoming just as rowdy as the band. On July 6, 1975, at a hometown concert at Jacksonville's Coliseum, the band's old nemesis, coach Leonard Skinner, introduced the band. Skinner, by the way, says he first knew about the band using his name when he heard a song announced on the radio.

The crowd loved the appearance of the former coach, but the show rapidly declined from that point. After a song or two, Ronnie's throat began to bleed. VanZant, understandably, decided not to continue. When the band announced that the show was over, bottles were thrown on stage and a small riot broke out. Sixteen Skynyrd fans were arrested. The *Jacksonville Journal* reported that 500 of the estimated 15,000 people attending the concert participated in the melee. A policeman was beaten and kicked and the estimated damages were $1,400. Skynyrd's onstage instruments were abandoned by their players and were badly marred before they could be rescued. The stage lights were also heavily damaged. Reports of the disturbance were not exactly the kind of press one would want publicized in their hometown paper. The paper went on to report that earlier in the evening a man was cut across the chest with a knife. Yet such episodes were part and parcel of the Skynyrd experience and most people probably did not think twice about it. Even their adversary Skinner was now a real-estate agent using his name to draw in customers. One of Jacksonville's hot spots was a bar located on the corner of San Juan Avenue and Roosevelt Boulevard known as The Still. In 1976, Leonard Skinner bought the bar and renamed it Leonard Skinner's.

Despite some hardships such as the riot and some personal injuries, Skynyrd continued to rock hard. They seemed to know that they were experiencing only the tip of the music industry iceberg. There was always more music to make and more of the rocking life to experience.

7

Nuthin' Fancy,
Just Skynyrd

AND THE BAND PLAYED ON . . . Lynyrd Skynyrd was playing the music *they* most liked to hear. Nothing wrong with that. If a few of the songs were considered somewhat commercial, was that a problem? Any fan of rock-and-roll liked to hear their favorite songs on the radio. The problem that the record company had with Skynyrd's music was that the songs were usually so long, which made them unsuitable for radio play. So, occasionally the songs were whittled down to radio-friendly lengths. But only if it suited the music and only if it suited the band. In the long run, while some of the songs were shorter, thus making them more "commercial," most were longer and made for jamming.

Robert Cristgau summed up his opinion of the band's appeal in the August 1975 issue of *Creem* magazine: "Lack of virtuoso is a virtue of this staunchly untranscendent band. Its music is structured vertically rather than horizontally, condensed rather than stretched until it disappears. When it rocks, three guitarists and a keyboard player pile elementary riffs and feedback noises into the dense combinations that are broken with abbreviated pre-planned solos, at quieter

moments, the spare vocabulary of the oldest Southern folk music is evoked or just plain duplicat-
ed. The standard boogie-band beat, soulish but heavier and less propulsive, is slowed down so
that the faster tempos become that much more cleansing and climactic. In other words, as
Ronnie VanZant explained to me amiably on the way to the limos at the Johnson City Holiday
Inn: 'We're more commercial than the Allmans.'"

Ronnie summed up what Lynyrd Skynyrd music was all about in the Los Angeles *Free Press*
when he told Bob Fukuyama, "Basically, people who listen to music don't know a fucking thing
about music. But they want to feel it, to get with it. They want us to put them in the mood. By
making it simple we reach a wide audience. It's worked for us, it's worked for Bad Company. All
they do is drive it right down your throats."

In between live appearances, arrangements for the band's third album were underway. The
record would be titled *Nuthin' Fancy*. The band would spend twenty-one fourteen-hour days in
the studio for this one.

Since Bob Burns had officially left Skynyrd claiming that he had no interest in either touring
or recording, a permanent drummer needed to be signed. Artimus Pyle seemed to be what
Ronnie was looking for, and the Kentuckian was warmly welcomed into the band as an official
member in December 1974.

Thomas Delmer Pyle was born on July 15, 1948, in Louisville to Mildred and Clarence
Pyle. Artimus was a nickname acquired in college. Music had always been an important part of
Artimus' life. His grandmother loved to listen to country music on the radio and his father often
conducted local bands. "I was outside of Jamestown, Tennessee, in a little town called Allardt,"
Pyle recalls. "Grandma would always have country, pure Nashville, Tennessee, country music
blaring over the radio with a lot of static. Real bad reception, just blasting through the house to
get everybody up for breakfast."

It was in this area of Tennessee, the home of famed World War I hero Alvin York, that
Artimus spent his formative years. One of the first things he remembers is running a bulldozer
for his grandfather Guy Williams' road-building company when he was eight. "It's amazing when
you're sitting on one of these big bulldozers," says Artimus. "You hear all these rhythms. And you
play along with them. I found myself kind of tapping along with them. I can still do that. I can
still make the sound of a V-8 engine with my hands."

Artimus also loved to ride horses and found their rhythm both soothing and exciting. "I
rode horses so the rhythms of a horse galloping underneath me, I can still simulate that with my
hands," he says. One of Guy Williams' friends was Senator Al Gore, Sr., and Artimus became
friendly with Gore's son, Al Jr.

Throughout his childhood Artimus could be heard pounding on pots, pans, and his mother's
Quaker Oats boxes. He was given a pair of bongo drums for his ninth birthday. He also loved to
sing and participated in a variety of musical activities including choir, chorus, and boys' ensemble.

"[My early influences] would be my father beating on the dashboard of the car," Pyle remembers. "Big bands, Glenn Miller, Tommy Dorsey, Jimmy Dorsey, Gene Krupa, Harry James, that kind of stuff. My dad was actually a leader of an orchestra sometimes. If the Masons or something in town would do some kind of a function, or they'd have a little band, Dad would use a long knitting needle as a baton. He would lead the orchestra. Dad would tap with his hand on the dashboard, keeping time with the music, and he'd sing a little bit."

A dream came true on Artimus' twelfth birthday when his father gave him a set of red sparkle Slingland drums. Pyle formed a garage band he called The Thom Thumbs and soon became part of his school's concert band. "They were red sparkle Slinglands with a calfskin head," he recalls. "Nowadays, of course, everything's plastic. But these calfskins, I'll never forget. They have no overtones, so when you play them, they just sound great. Plastic heads have a lot of lean to them. I'd give anything to have those drums back."

Pyle enjoyed playing the drums even as he grew older. His father was an architect and often relocated his family for business purposes. Artimus spent his teen years in Columbus, Ohio. In the absence of familiar friends, he turned to the drums. "As I went, along [came] the rock thing," Pyle muses. "Ginger Baker, Cream, and so many other bands [Baker] was in, and of course Keith Moon and John Bonham [influenced me]. I was [later] in a popularity poll in England. I came in third, behind John Bonham and Keith Moon. I always thought that was appropriate. I was as proud of that as I would've been anything, being in the company of those guys."

Artimus enjoyed the music but didn't give much thought to pursuing a career in music. After high school graduation Pyle enrolled in Tennessee Technical College in Cookeville, Tennessee. It was here that the baby-faced Tommy Pyle was nicknamed Artimus, after the virgin goddess Artemus. Within a short period of time, Artimus joined the Marine Corps. He excelled in the military and was named "Best Honor Recruit" in 1968. After aviation training, Sergeant Artimus Pyle was training as an E-5 sergeant and preparing to go to Vietnam when the war ended. His career in the Marine Corps was cut short, although the reason had nothing to do with the end of the war. Pyle's father was killed when his Cessna 150 airplane was hit from behind by a B-57 bomber over Albuquerque, New Mexico. Artimus was given an early release from the Marines. He eventually returned to the South to live, taking up residence in Spartanburg, South Carolina.

Some of the members of Marshall Tucker were childhood friends of Artimus' first wife, Patricia Williamson. "She kept telling me she knew these musicians," he remembers. "Well, I met George McCorkle and all of them and it was just like getting together and smoking a joint. So, I got to know the guys and everything. They invited me to a couple of shows."

Through Marshall Tucker, Artimus was introduced to musician Charlie Daniels. Charlie heard Pyle's skill at the drums and offered club work. Soon Artimus' reputation as an imaginative drummer grew. So when Bob Burns was contemplating leaving Skynyrd, Artimus' friends recom-

"Best Honor Recruit," United States Marine Corps, Artimus Pyle, 1968.

mended him as a replacement. "When Ronnie VanZant got the O.K. from Marshall Tucker and Charlie Daniels, hell, he hired me almost without hearing me," remembers Artimus. "He set up an audition for me with Ed King and Leon in Atlanta [at Alex Cooley's Electric Ballroom], but he didn't even show up. He said, 'Hire the guy.' He gave me a paper sack with $5,000 cash in it in Nashville. I couldn't believe it. Patricia and I got in our little Volkswagen bus and drove back to Spartanberg, South Carolina, with a paper sack with $5,000 cash in it. We were two of the happiest people in the whole wide world. We paid our bills, we bought us a Sony Triton TV set. We were fat city."

Artimus' first appearance with Lynyrd Skynyrd was a benefit for Jacksonville's Food Bank held at Sergeant Pepper's Club in October 1974. Pyle and his distinctive double bass drumming were well received. When Burns officially left the band in December, Artimus took over as Skynyrd's new drummer. When the time came to enter the recording studio for Skynyrd's third album in early 1975, Ronnie was confident Artimus was up to his standards.

The band was now headlining and had their own support acts. One of their favorites was still The Charlie Daniels Band. Charlie was older than most of the Southern acts of that time, having begun his career primarily as a songwriter and producer. Charlie was mostly known for his approach to country music, but he most certainly had the heart of a rock-and-roller. Many of his compositions were solidly based in boogie. Charlie Daniels was very much respected by Lynyrd Skynyrd.

"Charlie Daniels was our backup band for awhile," says Billy Powell. "We still love Charlie and all those guys. The keyboard player is Taz Degregorio. His name is Joel Degregorio, but [he was given the nickname] Taz, after the Tasmanian Devil. [He] used to be pretty rowdy too, but he's also been sober for years now. I named my second son after him. My second son's name is Joel Powell . . . Billy . . . his full name is Billy Joel Powell. Take off the Powell, you have Billy Joel. Take off the Joel you have got Billy Powell. We call him Joel, after Taz Degregorio. I named him after three keyboard players: myself, Billy Joel, and Taz."

"I love ole Charlie," said Leon Wilkeson. "I guess my favorite [band] would be the CDB. It's like Ronnie would later sing, 'There's a few good rockers in New York City, big L.A. never cared for me. So to all them Hollywood writer people, it just don't make a damn when you got good friends like these.'"

"[He's] a storyteller," says Johnny Van-Zant. "A really good storyteller and a good friend of Ronnie's. He's doing a country thing these days, which I think he fits into that. He's the only one of the Southern Rock bands that's actually been able to cross over and do that. And a gentleman, a great man."

Ronnie VanZant and Daniels grew to be great friends, with a strong mutual respect for one another's music. "Ronnie and Charlie were such good friends," says Judy VanZant Jenness. "They did a lot of stuff with Charlie. Charlie and Ronnie were very, very close. He probably enjoyed [playing with Charlie] more, 'cause he'd get to sit around and shoot the shit with Charlie. They just got along real well. [Charlie] is a nice man. He was just a great guy. I think he was experienced and he would kind of help guide them and stuff like that. I wouldn't want to say he was a father figure, but he was a little older and a little more experienced."

"We all basically came up the same way," says Charlie. "It was easy to relate to those guys. It's like somebody you'd known all your life, basically. You run into people sometimes that were raised in the same type of surroundings that you were, and basically in the same way, and you feel like you know these people. You just hit it off. And that's the way it was with Ronnie."

"Ronnie and Charlie were so close," says Artimus. "I have a vision in my mind of them right now. In a hotel, on the beds, facing each other, swapping hats. Charlie's hat came down over Ronnie's ears and Ronnie's hat just sat on the top of Charlie's head like a Deputy Dawg. I think it was Ronnie's birthday that night. They were partying. We must have done a hundred, a hundred-fifty, two hundred shows with Charlie."

Other supporting bands were friends as well. "We would play with [Marshall Tucker] a lot too," says Powell. "We were real good friends with them. It's just such a shame about [guitarist Toy Caldwell's premature] death. That really shocked me. We respected him . . . highly respected him. [We] had a good time with them."

"[Skynyrd] were just gung-ho and ready to get out there and do anything that they could to make it work," says Tucker's Doug Gray. "One time we had just played San Francisco with them, but we had to go to play San Diego. They called up and said Ronnie was going to have to wear [dark] glasses. He'd gotten beat up in this bar in San Francisco. [But he was] one of the best entertainers around."

In San Francisco the doors to Skynyrd's equipment truck had somehow been left unlocked. Ronnie had come across some locals in the truck, attempting to take some of the equipment. Of course he wasn't going to let them get away with that. A fight ensued and before any of the roadies arrived, Ronnie had a black eye.

Another band Skynyrd enjoyed was Little Feat. "We used to sit in the audience and watch them," says Ed King. The respect was mutual. Skynyrd would also do some dates with Ted Nugent and his band.

Skynyrd kept a respectful distance from sharing a bill with certain other bands. "Ronnie kind of knew Gregg and Duane Allman, but I never met 'em," says Powell. "We never really chummed around with them like we did some of Charlie's and Atlanta Rhythm Section's people, which we did a lot. We always thought [The Allman Brothers] were just as big as we were, and they kind of started sizing us out in their Southern way, that Southern Rock band thing. Whatever, but we never really got to know 'em real good, and we never played with them a bunch because we knew there'd be a dispute over who was going to headline."

Appearing on *Nuthin' Fancy* were three female singers who were brought together to broaden

The Ladies of Skynyrd: The Honkettes. Left to right: Leslie Hawkins, Cassie Gaines, Jo Jo Billingsley.

both the Skynyrd sound and appeal. Cassie Gaines from Oklahoma, Jo Jo Billingsley from Mississippi, and Leslie Hawkins from Jacksonville were dubbed the "Honkettes."

Jo Billingsley began her singing career singing in a local band upon graduation from high school and then joined a musical enterprise called Oil Can Harry. When a friend of hers, a roadie with Skynyrd, told her that the band was considering adding backup vocals, Jo was interested. She met up with Ronnie VanZant in Nashville and he hired her on the spot.

When the Honkettes later sang at Knebworth they caught the eye of every male in the crowd. They would bring an additional sauciness to the music on the album. "I think they're a necessity," says Billy Powell. "And their parts [are] always in the right places. I think they add to the sound. Skynyrd at first had no backup singers at all, and I don't think anybody missed them. I think they'd miss 'em now, if we tried to play live without 'em."

"I guess I was disappointed 'cause I thought they should've been called the Skynats," said Leon Wilkeson. "But actually, they added a lot. I remember when we started rehearsing with Deborah Jo Billingsley, Leslie Hawkins, and Cassie [Gaines]. [Now] it's not Skynyrd without the

Honkettes." (Over the years the Honkette line-up would change to include, at various times: Cassie Gaines, Leslie Hawkins, Jo Jo Billingsley, Dale Krantz-Rossington, Carol Bristow, Debbie Bailey, Debbie Davis, and Carol Chase.)

Kate Simon, writing for *Sounds,* would make particular note of the ladies: "The band aren't really into dressing that much, but the three lady singers counter-attack with a vengeance. Leslie is a vision in white, Cassie—who spent six months in Santa Fe and a year in Mexico—favors suede and dripping turquoise, while Jo is definitely in a Billie Holliday vein, turquoise rings on every finger, lots of boas, feathers in her hair."

The Honkettes were to find that being on the road with Skynyrd could be long and tiring. "There were two hundred bookings a year out of three hundred sixty-five days," remembered Jo Billingsley. "We rehearsed during open dates with very few days off. We hit every major and minor city three times in the United States as well as many other major cities around the world during the three and one-half years I was with the band. We flew in during the morning and flew out at night."

Al Kooper was once again asked to produce Skynyrd's album, and it was decided to return to Atlanta to do the recording. Initially, Bang Studios would be used. The enterprise would then move to Webb IV Studio in Atlanta. It was important to Ronnie and the other members of the band to keep up their momentum. "If we get off a good one this time, we're on easy street and cruisin'," claimed Ronnie. "We really want this one bad."

Kooper had some problems working with studio engineer Dave Evans. There were disagreements about technicalities. Additionally, Kooper knew the band didn't have a lot of songs to work on and decided to give them two weeks before entering the studio to come up with some winners. When he returned to the studio with the band, they did not disappoint him. The deep bass-driven "On the Hunt," the joyous "Whiskey Rock-A-Roller," and the tender "Am I Losin'" were ready to go. By the end of the brief recording period, everybody was mentally exhausted.

Nuthin' Fancy was released in the late spring of 1975 with little fanfare. The album was a good one, but not the great one for which the band had hoped. Kooper says that a lack of outstanding material and the mere thirty days of recording at Webb IV Studio in Atlanta with virtually no preparation made *Nuthin' Fancy* a classic example of how *not* to make a record. Limitations aside, Kooper feels the album turned out to be a good one and the members of the band were contented with the recording. *Something* must have gone right. "It was the best time I ever had in a studio," claimed Allen Collins.

Sounds magazine would note on May 21, 1975, however, "Unfortunately Kooper's firm set ideas and the band's natural development have unintentionally set themselves up in opposition, with Kooper wanting a sound that Skynyrd really cannot provide today. The result is that the album occasionally feels stretched, lacking in the hotter than hell feel that hallmarked the debut albums."

Regardless of the limited approval from the music press, the fans thought the album was just fine. Perhaps it was the general allure of the band. While stating in *Rolling Stone* that he wished the album contained more of what he had come to like from Skynyrd, Bud Scoppa described Lynyrd Skynyrd's appeal: "With three full-time electric guitarists, a piano player and a fireplug of a lead singer who looks like Robert Blake's Baretta in a hippie disguise, Georgia's Lynyrd Skynyrd presents an unusually broad front line."

Nuthin' Fancy featured some exceptional music such as the raucous "Saturday Night Special," the Jimmy Rogers–influenced "Railroad Song," "Am I Losin'" (said to be about Bob Burns), and the self-explanatory "I'm a Country Boy." The simple ditty "Made in the Shade" featured dobros, mandolin, and Ed King on Moog bass for some Delta blues; and "Cheatin' Woman" contained a unique twelve-bar structure. Another anthem was the boisterous "Whiskey Rock-A-Roller," and a driving assertion of rock-and-roll's calculated sensual indulgence was included with "On the Hunt."

"Made in the Shade" was a simple but straightforward song about life and life's expectations. The song was recorded one night after some of the band had left the studio. Ronnie had wanted to put the song down, so he enlisted the help of Jacksonville friend Barry Harwood, Gary, Ed, and Artimus who were still present. Harwood played mandolin, Rossington played flattop. A marching drum and a Coca-Cola crate were used for percussion. Ronnie was pleased with the end result.

Circus magazine particularly liked "Whiskey Rock-A-Roller," noting that "VanZant's voice rises above a careening wall of guitars and soars high on the melody in a way only Paul Rodgers vocals can equal." Ronnie must have loved *that* review.

The line-up of Lynyrd Skynyrd was certainly different than in albums past. While Ronnie, Gary, Allen, and Leon were still active components of the band, Ed King (excepting "Made in the Shade" and "Railroad Song") and Bob Burns were out. Ed hadn't been replaced at this point, and Artimus Pyle had come in on drums. Without Ed King some of the excitement was lost, along with a great deal of range. *Sounds* magazine's Billy Walker reviewed the album on April 12, 1975, and put it all in perspective: "They have managed to retain the powerhouse rhythms which don't let up throughout the album and the three-pronged guitar attack, when firing on all cylinders, is a joy to hear but that 'nail 'em to the wall' drive and aggression that made their debut set so good isn't here . . . . All in all a rather disappointing album. Disappointing because, rightly or wrongly, you expect a band like Skynyrd to wipe the floor with you every time."

Despite the shortcomings, *Nuthin' Fancy* included some of the most unadulterated Skynyrd music that the band had released to date. The band's rural roots were paid homage with "I'm a Country Boy," King and VanZant's "Railroad Song," and Jimmy Reed's "Big Lights, Big City." "Made in the Shade" harkened to classic blues and "Whiskey Rock-A-Roller" was classic Southern Rock. "Am I Losin'" is one of Ronnie VanZant's most heartfelt songs. *Pop Top* magazine noted, "'Am I Losin'" is an unusually gentle, plaintive ballad that comes right to the threshold of incandescence."

The album contained a major radio hit in "Saturday Night Special." The song had not originally been intended for the album. It had been recorded prior to entering the studio to record *Nuthin' Fancy* for use in Burt Reynolds' movie *The Longest Yard*, which was released in 1974. "They recorded [only] one song at Studio One [for that album] and I engineered it," remembers Rodney Mills. "It was 'Saturday Night Special.' They came in the studio to cut that for the Burt Reynolds movie, *The Longest Yard*. I didn't know what the movie was at the time but we were supposed to meet for this movie. We cut that all in one day, all in one night's time. I remember being pressed to get that done, but also remember at the same time the band went out and played live and did a couple of demos of songs that I think were kind of lost. We did two-track demos of a couple of songs and I don't think anybody ever found the tapes. I remember we looked for 'em later on, 'cause people remembered us recording them, but we never could go back and find 'em. I don't know where they got lost, or who's got 'em."

"Saturday Night Special" was used in the movie during a chase scene. A police officer chases an outlaw while the song plays on his radio. It would be considered a good placement for the song by Skynyrd fans. The song was also promoted in magazines in a unique way. Under the words "Saturday Night Special" a voluptuous woman in a garter belt was seen in the throes of passion embracing a giant handgun. The trigger of the gun was notably placed between her legs. *The Longest Yard* was a release of Paramount Pictures, and not the Skynyrd-related MCA-Universal. Evidently Burt Reynolds and the producers were Skynyrd fans. This was the first, but not the last, time that Skynyrd's music appeared in a film. The band was thrilled. They hoped to place other songs in future films.

Although Ronnie had been around guns all his life, he realized that there was a certain irresponsibility that gun ownership sometimes evoked. The song made no bones about a .44-caliber "Saturday Night Special" handgun being used for little other than rage-stoked violence. He wasn't, however, anti-gun. "[Ronnie] wasn't politically motivated, you know, he didn't get into these things," says Judy VanZant Jenness. "He just wrote about it in songs. He didn't go out and try to cram it down somebody's throat. Oh, O.K., here's my message, dig it or don't dig it, you know? We had guns in our house. He was a hunter, he had rifles. He actually bought me a little .38 Special, 'cause we lived out in a secluded area and he wanted me to have a gun for protection. He'd actually take me out and we'd do target practice. I think the area that he grew up in was kind of a rough area . . . ."

Despite any initial misgivings, the album reached #9 on the Billboard Chart. On the heels of the release of *Nuthin' Fancy*, another tour of the U.K. was arranged, and Lynyrd Skynyrd was back on the road by the summer of 1975. Skynyrd fans responded well to the new material. They had come to know that Skynyrd would always offer something special, and not the same, tired set list. Other bands liked to appear with Lynyrd Skynyrd for this reason, also. The band's ability to constantly offer new material was appreciated both by fans and by music professionals. The record seemed to truly represent Skynyrd's philosophy. This idea was detected by English reviewer Doug Collette. "What further differentiates Lynyrd Skynyrd's approach to that mode is the very same thing they have in common with their regional brethren: a virtual abhorrence to flash or frills. This LP's title would seem to say it all because for Skynyrd the music has total precedence over the sort of attitudinizing and posturing so prevalent elsewhere in rock and roll."

Yet reviews of some of the shows in the U.S. demonstrated the lack of musical excitement that those who panned the album pointed out. "Lynyrd Skynyrd played basic boogie to the half-filled Auditorium, which was O.K. for awhile, but eventually grew tiresome," wrote Peggy Mulloy Glad in the *Milwaukee Journal* at the end of May. "The group's two guitars, bass, keyboards, drums and vocals were used unimaginatively until the last number of the night, 'Freebird.' The song was nothing short of excellent as it shifted easily from a slow, moody sultriness to driving, soaring heights. But one exciting song in an hour-long set?"

Perhaps some of the crowds were disappointed, but most acts, even with a variety of crowd-pleasing songs, rarely rose to the eminence of a song such as "Freebird." Skynyrd's fans so loved the song that it was all that many of them needed to hear. "I got along with those guys really, really well," says Marshall Tucker's George McCorkle. "And me, I'm a very passive person. Ronnie was just the total opposite, you know. But I loved Ronnie. I thought Ronnie VanZant was the epitome of a rock singer. He'd fight ya . . . he'd drink with ya . . . he'd screw ya . . . It was like Ronnie was the real deal, man. Plus Ronnie could write songs. And perform 'em. That whole band, that original band, was scary when they were on. They carried the rock-and-roll side of Southern Rock. I think Ronnie wrote and talked to the average person. There is not a guy or girl probably that could not tell you they know 'Freebird.' Because there's something in that song for everybody. And I think that's a great thing to have said about you. And I think Ed King and those guys could write some stuff that talked to the average man. That's exactly what Southern Rock and everything did. It hit on the working man. That's what Ronnie VanZant did. Ronnie VanZant was the people's singer."

In the meantime, Al Kooper was having continuing difficulties with his Sounds of the South label. MCA knew they had a huge success with Skynyrd but Kooper's other acts didn't have the same mass appeal. While Skynyrd prospered, others on the Sounds of the South roster floundered. Kooper continued his support of Skynyrd but mourned the respect and support denied his other bands. "MCA stopped supporting all the other acts except Lynyrd Skynyrd," he says. "I had to get out. I'm a man of my word. I said I'd help those bands and I had my hands tied."

Being back on the road raised the same old demons. Too much drinking and too many drugs caused friction in the band and among the crew. Ronnie VanZant, as always, was at the forefront of the problem when he drank. "I was the one that could go to Ronnie and say, 'Ronnie, you need to get some sleep,'" says Artimus Pyle. "And Ronnie would go 'O.K.' Everybody else, he'd say, 'Hey, come here,' and then he'd talk their ear off for another two hours."

"I think all of the stories you hear about the fighting and stuff like that are very true," says Charlie Faubion. "No doubt whatsoever that all of that stuff was true. Because I knew that side of Ronnie. I didn't know that side of Allen and Gary. Gary I could see probably being that way but Allen didn't impress me as being a very aggressive person."

"Ronnie and Gary were actually best friends," says Judy VanZant Jenness. "Gary was probably the only guy in the band that we ever socialized with at all when Ronnie was off the road. He and Gary would fish together, they had that in common. We would do things with Gary. [But Ronnie] actually wrote more songs with Allen. Allen was an incredible guitar player. He was a different guitar player [from Gary]. He was flashier, he was faster. I think [with writing songs] it was just whoever came up with the idea at the time, or whoever happened to be there. The three of them wrote a lot of songs together."

Ronnie was at his best while creating his songs. "He would come up with the lyrics and melodies," says Judy. "It wasn't like they would do the music and he would have to put lyrics to it. A lot of times he would come up with the lyrics and they would put music to the lyrics. So he would have a melody in mind. But he didn't play piano or guitar or anything, so he didn't like to sit down, do that part of it. I think he knew where he was going with the song before he started putting the music to it. It would be difficult to just come up with a lyric without having an idea of what it was going to sound like. You gotta have a melody to go with it. I think he did a lot of that and then they would just put it all together."

Ronnie and Gary may have been the best of friends, but that relationship was in no way insurance against one of their nasty interband outbursts of violence. Returning to Europe in support of their latest album, a fight between the two broke out the night they arrived. The subject matter that touched off one of their most physically destructive battles yet was alleged to have been over the mispronunciation of the word "schnapps." Although the music was going well, the interband dissension was the same as always.

"We got over there and Ronnie got drunk one night," remembers Artimus Pyle. "He gored the back of Gary's hand. He busted a bottle over the head of our [tour] manager, John Butler, then he took the jagged edge and actually gored the back of Gary's hand. It was really scary. I had a major confrontation with Ronnie, the day after it happened. I busted his door down as a matter of fact. He came in the room and I was ready to whip his ass. His hands were bandaged too. I said, 'How can you do that to people you love?' And he says, 'I was drunk, I was drunk.' I said, 'That's bullshit. That's no excuse.'"

The result was two bottle-cut wrists for Rossington and a bruised windpipe and broken hand for VanZant. Great way to embark on a tour. Gary played "Freebird" that first night with his fingers and hands bleeding.

Gary Rossington, hands intact. Background: The Honkettes and Leon Wilkeson.

Ironically, Ronnie had told writer Scott Cohen that he was leery of other people messing up his throat or the hands of his guitarists. "Sometimes we attract rowdy people who want to take us on, but we don't want to fight because I don't want people stomping on Gary and Allen's hands so they can't play, or kicking me in the throat," he said. "That's why I want to bring along these two guys from Jacksonville with us. We already have some of the biggest and baddest [crew] around." Peter Rudge seemed to sum up the constant infighting when he said that the boys in Skynyrd are either brilliant or abominable, never anything in between.

Also around this time, there apparently was a confrontation that resulted in VanZant attempting to throw roadie Joe Barnes out of an airplane, which happened to be 13,000 feet in the air. Barnes had decided, evidently without consulting anyone, to throw away a disabled bar cart. When Dean Kilpatrick heard about the missing $500 cart, he was furious. VanZant heard the ensuing heated conversation between the two and asked Barnes to discuss the matter with him. Barnes allegedly told Ronnie that the cart was just no good. Ronnie's response was to grab

"Mistah Ronnie VanZant."

Barnes and attempt to open one of the cabin doors in order to toss the roadie out into the stratosphere. Although the attempt to send Barnes flying was aborted, Barnes somehow ended up with a stomach wound, allegedly caused by VanZant. His response was to file a $250,000 grievous bodily harm lawsuit against the singer.

The band found time in between the recording and release of the record and their next international tour to form and incorporate Lynyrd Skynyrd Productions, Inc. Gary Rossington would serve as the corporation's president. Share certificates were issued to the band members on September 15, 1975.

No one could really tell there was an offstage situation that was anything but just right after Skynyrd returned to England in the fall of 1975. England's *New Musical Express* set the tone for the concerts when they ran a paragraph on the coming Skynyrd dates. "Lynyrd Skynyrd return this week for a bill-topping tour in their own right. Although they still haven't made any noticeable impact on the British charts, their previous appearances here have been widely and wildly acclaimed, and they have built up a sizable following and a considerable reputation. What's more, their concerts will be even better for the inclusion of the Southerland Brothers and Quiver as support acts."

Sounds wrote that the members of the band "were reportedly in better form than on previous live appearances." The magazine review of their Hammersmith Odeon appearance noted that reviewer Tony Mitchell "was pleased to find that they live up to expectations both visually and sound-wise. In particular they got full marks for being the first American band I've seen to have a suitable [sound] for British-sized venues. Their power came from the orchestration and execution of their songs rather than from over-amplification."

The London *Daily Telegraph* liked Skynyrd just fine. "Nothing can be more basic than the blues, so Lynyrd Skynyrd, coming from their birthplace in the Deep South, stamp their biting, sometimes blistering country rock with a hallmark of authenticity. With an immaculate sound and light system to enhance the work of their lead vocalist, Ronnie VanZant, and his faultless musicians, this was indeed a night to cherish an American rock band in majestic flight."

Skynyrd was enjoying all that they had ever dared to dream as a band. They didn't let little things like passing out drunk or fistfights between band members get in their way. They were a rock-and-roll band, becoming a *premier* rock-and-roll band. So there was a small price to pay; the end result was more than worth it for the boys from Jacksonville.

8

Bullets Returned

BY THE END OF 1975, it was once again time to turn to the recording studio. The band bought Riverside Studio in Jacksonville to rehearse and record demos. Ronnie had come up with a song he titled "Gimme Back My Bullets" and felt that would make a good title for the album. The bullets Ronnie referred to were not those shot out of a gun, but rather the type awarded by *Billboard* magazine for successful, rising records. Ronnie knew that the band was extremely tired from touring and fairly uninspired to create and record new music. He was ready to do whatever it took to pump them up and get his dream back on track. He wanted to make the next recording experience enjoyable in hopes that the band would respond with the quality of music that they had been able to produce for the first two records.

Ronnie realized that even though the band's association with Al Kooper had been remarkably successful, there was a certain stress that came with working with Kooper. The band members were not always thrilled with the complete involvement Kooper offered. "We fought all the time," says Billy Powell about Kooper. "Constantly fought. It was almost like he wanted to be the keyboard player, the producer, the director. He wanted to be everything. We finally got fed up with it after three albums. That's when we released him."

The others in the band couldn't get along with Al Kooper because "he was a northerner," says Ed King. "They made it into a North vs. South issue. They just don't like Yankees and would revise history to make Yankees look like idiots." This sentiment was a professional issue directed at Kooper, as Skynyrd always seemed to like and respect their Northern fans.

Kooper also felt there was too much stress involved. Working with the domineering VanZant and opinionated band could not have been easy. When the time came to record, Kooper and the band mutually decided that it would be better if Skynyrd worked with another producer for this next album. It was time to think about who should be called in to handle the chore.

"Ronnie and I were friends," remembers Paul Hornsby, who had produced Marshall Tucker, among others. "I saw Ronnie at the Georgia Jam up in Atlanta Braves Stadium one year in the mid-1970s. This is after they'd done several albums. 'Hey, man,' he says. 'I'm working towards getting you to produce our next album. But, it's a democracy in the band. Unfortunately, I'm always outvoted or something, you know?' If he had had his way, we would have worked together."

Eventually it was decided to call in Tom Dowd. Dowd had successfully produced The Allman Brothers Band and Eric Clapton. He had worked successfully with R&B-producing legend Jerry Wexler, and was considered one of the most innovative producers of the time. Lynyrd Skynyrd wanted to see if he could create a little magic with them. They thought he might just be the one to take up where Al Kooper had left off. "The guy's a master," said Ronnie. "He makes you feel real comfortable in the studio."

Dowd decided to check out Lynyrd Skynyrd before committing to producing them, and so caught their set at the Santa Monica Civic Auditorium in the month prior to the dates the band wanted to record. The opening act was Peter Frampton. Frampton's popularity was soon to explode with his album *Frampton Comes Alive*. Dowd liked what he heard and asked the band to step into the studio with him while they were still in L.A. to see if they would work well together. Skynyrd believed that Dowd could help them recapture the seductiveness of their first two albums, and Dowd apparently did too.

Billy Powell was excited about the upcoming recording session and now had a seasoned perspective on his contributions to the band. "You don't hear a whole bunch of rock-and-roll bands that have outstanding [piano] solos like I do," he says. "I call [them] my hit-and-run solos. They're real fast. Billy Joel does it and every once in awhile you might hear a band with a good piano solo in there but I did them all the time. Just a whole bunch of piano solos. It wasn't easy because we used to be called the three-guitar army. The three guitars were what really made the band famous, besides Ronnie's vocals and the lyrics and originality. I had to fight to get a part to go in between three guitars. Al Kooper helped me out a lot, our first producer. He helped me out a lot on that. He helped me [with] the knowledge of playing in between the lines, don't step on everybody else's parts, like I kind of did when I started out. I didn't care. I had to play in between the lines, and I think that established the band not only as the guitar army but [the band as having] a real good keyboard player. And it's like a trademark now. There's a lot of people who like the piano parts more than anything. Of course, they're usually keyboard players. I just attribute it to taking lessons is all. If I didn't take those lessons, I'd have never been able to do those kind of solos real fast, 'cause a lot of 'em are actually one-handed solos. A lot of the solos I did was one-handed, where I'd sit on my left hand so I wouldn't interfere with my right hand."

The album was recorded in bits and pieces. Whenever the band would come up with a couple of songs, they would call Tom Dowd and tell him they were ready to go into the studio. After laying the tracks, they would do several more gigs and come back again ready with another couple of songs. The album was by no means recorded in one lengthy, nonstop session, but rather over several weeks.

The band was finding that recording with Dowd was quite different from recording with Al Kooper. Dowd said that he would sometimes purposely give the band bad advice in order to test them to see if they were actually committed to the sound they were producing. Nine times out of ten they said they liked it better their way. That was actually what Dowd wanted to hear. He wanted a full commitment to their songs, to their music. Although the band was used to more involvement with the producer, they were fine with recording in a different, less involved manner.

Things were not all that terrific in Skynyrd's personal camp. During the recording Gary Rossington was injured once again, this time in a car crash in Jacksonville. It was just the latest in a long line of many reckless accidents for the band members. Most band members continued to drink and by now the use of serious recreational drugs, such as cocaine, Quaaludes, and amphetamines was becoming a problem within Skynyrd. The boys were high on life, but often on something else as well. Many times this resulted in musical aggression, as witnessed by their brutal guitar approach to some of the songs on the album. The band members seemed to adhere to the "live fast—take the consequences" doctrine of rock-and-roll, and this credo was reflected in the music released on *Bullets*.

While the songs still represented the established Skynyrd sound, many of the songs the band recorded rocked even harder than in the past. The guitars were heavier and the vocals brusque. And, again, many of the band's true-to-life experiences were played out in song. One example of this was the song "Cry for the Bad Man." Here were lyrics concerning greed and monetary exploitation. There was speculation that the song was about former manager Alan Walden, but that seems a bit harsh. Ronnie VanZant always refused to say whom the song was really about.

"Gimme Back My Bullets" had meant to express the band's desire to return to the top, but many of their fans misinterpreted exactly what Ronnie was singing about. The song turned out to be popular on the radio, and when the fans heard it in concert, they pelted the stage with a variety of types of real and live bullets. It started to get dangerous up onstage. Although Ronnie explained what they meant by "bullets" in radio interviews in an effort to clear up the misinterpretation, the band had to stop performing the song in concert lest someone get seriously hurt.

One of the songs that stood out on what was mostly a lackluster album was "Roll Gypsy Roll," an involving song about the romance of a nomadic life. Ronnie VanZant was very clearly the gypsy mentioned in the song.

The invigorating and hard-edged "Double Trouble" was another of Skynyrds' art-from-life songs. The song came about one night when Ronnie and Gary were sitting in a jail cell after a run-in with local rednecks. Ronnie realized that this was his eleventh time being thrown in jail for rowdiness, fighting, or being drunk in public. Rossington looked at VanZant and told him the cause was simple—he was "double trouble."

Regardless of who was in the producer's chair, the band members continued to have their own individual approaches to recording. During a visit to the recording sessions, writer Andy McConnell made the observation that Allen Collins was very serious in his approach to music, but never missed an opportunity for a laugh. McConnell noticed on the other hand that Gary Rossington rarely seemed to smile. It is interesting to note how different people respond to the stress and enjoyment of living out their dream.

The way the sessions were approached and recorded initially seemed successful. *Bullets* climbed quickly into the Top 20 when it was released in the spring of 1976. The album resulted in the band's fourth gold record. The bullets were returned.

Although the album was well received, something seemed lacking in the record's presentation. The tight recording unit that Skynyrd had become seemed almost to have become a thing of the past. It seemed the change of producers, however talented Tom Dowd might have been, was not necessarily a good thing. Al Kooper agreed. "When I heard it [*Gimme Back My Bullets*] I said, 'Come on, kick my ass,'" he recalls. "[But] I hated it. It lacked *me*. Nobody fought over the songs. Half of the songs I would have thrown out."

Hit Parader also noticed the absence of Kooper as producer. Jean-Charles Costa wrote: "Unlike many of their regional counterparts, Skynyrd thankfully resist the temptation to 'sweeten' up the music with string sections, blaring bass or overworked synthesizers. An occasional backing chorus, slipped in with muted efficiency—'Double Trouble'—and the slightly toned-down but more focused production of Tom Dowd are the heaviest concessions they make to stylistic progression."

Rolling Stone seemed to be somewhat of a fan of the band but in the end they couldn't really give the new album much of an endorsement. David McGee seemed to agree with Kooper. "Dowd gets credit for coaxing uniformly uninspired performances from the musicians . . . but neither he nor they can overcome such poor material, fully half of which I couldn't have imagined Lynyrd Skynyrd recording two years ago. There is inertia here. Lynyrd Skynyrd is a good band in limbo."

A review of *Bullets* in *Stereo Review* was also lackluster. "Lynyrd Skynyrd is a tight band, but awfully definite about being a second-generation Southern Blues-rocking band—it doesn't seem to try anything that hasn't been market tested in or around the region. Still, it's competent, not hard to take, for all my carping, and if this leads some kid to wonder about sources back beyond The Allman Brothers, it's done some good."

After the recording it came time to tour again. Although the band had played well with their current line-up in the studio, they missed the power and excitement of the third guitar that Ed King had brought to the Skynyrd sound. They talked it over and decided to actively look for someone to step into the place left vacant by the departure of King. Several guitarists, including Leslie West, were auditioned. No one seemed to fit.

Time was of the essence. It was time to promote the new album. The reviews of this latest tour were good. When Skynyrd played Winterland in March, the lack of a third guitarist wasn't necessarily felt, and esteemed music critic Phil Elwood was impressed with their show. "Vocalist Ronnie VanZant with Lyn Skyn has a masterful touch: he is an electronic singer, a firm enunciator of lyrics, a ringleader, m. c., stage manager; he's rather short, pudgy, cool and domineering . . . also marvelous. Skynyrd plays with abandon but the show is tight, and well choreographed—they are so strong that even Allen Collins and Gary Rossington, on dual lead guitars, don't overwhelm the ensemble sound."

When the band played Boston's Orpheum in early April, that show also was well received. *The Boston Globe* wrote, "The guitars dominated the sound, punctuating VanZant's vocals in modified country riffs, with Rossington often indulging in long, fancy pickin' solos while Collins laid a loud, heavily chorded base. With the Confederate flag unfurled behind them, the sextet delivered almost two hours of simple, satisfying 'meat and potatoes' rock." Still, Lynyrd Skynyrd had known the thrill of the three-guitar army and wanted that component back in their music.

When the band moved to New York City to play at the famed Beacon Theatre with The Outlaws, there also was little mention of the down-to-two-man guitar lineup. Ronnie's command of the show was noted by reporter Kris Di Lorenzo: "Despite Van Zant's minimal vocal energy, he obviously rules the Skynyrd roost, displaying camaraderie by flinging an arm around someone's neck, baptizing Billy Powell with whiskey, or pouring ounces of Jack Daniels down Rossington's throat while Gary played bravely on without batting an eyelash. VanZant stalked the stage barefoot, watching hawk-like each member's solo; no one got too big for his britches or played one note too many . . . . [During 'Freebird'] Collins and Rossington kept steamrolling along while Ronnie grabbed them by the scruffs of their necks, tugged them by their Rapunzel hair to the spotlight front center, and held them there while they played their asses off."

New York's *Newsday* was impressed with Skynyrd, despite being a "Yankee" publication.

Wayne Robbins wrote: "Lynyrd Skynyrd has no pretenses about who they are or where they come from. Maybe that's why at this point it has transcended its regional identity to the extent that Lynyrd Skynyrd is no longer merely a Southern band but a great American band." The band must have been delighted to read that review.

Even the supercilious *New York Times* seemed to endorse the Beacon show, albeit in words not often used to describe Lynyrd Skynyrd. John Rockwell wrote, "Like all rock, the kind purveyed by these bands builds whatever complexity it aspires to over the most primordial of basics. In Lynyrd Skynyrd's case the ground is often a four-bar repeated ostinato in the bass, against which the occasional 12-bar patterns in the blues songs sound like extreme celebration. It might sound boring, especially given the predilection of Ronnie VanZant, the group's singer and chief songwriter, for short, choppy phrasing. But it lends the band's material a solid, hypnotic underpinning well suited for clever cross rhythms and melodic ornamentation for the guitars, piano and drums."

Skynyrd's show with The Outlaws and Montrose at the International Amphitheater in Chicago was well received although, according to the *Chicago Tribune*, a tad rowdy. "Lynyrd Skynyrd . . . is a band that makes no bones about the fact that they like to drink, and it's true that their foot-stomping Southern-style rock goes down better if you're a little wrecked. As it turned out, though, things went pretty peacefully. But loud."

The *Chicago Sun-Times* liked the show too. Their reviewer was particularly taken with the band's personality. "VanZant, a compact, heavy-set man, makes no effort to be charismatic or eye-catching, giving the appearance of controlled explosiveness and generating more power than many a flamboyant performer," wrote Al Rudis. "The only wild man in Skynyrd was Collins, whose rubbery body stretched itself every which way he played."

When Skynyrd played the Memorial Auditorium in Dallas in late April 1976, dozens of people attempted to climb up on the stage during the encore. The show was exhilarating and memorable. Wrote Pete Oppel for the *Dallas Morning News:* "Skynyrd is not a visual band—its mere stage presence cannot excite. But its audio impact in concert is much greater than it is on vinyl. In other words, Lynyrd Skynyrd is a band that must be heard, rather than seen to appreciate; but you must hear the band in concert to appreciate the complete mesmerizing effect of its music."

Some dates in Great Britain were booked on the heels of the successful stateside tour. Skynyrd was amused to once again play the Apollo Theatre in Glasgow, this time with a band they considered to be the epitome of laid-back: the Eagles. The Eagles surely knew how to indulge in the rocker lifestyle of drinking, drugs, women, and destructive fun, but there were some in the California band who enjoyed themselves and added some juicy tidbits to their rock-and-roll journals from hanging with their American brothers from the South.

Ronnie, Gary, and Allen continued to be bothered by the fact that there was no third guitar. They had auditioned several hot guitarists, but none seemed to be the exact fit the band was looking for. They questioned how to go about finding a guitarist who fit both their personal and

Artimus Pyle (left) and Ronnie VanZant, Ontario Motor Speedway, 1976.

musical profile. The answer, ironically, proved to be right in front of the band all along. Backup singer Cassie Gaines suggested to Allen Collins that he and the boys might want to listen to her brother Steve. She told him that Steve was an extremely proficient guitarist and had his own successful band. Cassie suggested the band meet with Steve when they next played Kansas City. The venue wasn't far from Steve's small farm near West Seneca, Oklahoma. As luck would have it, Steve's band wasn't playing the night Skynyrd hit Kansas City and he was available to show them what he could do.

Cassie Gaines was born on January 9, 1948, and had been one of Skynyrd's Honkettes since early 1975. Cassie had auditioned for the group after being introduced to the band by her friend Jo Jo Billingsley. Cassie had earned a degree in physical education from Memphis State University, but singing was her first love. While at Memphis, she had sung semiprofessionally in a production of the popular musical *Hair*. She knew then that she wanted to pursue a career in music.

Cassie's comments about her brother's capabilities raised the band's curiosity. Steve Gaines had been born September 14, 1949, in Miami, Oklahoma, and became interested in playing the

Guitar/songwriting ace Steve Gaines.

guitar after attending a Beatles concert in Kansas City. Steve and Cassie's parents Bud and La Rue supported the musical interest of their children.

Steve had majored in art, first at Northeast Oklahoma College, and then at Pittsburgh College in Kansas. Although his art would remain a strong second priority, playing the guitar soon became his passion. Steve's first band was the Ravens, a band successful enough to record at Memphis' famed Sun Recording Studio. Steve played with RIO Smokehouse in 1972 and eventually hooked up with Rusty Day and Detroit, a band that had played with Mitch Ryder. Steve cut some tracks with producer John Ryan while working in Detroit.

After Gaines left Detroit to return to Oklahoma he formed the band Crawdad. Crawdad recorded at Capricorn Studios in Macon and at Leon Russell's Shelter Church Studio in Tulsa. These sessions would later surface in a Steve Gaines solo album titled *One in the Sun*, which was released by MCA Records in 1988. Crawdad included Terry Emery on keyboards, John Moss on guitar and background vocals, John Seaberg on bass and vocals, Ron Brooks on drums, Tommy Lockey on horns, Bruce Blair on keyboards, and Chip Miller on congas.

Steve certainly liked the music of the band and the other players, but he was growing weary of playing small clubs. He was in charge of writing the songs, singing the songs, playing the songs, and booking the clubs. That was a lot of work. It was hard to do any one thing as well as Steve would have liked. He was anxious for a change. Steve had married his longtime girlfriend Teresa Lawliss. Steve had met Teresa when he was fifteen years old, at a baseball game. The Gaines' daughter, Corrina, named after a song from Taj Mahal's album *The Natch'l Blues,* was born to the couple in 1974. With a family to support and a need to elevate his musical contributions, Steve was ready to take the next step in his career, whatever that might be.

On May 11, 1976, Skynyrd had their Kansas City soundcheck and Cassie introduced Steve to the band. They agreed on jamming together for one song during their set, an invitation based solely on Cassie's recommendation. Steve was delighted. He had hoped to audition at the soundcheck—certainly not at the actual show.

Gary Rossington and Allen Collins were expecting Steve to be a "Holiday Inn lounge player," but since they thought a lot of Cassie, they agreed to give him a shot. Skynyrd's soundman Kevin Elson was directed to use discretion when Steve took the stage. "The band said to me, 'Look, this is Cassie's brother,'" Elson recalled. "'We're just going to let him play. If it's good, fine. If it's not, turn him off.'"

Steve appeared not at all intimidated, despite the fact that all he had for power was a small Fender Twin reverb amp. When he played, the sound was so low the band could hardly hear him. Then Steve tore into "T for Texas," putting a unique slide on it. What the band could hear, they liked. They all agreed that they wanted to hear more from this guy. Some offstage jam sessions followed.

Gaines impressed Skynyrd immensely with his powerful and unusual guitar work. The band began to talk about the possibilities if Steve were to provide that third guitar. At the end of May, Steve was told by Ronnie VanZant to report to Myrtle Beach, South Carolina, for work. Steve Gaines was now a member of Lynyrd Skynyrd and a participant in their next album, a live recording. His soulful gold-top Les Paul and raunchy Stratocaster were welcome additions to the Lynyrd Skynyrd sound. "Stevie Gaines actually had a pretty unique style," says Rodney Mills. "He had a style of playing slide guitar which was totally different from Gary Rossington's."

Those in and close to the band couldn't help but compare Steve Gaines' style to the others in the band. "Gary is very signature," said Leon Wilkeson. "[Gary's] more laid-back, rhythm-y. He wasn't like a rapid-fire lead guitarist like Allen was to me, but his signature was equally as important to the Skynyrd sound. I have a blast. I get to stand next to him and have fun." Gaines' zippy, intricate guitar playing would provide an interesting complement to Gary's playing and would expand Skynyrd's sound.

A lot of the Skynyrd sound had to do with what Ed King had brought to the band. Yet the band didn't think there would be much problem getting Gaines to make contributions of his own. "[Ed] could do just about anything," says Billy Powell. "He was always the grouch. We called him Deputy Dawg 'cause he kind of resembled him. He was the grouch of the band, even though we loved him."

"To a certain extent Stevie was a very fast player and Ed King was a very fast player," muses Rodney Mills. "On some of the songs that Steve was playing, they weren't wanting [Steve] to go in there and change Ed King's parts. Stevie picked up on that. That's kind of the way it should be, because some of that stuff is signature."

The next exciting event, and the first major appearance for Steve Gaines, was when Lynyrd Skynyrd was invited to play at the celebrated Knebworth Festival in England on August 26, 1976, as one of the opening acts for their boyhood heroes, The Rolling Stones. They were excited about sharing the bill with Creedence Clearwater Revival, The Don Harrison Band, Hot Tuna, Todd Rundgren, and others. "There was 250,000 people there that day," says Artimus Pyle. "There were no drug overdoses, it was in the middle of an English drought. There was dogfights above the crowd by old WWI aircraft. Simulated dogfights. There was hot air balloons . . . it was just a beautiful day."

"That was awesome," remembers Billy Powell. "250,000 people. I guess that right there was one of the signs, finally, telling me, man, you definitely have made it big now."

Artimus Pyle later stated that Lynyrd Skynyrd kicked The Rolling Stones' ass that day. "I felt as though we did," he says. "They came out two hours late and drunk, but, you know, of course, that's the Stones."

Pyle's bandmates agreed with him. "The rumor went around that we smoked The Rolling Stones," says Billy Powell. "[The Stones] made the audience wait so dadgum long before they came out. By the time they finally came out, a lot of them were on Quaaludes. I know this for a fact. The audience was so tired and drunk . . . drunk, or stoned, or tired, you know, tired of waiting. The enthusiasm wasn't anything like it was when we were up there."

Several film clips from the show later appeared in *Freebird . . . The Movie* and it looks as if Pyle and Powell's assessment is fairly accurate. "The Rolling Stones did not intimidate them," says Judy VanZant Jenness. "They probably enjoyed playing with people like Charlie Daniels more than [the Stones]."

Skynyrd was hot in more ways than one that day. The band played as a tight unit and the music was a direct hit. Ronnie strutted the stage as if he owned it and the other musicians forcefully made their presence known. Allen Collins, in particular, made quite a visual impact that day. "Allen would jump seven feet in the air," remembers Artimus. "He looked like a big daddy longlegs. And that energy that he possessed on stage and that raunchy guitar playing. Those long fingers, you know? That boy was born to play guitar."

Leon Wilkeson laughed when he was asked what he remembered most about the Knebworth Festival. His reply was that "my cord was too short." He was also confounded when people around him pegged a nickname on him. "Everybody was calling me 'interpol' all day," Leon recalled. "I thought, what does interpol mean? [They said,] 'International Police, you dummy. You got an English bobby hat on and an American cop shirt on.'"

The band seemed oblivious to everything but their music. Steve Gaines simply got down to business and played his heart out. Skynyrd was a tight seven-piece band once again.

The band had almost as much fun hanging out in the backstage area as they did playing. "I met more musicians that I always wanted to meet at that one concert than any ever before," says Billy Powell. Paul and Linda McCartney, Rod Stewart, Jack Nicholson, The Stones, Jon Anderson, Eric Clapton, Billy Preston, 10 cc, Todd Rundgren, Creedence Clearwater Revival, and many other celebrated rock stars could be seen relaxing and enjoying the music. The atmosphere was like an insiders' party.

"It was an incredible day," says Pyle. "Incredible music and just brushing shoulders with Jack Nicholson and Paul and Linda [McCartney], and I met the Stones and all the people from the business that were there. I remember looking through a window out of our dressing trailer, and looking into this tent where Mick Jagger and Gary Rossington and Ronnie were sitting. They were smoking hash. They were tapping a pipe. I mean this was years ago so I know it wasn't crack, or whatever they smoke in that. They were passing this thing around, and I remember sitting there in my dressing room looking through the window and going, 'Man, I'd like to go over there and smoke hash with Mick Jagger.' But I didn't. I said, 'Nah . . . I'll just watch.'"

"I smoked some pot with Jack Nicholson that day," says Billy Powell. "He was in one of the trailers. Just him and Leon were in there by themselves. I walked in and Leon said, 'You'd never guess who's here smoking a joint with us.' I said, 'Who?' He had his hat on and sunglasses. Leon took his hat and the sunglasses off of him and I went, 'Whoa, Jack Nicholson . . .' Cool guy, too. I met Billy Preston, went up there and went 'Hey BP, I'm BP, man.' And Paul McCartney's probably *the* nicest superstar I've ever met. He'd sit and talk to you like he's known you for ten years . . . him and Linda both. Jon Anderson of Yes was there, Rod Stewart, some of Clapton's people. 10 cc, the Stones . . . they were walking around and stuff. They're pretty nice to you. The Who are real nice people. I think they've gotten over their tearing up stages."

"I got to meet Stu Cook and Cosmos, the original bass player and drummer for Creedence," remembered Leon Wilkeson. "Jack Casady, my hero, was there, playing a Gibson Flying V bass. I said, 'What happened to your Olympic?' He said 'I had to trash them.' I was going, 'Wow, I thought you and Phil Lesh, the bass player for the Grateful Dead, were like big heavy endorsers for Olympic bass guitars. What are you doing playing a Gibson?' 'Oh I had to trash them.'"

There were some additional adventures for some of Skynyrd's group. "There was a scaffolding sitting on the side of the stage," Pyle remembers. "I looked up and saw Paul and Linda [McCartney] sitting up there. So I climbed up on this scaffolding. I got my courage all up and sat down beside Paul and scooched in. He made room and I said, 'Did you like our set?' And he goes, 'Oh yeah, I loved your set . . . I loved that "Freebird." That was great.' And Linda's like, 'Yeah, yeah, that was great.' And I said, 'I know you guys have kids, and I just wanted to let you know that I have children and you know, my favorite song, Paul, is "Maybe I'm Amazed." And he goes, 'Wow. That's a good favorite to have. That would be a good one.' His legs were crossed underneath him on the scaffolding and he reached up and grabbed hold of the scaffold bar to pull himself up and let his legs dangle. As he did that, he smashed his head into the scaffold bar. He literally slumped forward and knocked himself out and saw stars. And we were thirty feet above the stage. I grabbed him with both arms . . . Linda grabbed him with both arms. And [we] pulled him back. He shook his head . . . he looked at me . . . directly in the eye and said, 'Us old gunfighters have hard heads, don't we?' I'll never forget that as long as I live. I looked at him and I said, 'That's right.' I didn't know what else to say. I remember them sending Christmas cards to me for the two years after that . . . and Linda sent me a beautiful black-and-white book [of her photographs]."

Appearing on the bill at Knebworth was certainly good for Skynyrd's growing and luminous reputation as a musical force. Those in Great Britain and Europe were anxious to see them again. They played a variety of dates while overseas and had a terrific time. "People told us that audiences here are critical," said Ronnie VanZant. "Well, that's good. In the States, the show goes on, the whiskey bottles fly, and everybody has a party. People told us that here the audiences take you for what you're worth. Well, I'll give you my opinion of that after the tour. I'm really looking forward to it."

Artimus Pyle remembers that the band members and crew were thrilled to visit so many exciting international locales. "Paris, London, New York, everywhere . . . " recalls Artimus. "Dean [Kilpatrick] and I would get out and walk. Dean and I were the best of friends. We would walk and walk until we dropped and then we'd just fall into a cab. You know, if we didn't speak the language, we'd just give the driver a matchbook. And he'd take us back to the hotel."

The band always managed to have adventures while they were abroad. Some of them were fun while others were more difficult. "[There was an] MCA rep, Fabrice, he was French," Artimus remembers. "He knew that I loved motorcycles and left me a Harley Davidson Motorcrosse motorcycle to ride around Paris. So I jumped on it and took off and didn't even think of a helmet. You're supposed to have a helmet. I rode for three hours without a helmet. Finally the gendarmes pulled me over and arrested me. [At that time] there was a press conference and a photo session. Well, Dean went to the photo session and played me. Because he had the long hair just like me, but he didn't have a beard. What they did is they put a scarf below his nose. I'd give anything to have a copy of Dean playing me in a photo session."

Dean was definitely one for practical jokes. On another occasion he and Skynyrd roadie John Butler briefly shared an apartment on Confederate Point in Jacksonville. On Halloween, the two rowdies decided to have some fun. They staged a fake murder, complete with ketchup "blood" on the steps in the hall at the apartment building. They were promptly evicted.

The Knebworth Festival was not the only engagement where Skynyrd would have the opportunity to party with other rock stars. "One day we played with Rod Stewart and Alvin Lee from Ten Years After." remembers Artimus. "We were playing at the Roosevelt Stadium. It's torn down now . . . over in New Jersey . . . big stadium. I walked into my dressing room and Mick Jagger and Bianca were sitting on the little couch thing. So I sat down, and we're talking, and the next thing I know Mick goes into the bathroom. But Ronnie's in the bathroom too, with Peter Rudge. And guess what they were doing in there. So they were all three in the bathroom and I sat there and talked to Bianca."

Sometimes the band would be flattered to realize that famous people were also big fans of theirs. "I remember that day [at Roosevelt Stadium] because Linda Blair was a good friend of the band and she came that day," recalls Pyle. "She had just gotten her driving license . . . she was sixteen. She was hanging out with Skynyrd. She was world famous at that point. She had a thing for Dean [Kilpatrick]. We were all sitting in a room in New York City, about fifty stories above Times Square. We were sitting there and Dean asked me to do his neck, 'cause I'm like a chiropractor. If you need your back popped or your neck popped, I can do it. I'm very careful and I don't hurt people. So I walked over and felt his vertebrae and made sure and very gently went click, and popped his neck. Well, Linda Blair asked me to do it to her. So I went over, I felt her vertebrae and I put her chin in my hand and I was just kind of working her head back and forth. Then I suddenly noticed that Gary and everybody in the room was staring at me. 'Cause I was moving Linda Blair's head. So I did her neck and it popped real loud. Everybody in the place . . . there was Dean, and me, Gary, I think Linda's sister . . . I think her name was Debbie or Cindy or something. She was in the room and everybody went 'Ooowww,' you know, when I popped Linda's head. I was thinking, 'Oh, God . . . .'"

Kilpatrick was once again attracting the women. "[Linda] made a beautiful coat for Dean," says Artimus. "A big patchwork coat. Or she bought it or something. Linda was very talented."

The band seemed at its apex. The excitement in the music community and from those who supported Skynyrd at home was tremendous. The boys in the band were rock stars. They continued to live large. Sometimes too large. Their earlier flirtation with debauchery returned and it seemed difficult to stop. The drinking, drugs, and fast living began once again to consume Skynyrd. Televisions were thrown out of windows, groupies were hanging around day and night, cherry bombing was rampant, and practical jokes of all kinds were played and enjoyed. Driving fast and recklessly continued to be a favorite pastime for some of the band and crew. Gary Rossington injured his hand again in a car crash right before the band began efforts for their next album, but even that didn't seem to slow down the Skynyrd machine. They moved into Riverside Studio and prepared for the next album.

Despite the forward momentum of the Skynyrd organization, Ronnie VanZant was having

Judy VanZant with Melody.

second thoughts about remaining with the band. He was tired and actually physically sick from all the years of hard living, traveling, and partying. He considered quitting the band and devoting his hard-earned leisure time to regaining his health and enjoying his family. Judy and Ronnie's daughter Melody Rene had been born in September and Ronnie wanted to see her grow up. At the rate he was going, that might be impossible.

VanZant did take some time off during the winter months of 1976 and was able to rebound somewhat, but Lynyrd Skynyrd was in his blood. He began to devise a plan whereby he could regain his health, take some additional time with his family, and still perform with the band he had worked so hard to bring to success. Ronnie acquiesced to Gary and Allen's pleas to stick it out, but VanZant was ready for some serious changes.

Ronnie had been unhappy with the last album and was anxious to give the listening public the Lynyrd Skynyrd quality product they had grown to know and love. He felt that the material on *Bullets* was too predictable. He wanted the next album to truly capture the band's essence—he wanted it to be live.

9

One More from the Street Survivors

LYNYRD SKYNYRD made plans for a double live album which they would title *One More ~~For~~ From the Road*. When it came time to pick a name for the album, "Ronnie said the way to name a record is, well, another shot before we go . . . one more for the road," says Johnny Van-Zant. "He was always coming up with things like that."

The album would contain at least fourteen songs, and plans were set in motion to record during one of Skynyrd's energetic shows. The first attempt was to be over Spring Break in 1976, but it was difficult to bring the band together, as they were enjoying some hard-earned personal time. They decided to wait a couple of weeks. When that time had passed, the band thought they would try again, but Artimus had broken a leg parasailing. The project again was put on hold.

Eventually, by the first week in July, everything fell into place. The album would be recorded on July 7, 8, and 9, during a three-night stand at Atlanta's famous Fox Theater, which concert promoter Alex Cooley was trying his best to keep from being demolished. There were a variety of fundraising efforts to save the deteriorating art deco landmark. Cooley, who had long supported Skynyrd, asked if they would be interested in doing a benefit concert. "They were going to tear it down, if we didn't raise the money for it," says Billy Powell. "When we heard they were going to tear it down, we just said, 'Uh uh, man. No way.' [Alex Cooley] came to us and said, 'Hey, you do some benefits we could maybe save it.' Hasn't been torn down yet."

"We started the Save the Fox Foundation," said Leon Wilkeson. "We were the first donators. We helped establish that foundation. The Save the Fox Foundation address was included in the album information."

Skynyrd decided that being back in the heart of Dixie for such an event provided a wonderful opportunity to record their live album. Skynyrd viewed the show not only as an excellent opportunity to record a live performance, but also as a way to thank their Atlanta fans for their continued support. They were more than happy to play three shows in Atlanta. All the shows were virtually sold-out, according to the *Atlanta Constitution*. There were over 4,500 people in attendance. Tom Dowd was asked to produce the album.

Fan Steve Powell was in the audience that first night and remembers how well the Atlanta crowd related to Skynyrd. "The most vivid thing I remember was during 'Sweet Home Alabama' when Ronnie says, 'Southern man don't need him around anyhow,' the huge Confederate flag unfurled," Powell recalls. "The crowd went absolute nuts. The roar from the crowd was so loud it literally drowned out the music from the stage. I also remember seeing Steve Gaines on the stage and wondering who he was. I felt that no one could replace Ed King. During 'T for Texas,' I quickly realized that Mr. Gaines could play and hold his own with Gary and Allen."

Steve Gaines was a little awed by the reception the band received, but focused on his playing and quickly captured the audience. Although the addition of Gaines was accepted by Skynyrd fans, Ed King had been a valuable contributor to the band's sound and continued to be missed. "[Ed] was such an important part of the development of that band," claims Jeff Carlisi. "From playing all the bass parts on the first record, you know, before Leon came in there, and to having the original idea for 'Sweet Home Alabama.' He was so important, such an integral part."

The fans realized that they would have to do without King and were naturally very curious about the man who had replaced him. They were elated to see that the new guy in the band had his own chops and his own attitude. He was, simply put, excellent. Ed King would later say himself that Steve Gaines "was brilliant." Ed wasn't bitter or jealous about Steve Gaines taking his place in Skynyrd. He felt that Gaines was an addition rather than a replacement. "I couldn't play his parts and he couldn't play mine," King says. It was Gaines' turn to shine. Both he and King would forge their own legacy within Lynyrd Skynyrd.

"He was pretty talented," said Leon Wilkeson of Ed King. "But I'd rather talk about Steve Gaines. He hoped [to] create some kind of movement in the right direction for the band, and he incredibly did. Very humble. What a guitarist. Ah, just incredible. Him and Allen . . . was that ever a guitar match made in heaven. Man. But, you know, everybody who has been involved have contributed to Skynyrd. I guess I should say in all fairness, from Ed King on down."

One More ~~For~~ From the Road, released September 13, 1976, was an immediate success. It quickly climbed to #9 on the charts and resulted in the band's first platinum album and the fastest-selling and largest-selling album of their career so far. Atlanta Mayor Maynard Jackson made the members of Lynyrd Skynyrd "honorary citizens of Atlanta." Ronnie VanZant and Allen Collins would, in turn, present a platinum record of the album to the mayor and a check in the amount of $5,000 for the Save the Fox Foundation.

Hot once again, the new, live, version of "Freebird" climbed the chart on its own. "Freebird" had always been Allen Collins' baby. He was proud of the song and was constantly seeking to play it the best it could possibly be played. Every time it was recorded on a Skynyrd album, Allen would ask for countless takes to perfect it.

The band was well pleased with the outcome of *One More*. Even though Steve Gaines was still new to the band and had to learn the notes of each and every song, Lynyrd Skynyrd was tighter than they had been in a long time. They breathed new life into some of the songs on the album and came across as a professional, well-tuned unit. *One More* was a live-album masterpiece.

In addition to their hits, other songs included were "The Needle and the Spoon," "Crossroads," and "Searchin'." John Milward, in the November 4, 1976, edition of *Rolling Stone,* wrote, "Skynyrd has never aspired to be more than a tough rock and roll band and their live set—which draws more than half its material from their first two albums—lives up to that. Penny for penny, *One More From the Road* offers a prime cut of guitar rock."

Immediately following the recording of *One More,* Lynyrd Skynyrd was asked to participate in a benefit concert for presidential candidate Jimmy Carter at Florida's Gator Bowl. The *Atlanta Journal* predicted that proceeds from the concert, along with matching federal funds, would amount to $500,000, a record sum for any presidential fundraising event up to that time.

The Marshall Tucker Band and Wet Willie shared the bill, along with a handful of other acts. Skynyrd had been looking forward to seeing their friends and enjoying the benefit. "Gary Rossington and I both drove our matching Jeeps to the gig," remembers Artimus Pyle. "And when we pulled up backstage, we came up and hit nose to nose. We put 'em nose to nose and went 'clink' together, like toasting." Lynyrd Skynyrd had come a long way. Now they were performing on behalf of the future president of the United States.

Although they had prepared for the gig, at the last minute Skynyrd was unable to perform as a band. Ronnie was suffering from severe vocal strain from recording the shows at the Fox. "Ronnie's voice was kaput," recalls Artimus. "He had been pulling notes for all time. He knew that this was going to be a live recording, and he was really working hard to pull all the notes and get 'em right. So his voice was shot. He was there that day, but we did not perform as a band. Allen got up and jammed, and Gary got up and jammed, and I got up and jammed, and a couple of other people, but we did not play as a group that day."

"Ronnie just could not sing," remembers Artimus. "His voice was gone. He was actually there, backstage in a trailer. And there [were] rumors that we didn't play because Ronnie was too coked out, or Ronnie was drunk, or all this other stuff. And then everybody that played that day, Wet Willie and all the other bands, they all got a signed picture of the president and we didn't. I felt real bad about that. [Because] we *did* play. It was in Jacksonville, Florida, at the Gator Bowl. Why do you think most of the people were there?"

Lynyrd Skynyrd was in as much demand as ever, but the boys in the band were exhausted. Nonstop touring and recording had finally taken their toll. "I was abusin' myself on the road," said Ronnie VanZant in a later interview with Jim Jerome for *People* magazine. "Because after all, if it ain't fun, it ain't worth it. If you're into drinkin' and tearin' up hotels, blowin' gigs, that's fine. But it'll take years off your life too. I ain't as old as I look and there are plenty of false teeth in our group. There's been treatment by doctors and hospitalizations for our drinkin'. We were doing bottles of Dom Perignon, fifths of whiskey, wine and beer, and we'd all have to puke once each before goin' on stage. We couldn't even remember the order of the songs. Some guy crouched behind an amp and shouted them out to us. We once looked at tapes of shows—man, we was sloppy drunk. I couldn't believe kids applauded for that shit."

A decision had to be made. As much as the band needed to keep its momentum, Ronnie decided that the only way they could save their musical muse, to say nothing of their sanity, was to deny the call of the road, stay home for a while, and recharge themselves. The band whole-heartedly agreed.

Although it sounded like a great plan, the band could not follow through immediately. They were already committed to perform at four sold-out concerts in Tokyo and one in Osaka, as well as a return to England in early April 1977. In late April and early May the band toured the Southeast. In the summer they played for 100,000 people at JFK Stadium in Philadelphia, and other huge crowds in Oakland, Chicago, and Anaheim.

Skynyrd traveled to Japan to play their music for their Japanese fans, but the trip was also a fun one for the band. They were especially taken with the reception they received on the streets. "The fans would come up to us and stop about three feet away and then bow and every time they wanted an autograph they would give us a little gift," remembered Jo Jo Billingsley. "I was really touched by that. They would hand us a little gift as a thank-you for signing an autograph."

There was an ugly incident at a restaurant in Japan, but at fault were some Germans who had insulted the female members of the Skynyrd party as well as the band. A fistfight developed and the police were called. No charges were pressed and the band was free to conduct their business and go home.

When he finally returned from the road in late June, Ronnie fished, hung out at Whitey's Fish Camp, relaxed around his Brickyard Road home with Judy and Melody, spent time down at Ray's Coffee Shop, or meandered over to Price's store to pick up his mail. Whatever he chose to do, he just let his creative mind wander. The band and crew took a short vacation in Maui, where they were joined by their wives and girlfriends. Also along were writer Cameron Crowe and his girlfriend Mary Beth Medley, who worked for Skynyrd's management, Peter Rudge's Sir Productions. (Crowe would later partially base the band in his hit movie *Almost Famous* on his experiences with Ronnie and Lynyrd Skynyrd.)

Calling a hiatus had been a smart move. By the time Skynyrd returned to the studio in August to record their next album, they were in top form. The new material was every bit as good as previous recordings, if not better. The new record would contain exceptional songs from the magic satchel of VanZant, Rossington, and Collins, plus those of newcomer and extraordinary songwriter Gaines.

Ronnie VanZant had changed in his outlook to both his life and to his music. Professionally, he knew now that he was a better-than-average songwriter and he had made a study of the music business and what it meant to him and to his band. Personally, he was weary of leading the pack when it came to rowdiness and self-destruction. It was time to grow up. Ronnie was not only ready to get his personal act together, he was ready to lead Lynyrd Skynyrd in creating an album that would not only make them proud, but also make them a household name. Ronnie was ready to take on The Rolling Stones.

The band had developed a certain sound, much of it formed from early influences. "They were checking out the English bands and stuff like that," says .38 Special's Danny Chauncey. "You go back and listen to early Skynyrd and you can tell. You can hear that. Skynyrd's version was kind of English Rock with a Southern accent."

"When you listen to Skynyrd music, it kind of changed," says Judy VanZant Jenness. "You can see influences of different people that they listened to. Like in the early stuff, in my opinion, you could hear a lot of the English bands. Allen was highly influenced by Eric Clapton and a lot of it you could hear in his playing. Gary was influenced by, and Ronnie always teased him about it, Pink Floyd. There was a period where they were really into Bad Company and Free. You can kind of hear some of that in there. Ronnie's heart was always in country music, so you can hear some of that. Then when Steve Gaines came in, it kind of changed to a little funky kind of stuff—bluesy funk. But maybe it's only 'cause I know all that, that I can hear all that. Then the sound changed because there were changes in different musicians. That's automatically going to change its sound a little bit. When Ed King left, and there was two guitars, and then Steve came in, it changed then too."

Even though the band felt artistically refreshed, the recording was not without its problems. The band would once again use the talents of producer Tom Dowd, and Dowd had persuaded them to record at Criteria Studios in Miami. This change of venue seemed not to agree with Skynyrd. Every studio has a distinct sound, and what Skynyrd was hearing on the playbacks was not *their* sound. As the album progressed, the band became more and more dissatisfied with the way the tracks sounded.

The band's soundman Kevin Elson arranged to fly up to Atlanta with a safety (a recorded copy of the multitracks), to consult with Rodney Mills and see if the veteran engineer could help ascertain what the problem was. "They were dissatisfied with some of the sounds they were getting," remembers Mills. "So we went through this trial thing. . . . [Elson] said, 'We can get a much better drum sound up at Studio One, than what you guys are getting down here.' So it was kind of like, 'Prove it.' So we made a rough mix of it, and Kevin carried it back down there and they just stopped the whole album. Ronnie says words to the effect of 'Well, we're gonna go back home where we started all this. This album is too important. It's the most important album we're going to record at this point.' They all felt real strong about coming back there where they recorded their first album and they wanted me to work with them. I was road managing The Atlanta Rhythm Section full time plus still working the studio when I was not on the road. So, I made a decision to quit that and just go back to the studio full time. I wanted to work with Skynyrd, too. So I left my job with The Atlanta Rhythm Section and took a fifty-dollar cut in pay with no promise of anything from Skynyrd or anybody else. I just wanted to go back to the studio. That was my first love. And I always wanted to work with them on that album. We thought we were doing a lot of real special things on that album."

"'We love Tom Dowd,'" Mills remembers Ronnie telling him. "'He's a wonderfully creative genius. The things he does with us as far as arrangements and things are just wonderful, but we don't want him to mix the record.'" It was a sticky situation. Ronnie explained to Dowd that the band was pleased with the work Dowd had done, but that they wanted other people involved in the mixing. "We did a lot of that record without Tom Dowd there," remembers Rodney Mills. "We recut a couple of tracks that they cut down in Miami. Dowd came in at one point and worked for a while with the band. And one night Ronnie got a little bit of drink in him and he kind of picked that moment to tell Tom just how important this album was to him and to everybody in the band. This was their life. He just felt it was too important for him to try to get the very best out of this from everybody involved. He appreciated Tommy and all the stuff he did in the studio and everything, but there were other people that did things pretty well and he wanted to utilize them. He wasn't telling Tom to get out or anything like that. I don't know whether [Tom] got his feelings hurt, or what his impressions were from that. This went on for like two or three hours. And the next morning, Tom packed his bags, checked out of the hotel, and went back to Miami."

Dowd possibly decided to end his participation in the project. The rest of the tracks would be mixed and produced by Rodney Mills and Kevin Elson. "We got to the studio and we kind of said, 'Where's Tom?'" remembers Mills. "So they called down and they said, 'Well, Mr. Dowd's checked out.' We didn't know what to do for a little while. We said, 'Well, we're here, what do you think we should do?' I don't know whose idea it was . . . 'Well, maybe we should just go in there and work.' I just remember we continued to work and we pretty much finished the album without Tom Dowd being there. At least a third of that album was done without Tom being there. It was Kevin Elson and I who did pretty much the remainder of the work on the thing, and we made the original mixes on the album. Ronnie was there [but] everybody else went back home to Jacksonville. Ronnie finally went back home to Jacksonville and just left it to us. When the album came out, Tom Dowd didn't want his name on it because he didn't have the final say on everything. When we got through with that album, Ronnie told me how much he appreciated everything I had done and he wanted to get me a royalty on the album. [That] didn't happen but Ronnie says, 'I want to give you some money for the work.' I wasn't expecting anything. I never got a bonus or anything from anybody for doing anything. This was the first time that somebody just seemed like they genuinely appreciated the effort . . . you put your heart into it and everything. And that probably had more to do with me kind of furthering my career than anything that happened up to that point."

Tom Dowd remembers it a little differently. He says that he was producing Skynyrd and Rod Stewart at the same time, in addition to getting married. His time was strung out pretty tight. He followed the band to Doraville when they decided to leave Criteria. He says that bassist Leon Wilkeson had an accidental drug exposure that caused production to be halted for a period of time, and when the recording resumed, he wasn't informed. It wasn't until the record was being mastered at Capitol Records that he was aware that Skynyrd had finished the album without him. After mastering most of the album at Capitol, the band returned to Georgia where they resumed mixing the rest of the album. Dowd says that he was busy then with Stewart and couldn't join them. The first printing of the album cover did not note Tom Dowd as producer although he says that, at the time of the plane crash, the band had told MCA to include his name when the cover was reprinted. The name of Dowd's engineer, Barry Randolph, does appear.

The band was proud of their effort, and they were anxious to unleash it on the public. "Everybody realized the importance of that album," says Mills. "I think that Skynyrd evolved on that album quite a bit. A new personality emerged out of that thing that I think made a real difference in their sound on that album."

The album was to be titled *Street Survivors*. The cover art, a photograph shot on the back lot of Universal Studio, in Universal City, California, presented the band emerging from red-hot flames. The implication was that Lynyrd Skynyrd had survived the hell they had created for themselves and had emerged triumphant to rock-and-roll once again.

When they had first started recording, there was a problem with the content of the album. MCA president Mike Maitland had told Ronnie VanZant and Tom Dowd that he wanted more radio-friendly songs included on this Lynyrd Skynyrd record. He wanted songs that came in no more than three minutes long. Skynyrd's songs usually far exceeded that amount of time. The band was not interested in tailoring their music to fit radio's needs. It didn't matter to them if they had hit singles or not.

Dowd timed each song as it was completed and Ronnie attempted to appease Maitland and give him one or two three-minute singles. But Ronnie hated it. He vowed to never give in to such an unpalatable demand again—his music was *his* music. Lynyrd Skynyrd was *Lynyrd Skynyrd*. Skynyrd was known for its lengthy, expositional compositions—not ditties, not lite music.

Those who heard the early pressings of the new album in early October were impressed with the amalgamation of the selected songs. Although Steve Gaines was new to the group, he was allowed to fully participate and contribute some of his own compositions to the album. "I Know a Little" was an energetic and rambunctious boogie that displayed Gaines' vigorous guitar work admirably. Gaines demonstrated his affection for R&B guitar and bluesy delta delivery with "Ain't No Good Life."

Although Gary Rossington and Allen Collins could certainly be counted on when it came to superior guitar wizardry, Gaines brought an additional dimension to the already powerful multi-guitar offensive for which Skynyrd was known. His hypnotic bridges and fret leaps revealed a proficiency much advanced for the young man's physical years. "I think [Gary and Allen] were supportive," recalls Rodney Mills. "I think also, at the same time, [Steve's] presence in the band pushed them. I can remember Allen and Gary both working real hard on their solo stuff on individual things to make it a little bit special. Like 'That Smell.' I know they all had individual parts in there. Gary must have come back to his solo section of that thing like two or three different times to get it the way he wanted it. He kept working at it. Allen would come in to do a guitar solo and there was just some magic moments when he played something and everybody was like, 'Wow, that's really, really good.' Billy Powell played a couple of piano solos on things and everybody just kind of looked at each other and said, 'Well, it just don't get any better than that.' Those guys were a real rock-and-roll band in that they grew up together, they didn't slowly evolve into a band. They developed themselves from almost the moment they started playing instruments. They were a little bit different."

As much as he had established himself in the past, with the addition of Steve Gaines, Allen Collins would really shine on *Street Survivors*. "His guitar playing was very stylistic of himself," says Mills. "He had that Fender Stratocaster sound or a couple of other guitars he played. Allen just burned as far as the way he felt about his music, the way his personal life was, and the way his professional career was . . . he just burned. He was just wide open all the time. I think sometimes it got him in trouble. [When] you saw him on stage, it's like you kind of absorbed the energy that came out of him. Much more so than probably anybody else in Skynyrd at that time."

Gaines may have been artistic, but he also knew how to enjoy a song. There were zealous, momentous songs and there were fun tunes. His duet with Ronnie on their rollicking cowritten tune "You Got That Right" revealed a glimmer in VanZant's approach to his music that had not always been evident in the past. Ronnie was good at sarcasm and often delicately, if not pointedly, exposed the underbelly of the rock-and-roll beast, but it wasn't often he actually cut up on a recording. His light approach to some of the songs would inspire his guitarists. "'You Got That Right,'" said Leon. "That's Steve and Allen showing off."

The first single to be pulled off the album was a rather macabre rage against self-destruction called "That Smell." The song emphatically took issue with the "smell of death" which had enveloped the band in the not-too-distant past with the car accidents that Gary Rossington, Dean Kilpatrick, and Allen Collins had been in the previous year. A drunk Collins smashed his car into a parked Volkswagen Bug. Rossington passed out at the wheel of his Ford Torino, knocked down a telephone pole, crashed into an oak tree, and hit a house while driving in Jacksonville. Kilpatrick drove into the back of a Trailways bus, and due to his internal injuries, his spleen had to be removed. Ronnie VanZant was not amused, and was more than a little concerned for his brothers.

Allen Collins' driving record was so marred with accident reports, speeding tickets, and DUIs that his license was suspended on several occasions. Allen had a solution for being rendered carless. He bought a speedboat and traveled up and down the St. John's River and tributaries. Allen would tie up his boat at the end of King Street, where he would meet up with Dean Kilpatrick. Dean would then drive Allen over to the Grand Phaloon, the local hangout, on Park and King Streets. The plan worked well until the night that Allen neglected to tightly secure his boat to the dock. His boat was spotted by a bridge tender as it drifted along under the Mathews Bridge. More trouble for Allen. . . .

Ronnie VanZant countered the darkness and gravity of "That Smell" with a homage to the band's groupies in "What's Your Name," which he cowrote with Gary Rossington. The inconsequential "Georgia Peaches" was another musical escapade penned with Gaines that brought lightness and fun to the album. VanZant's previously impertinent approach to love found and lost was replaced by a poignant appreciation of devotion and commitment in the heartfelt lyrics of "I Never Dreamed." The tender and aching music and lyrics of "One More Time" also introduced listeners to the deeper recesses of Ronnie's heart.

A more carefree, gentle side of Ronnie VanZant was definitely emerging in the lyrics of his songs. Ronnie was still capable of making his point, however, and he remained committed to imparting his opinion of social injustices, if not on this album then on future albums. Yet, with age, Ronnie seemed finally to realize that a serious musician could also poke fun at himself. Skynyrd's affection for frolicking with promiscuous women in smoke-filled bars was represented on the album by Merle Haggard's "Honky Tonk Night Time Man." The songs were well balanced and the album had a symmetric flow.

The mix of songs, as well as their performance, was well received by most everyone. Rick Clark would later write in *The All-Music Guide to Rock*, "The contrast between Gaines' clean lead style, Collins' flash, and Rossington's thick-toned lyrical phrasing is something to behold. Without a doubt, it's Skynyrd's most cohesive body of work since *Second Helping*."

The final product and its reception were even a surprise for some who worked on the recording itself. "I felt that they'd come up with a few songs I thought weren't necessary," says Rodney

Mills. "I didn't really perceive them as being hits. I just thought they were great songs. Ronnie was a great writer and he had a great way of kind of painting a picture with his words. Much more so than I think anybody ever gives him credit for. He's one of the better songwriters that I know of. Ronnie wrote about real-life stuff. He put it in a song. And I think that the whole band had just come off this thing where they realized that if they didn't put out an album that did pretty well, they didn't know where their career would go at that point. Everybody realized the importance of the album. They had a brand-new member of the band—Steve Gaines—and it wasn't like they just got a member of the band and he just kind of didn't contribute that much. They totally embraced him. The ideas he had and the songwriting ideas he had, his style of guitar playing . . . everything was incorporated into Lynyrd Skynyrd."

Steve himself was surprised and delighted with the amount of input he was able to have on *Survivors.* He didn't expect to even have any of his songs used. He was immensely flattered that the band considered him their equal. He looked forward to a new and exciting musical career with Lynyrd Skynyrd.

Steve Gaines' involvement in the album was noted by everyone who listened. After the initial surprise that Gaines seemed to be a vital presence in the band wore off, people realized that Ronnie VanZant was making a statement about the future of Lynyrd Skynyrd. "I think it was the first album that Ronnie kind of gave some of the songwriting as well as lead singing over to somebody else besides himself," says Mills. "[Steve and he] did a duet on the album, which Ronnie had not done a whole lot with anybody in the band that much before. I think Leon maybe had done some stuff before. But Ronnie looked at Steve Gaines kind of as his equal and Ronnie had a lot of respect for that kid. I wasn't there when they first saw Steve that made that first impression on [Ronnie], but Ronnie would be quick to tell you [that] this kid was special. There were no ego problems. Steve'd sing something and Ronnie just said, 'Man, that guy's great,' and just be totally behind him 100 percent. I think Ronnie, I don't know whether consciously or unconsciously, just decided here's somebody that's got a lot of talent and we need to exploit this too. Or let it be known, or let it be heard, whatever. I don't know all the processes [that] went behind in Ronnie's thinking on that, but it wasn't like here's this new guy in the band and we're gonna kind of let him out a little at a time. The very first record this guy done with them, and he was in the spotlight."

Knowing the intricate internal politics of those boys in the band naturally gives rise to questions regarding how the others perceived Steve Gaines. "I don't think anybody was surprised," says Mills. "I think Steve had been playing in the band long enough for everybody to really have a lot of respect for him, as far as he was equally as good a guitar player as anybody in the band. I think everybody kind of liked that, 'cause Gary had his own style, and Allen had his own style, and when Ed left the band, it was kind of like they had to pick up the pieces. Then all of a sudden here comes this guy that could very easily pick up the Ed King pieces that they were having to do. I thought Stevie Gaines actually had a pretty unique style. He had a certain style of play-

Steve Gaines taking center stage.

ing slide guitar that was totally different than Gary Rossington's. But to a certain extent Stevie was a very fast player and Ed King was a very fast player."

Then, of course, there was the question of how Steve felt that he fit into the already established and internationally famous band. "He seemed like he had fairly good studio savvy when we recorded," recalls Mills. "Here's this kid, you know? A lot of musicians at that time [were] struggling, trying to get something to happen. Then all of a sudden [he's] thrown right in the midst of a group that really had sold millions and millions of records. [Steve] got an opportunity to go in the studio and record something. He didn't just come in and do a part here and there. He was an equal part of it. As far as my memory [of it] I think he handled it real well. I think there was little bit of this kind of wide-eyed [thing] when things would come together and sound good. I don't think he had the complete knowledge of how to put everything together, but I think certainly those guys had a lot of studio experience and savvy and everything else. I think that all helped."

All in all, Ronnie and the other members of the band thought *Survivors* was one of the best studio albums they had done. They had attempted to create an album that showcased a variety of musical genres, and they had succeeded. Now they would wait to see how the public received that effort.

Street Survivors showed Lynyrd Skynyrd at its best: talented, professional, and contemporary. This would be the Skynyrd that would influence up-and-coming musicians and bands, from the sound-alike Molly Hatchett to future artists, such as the Black Crowes and Travis Tritt. One of the bands most influenced by Skynyrd in a more personal way was an entity very close to home: .38 Special.

Rodney Mills would go on to produce other bands, including .38 Special. Even though .38 had Donnie Van Zant and other Skynyrd friends, its musical style was more mainstream and radio-friendly. ".38 Special is not Skynyrd . . . was never Skynyrd . . . didn't write songs like Skynyrd," says Mills. ".38 Special had a tremendous amount of respect for Lynyrd Skynyrd. And every now and then we would kind of emulate a lick here and there, and we would kind of know it and we'd say, that's O.K. If we can't do it, who can? They totally resented anybody else doing it though. They did not like the fact that the other bands from down around Jacksonville sounded like Skynyrd 'cause they looked at it as total rip-off and not original at all."

Yet Donnie Van Zant, Ronnie's brother and one of .38's songwriters and singers, was very much influenced by Skynyrd. "Skynyrd had to be my biggest influence," Donnie says. "And the reason I say that is because for me even wanting to get into the music business was wanting to be like big brother to begin with. I actually remember when they were called The One Percent and they used to rehearse right there in my mother and father's living room. I remember looking at Ronnie and going, 'Man, it looks like he's having a ball here. Maybe I can do this.' So he actually was responsible for me even getting in the music business. Just the way he wrote. He wrote songs from his heart, living songs. I think I learned an awful lot from him. You write from your heart. You can't make that stuff up or it's not going to be believable. That you write songs that move you spiritually and emotionally. If you can't do that, you can't expect it to do it for someone else. That's what I got from Ronnie."

Not only does Donnie feel his talent development came from his older brother, it was Ronnie who actually encouraged him to develop .38 Special and put it on the music map. "I had been through so many bands breaking up and all that, as a teenager and in my young twenties, that I came at a time in my life where I really didn't know whether I wanted to be in the music business or go after something with a little more security," explains Donnie. "And at that particular time I'd had an offer from a couple of railroad companies, [one] called Seaboard Railroad and

I think the other one was called East Coast Railroad. I went to Ronnie and I just hit him with a question. I said, 'Man, would you go with the security of this railroad here? I've been through so many bands breaking up and all that, that it just don't look like it's going to happen, you know?' He actually laughed at me and told me that I had music in my blood, whether I realized it or not, and that I probably would regret it the rest of my life if I really didn't try it one more time. So that's when I got .38 Special together with Don Barnes."

Still, getting .38 Special off the ground wasn't easy. Like any band, there were the requisite dues to be paid. While Ronnie VanZant encouraged his brother's music career, he was also honest. "Ronnie came out and listened to us at this particular club in Jacksonville," Donnie recalls. "I said, 'What do you think?' He says, 'Come back and see me in about five years.' I says, 'Oh well, thanks a lot!' But he held true to his word. It was about four years later and I went back to him and said, 'Hey man, we're pretty tired of this. We got something new to offer you here.' So we played him what we had and he liked what he heard and introduced us to a few people. Then we got introduced to Jerry Moss of A&M and that's when it all started for us."

"Before we were successful we got reviews saying 'Oh, another Southern Rock band and following on the coattails of the brother," says former .38 guitarist Jeff Carlisi. "All of a sudden, we started getting on the radio and we had our own style of music and hit songs. Then all of a sudden people started saying, 'Hey, the new band that's carrying the banner for the South."

.38 Special enjoyed immense radio popularity and still have a lucrative career, occasionally releasing new product and touring almost nonstop. Donnie Van Zant is a popular rock-and-roll figure. "I've always thought Donnie was the nicest of the three brothers, when I was in the band [Alice Marr] with him there for awhile," says Billy Powell. "[He and Johnny] both got real good manners."

.38 Special would go on to be a multimillion selling band, but in the meantime Lynyrd Skynyrd was looking for a huge hit with *Street Survivors*. That meant, of course, that they needed to get back on the road. However, after accepting the changes in the organization and winding up what he felt was perhaps the best album of Skynyrd's career, Ronnie VanZant felt it was necessary to take another short respite before heading out. He retreated to his home on Doctor's Inlet where he instigated a regimen of jogging two hours a day and adhering to a high-protein diet Judy had suggested. He took time to play with Melody, and to fish. He enjoyed poking around the 1954 white Mercedes he had found in a junkyard and poured thousands of dollars into renovating it. Ronnie even bought twenty-nine acres of land in Tennessee's hill country as a future getaway. Life was good.

Recording the album had been a gratifying professional experience for Lynyrd Skynyrd. MCA had some great news for the band: *Street Survivors* would ship gold when it was released on October 7, 1977. Within days of the album's release, the time had arrived to promote their new artistic project. Skynyrd launched the first leg of a worldwide tour to promote *Street Survivors* by hitting the stage on their own turf: the South.

10

A New Beginning but the End of the Line

THE INITIAL DATES of the tour in mid-October 1977 went extremely well and Skynyrd was welcomed to concert halls and arenas with open arms. The band had lost no professional momentum by choosing to focus on their music and families rather than the rock-and-roll lifestyle over the past months. The tour promised to be just as exciting to Skynyrd as it would be to their legions of fans. Even Ronnie VanZant's dream to headline at Madison Square Garden was about to come true. The date had been set. Ronnie thought playing such a prestigious venue surely indicated that Lynyrd Skynyrd had finally arrived.

This tour would start off on a much sounder footing than tours past. The tour would be more leisurely with rest days in between some of the dates. The band was looking forward to actually enjoying themselves for a change. The members of the band and the crew had eaten themselves alive with the resplendent immoderation of rock-and-roll life on the road. In preparation for the tour, the boys had been making it a priority to keep the drugs and alcohol at a minimum. This time cocaine, Quaaludes, and innumerable bottles of whiskey and beer would not be consumed on a regular basis. Lynyrd Skynyrd was ready to get down to business. The band was

Back on the road. Left to right, standing: Artimus Pyle, Gary Rossington, Ronnie VanZant, Allen Collins, Steve Gaines. Seated: Leon Wilkeson, Billy Powell.

tight and they were ready to rock. Ronnie often verbalized his belief that he and the band were just "street people" who wanted to play their music for no reason other than to have it be enjoyed. Now, with their heads free of synthetic stimulants and unhampered by drug-induced moodiness and paranoia, they were in a position to enjoy themselves. They would call their cur-

rent road trip the "Tour of the Survivors."

Road Manager Dean Kilpatrick had proven invaluable to Skynyrd's daily life on the road. When he had been sidelined the month before because of a pernicious van accident that resulted in the loss of his spleen, the band grew concerned. Dean brought so much to the road experience that it was hard for Skynyrd to think of doing a major tour without him.

"I had rented a van," recalls Artimus Pyle. "One of these big fifteen-passenger vans. I believe it was a Dodge. Somehow the band was using it and I was driving it. I loaned it to Dean one night. Well, he was doing Quaaludes and he ran into the back of a Continental Trailways bus on the off-ramp coming across the St. John's River. He hit the back of this bus. He was hurt very badly. They had to take his spleen out. 'Course the band, under tragic circumstances we find some way to kid about things, and I think they were calling him Disco Dean with he ain't got no spleen. We were kidding him about it."

Yet Kilpatrick said he was ready to go on the road and recovered enough to assume his mandated position in the tour operation. Everything seemed to be coming together for a notable tour. By the time the first date of the tour rolled around on October 13, 1977, Lynyrd Skynyrd was ready to rock-and-roll.

There had been some discussion about no longer using the Honkettes and lightening the personnel load. There had been some talk about just "using the guys." Yet the music didn't seem right in performance without them, and one by one the band hired the three young women back. The last to rejoin was Jo Billingsley, who had taken ill and was recuperating at her mother's home in Mississippi. When Ronnie called her she at first hesitated, then agreed to join the band when they played Little Rock a few days later.

The tour got off to a great start and Skynyrd was in good spirits. *Street Survivors* was a hit

The Lynyrd Skynyrd Guitar Army, 1977.

and the new material seemed destined to take its place right alongside classic Skynyrd. Ronnie had sworn off excessive alcohol intake to get in shape for the road. The results were obvious in his approach to his performance. The first four shows, in Statesboro, Georgia; Miami; Bayfront Center in St. Petersburg; and Lakeland Civic Center in Lakeland, Florida, had gone exceedingly well.

The fans had experienced changes in personnel over the years, so it wasn't difficult for the audience who had yet to see him to adapt to the addition of Steve Gaines. They were surprised with the key position Steve played on stage. Ronnie VanZant had never before shared lead vocals.

Steve had only been in the band a very short time, but it was apparent to everyone how much Ronnie respected him, both on- and offstage. "[Billy Powell] lied about the fact that no one stood up to Ronnie VanZant [on VH1's *Behind the Music*]," says Artimus Pyle. "I pulled Ronnie off of Billy, Leon, Gary, and Allen, countless times. Ronnie didn't mess with me and Steve because, number one, he knew he couldn't whip my ass, and Steve, he had a great amount of respect for Steve. He'd leave the stage in front of 200,000 people and let Steve sing a song. Hey, that tells you something about Ronnie's confidence in himself and also about Steve's abilities."

Not only was a new musical approach being attempted in performance with the duets and

Gary Rossington and Steve Gaines in sync.

intensive boogie-woogie, but Steve was playing his own material with a guitar vengeance that hadn't been seen by Skynyrd fans in some time. Steve had much to offer the band. He easily solidified the position he had forged on the album *Street Survivors* on stage in front of thousands of dyed-in-the-wool Skynyrd fanatics.

When Skynyrd played the Sportatorium in Hollywood, Florida, on October 15, the opening band was a band from Scotland called Lake. The audience did not know quite how to respond to them. But by the time Skynyrd took the stage, all was as it should be. "The concert was fantastic," fan John Stucchi recalls. "They played all the favorites and all the great new songs. When Ronnie announced that they had a new member, the first thought that came to mind was, he's the new kid in town and is going to have to pay his dues. But when Ronnie cut him loose, you knew that Steve was no ordinary musician. Right away I could tell he had a big influence on the new music. It was his sound that captivated me. I was very impressed and enjoyed every note. I couldn't help but wonder if the other members were a bit jealous but they seemed to have a great deal of respect for him."

It was clear to see that Steve Gaines was having the time of his life. Leon Wilkeson remembered Steve saying that his involvement with Skynyrd was similar to a "Disneyland tale." Leon could see right away that Gaines and Allen Collins were indeed a "match made in heaven." Steve himself said, "This is like the start of what I want to do. This is the beginning. I hope that I can be good enough to keep on going. This is all I ever dreamed about, you know? Just doing this."

In the meantime, the established members of the band enjoyed receiving their due recognition also. "[Allen] was a very talented guy," says Charlie Faubion. "He used to hold those crowds in awe of the way he played, his stage presence and everything. I know Gary is a good musician but I think Gary learned a lot from Allen. 'Cause to me when you saw that band in the early days, it was Allen. Allen had the stage presence, his music stood out amongst all the rest of 'em. And Ronnie, and of course Gary, writing songs together and everything. To me, Allen was every bit [as much] a songwriter as Ronnie was." And now Steve Gaines would bring yet an additional voice to the band.

On October 19 in Greenville, South Carolina, at the Greenville Memorial Auditorium, Skynyrd was welcomed back with extreme excitement. The fans hollered and boogied until they had nothing left to give. "It was a fabulous performance," remembered fan Pat Matthews.

"The show that night was simply incredible," recalls writer/musician Michael Buffalo Smith. "Artimus—from just up the road in Campobello—played his heart out; Gary, Steve, and brother Allen blazed across the fret boards of their guitars; Leon, "Thumper," was right on the money as always, delivering bass lines that always went far beyond what the bass usually contributed to a rock band. Billy played piano with the class of a Carnegie Hall pianist and the heart of a rebel; Cassie and the other ladies smoked the backing vocals, and right out front was Ronnie VanZant, one of the most amazing showmen I have ever witnessed. They were great. And I was fortunate enough to be backstage and meet most of them after the show. I'll never forget the moment, shaking hands with Ronnie, seeing him smile, and reflecting on the gentleness of this man who was known for his fisticuffs and hard living. He made a fan for life in me that evening, as he did with many others."

There was, however, an early hitch in the band's enjoyment of being back on the road. The band was extremely unhappy with the airplane that had been chartered from the L&J Leasing Company of Addison, Texas, for the American leg of the tour. Because of all of the infighting, it had been getting more and more difficult to book passage on commercial airlines. It wasn't uncommon for the band members to have fistfights while in the air, and the guys wouldn't promise to keep their hands off each other. All they needed was a big lawsuit filed by one of the airlines or fellow passengers. After many warnings by Kevin Elson's wife, who was a stewardess, and other flight attendants who encountered their rowdiness, it became an accepted idea that chartering the band's own small aircraft might be the way to go in the future.

Lynyrd Skynyrd had been scheduled to lease Jerry Lee Lewis' plane for their use during the *Street Survivors* tour, but something happened and the deal fell through at the last minute. The replacement plane, a $100,000 Convair 240 built in 1947, was in many ways inferior to what the band had been promised. Zunk Buker, whose father handled flight operations for Aerosmith, says that his father refused to fly the airplane when it was offered for charter to that band. Yet L&J Leasing assured Lynyrd Skynyrd that the plane was in fine shape and attempted to make it more acceptable to the band. "They painted Lynyrd Skynyrd on the nose of the plane," recalls Artimus Pyle. "How can you resist that?"

The Convair 240 made some troubling noises on the way from Lakeland, Florida, to Greenville, South Carolina. "The right engine backfired a lot," remembered Skynyrd sound technician Kenny Peden. "We watched it catch on fire . . . had a flame about six feet long out the engine."

When pilots John Gray and Walter McClary were asked about the fire they assured everyone that there was nothing seriously wrong. The band had no choice but to defer to the expertise and training of the pilots. But when the plane landed in South Carolina without incident the band was greatly relieved.

Ronnie had been talking to the other guys about the possibility of buying a new Lear jet for themselves and a new tour bus for the crew. The band liked that idea because then they wouldn't have to rely on leased, and often antiquated, transportation. But for the time being, they were stuck with this plane as they traveled to their next venue, in Baton Rouge at Louisiana State University's Assembly Center.

Several of the band members were extremely uncomfortable about using the Convair. Jo Billingsley had talked to Allen Collins by telephone about a disturbing dream she had had before rejoining the band that the Skynyrd plane had crashed. She begged him to relay the dream to the others and pleaded with him not to fly in the plane. Cassie Gaines told Ronnie VanZant that she would rather ride in the equipment truck than on the plane, but eventually she changed her mind. Roadie Joe Osborne made reservations on a commercial airline but later changed his mind and stayed with the band and crew. Members of the band asked Dean Kilpatrick and tour manager Ron Eckerman to talk with the pilots and obtain a solid guarantee that the airplane was safe. On the morning of October 20, 1977, they planned to do just that.

Eckerman was surprised to find the pilots Gray and McClary gone when he knocked on the door of their hotel room in the morning. A message had been left at the desk informing the road crew that the pilots had gone to the airport to work on the engine. The band and crew were told to meet them there at the appointed departure time with an assurance that everything would be just fine.

The band accepted the word of the pilots that whatever may have been wrong would be fixed before the scheduled departure. Just as they started to relax a little and worry less about the plane, they found themselves in the hotel lobby waiting an exceedingly long time for their customary limousines. The band grew agitated and finally decided to forget the limos altogether and hire some alternate transportation. The band and crew crammed themselves into five cabs and headed for the airport.

Walter McClary met the band and crew at the airplane, explaining that there was a problem in the right engine with the magneto—a small generator in the ignition system. McClary was calm and assured them that things would be fine for the flight. He reassured them that a mechanic was scheduled to meet them in Baton Rouge to repair the airplane so they wouldn't have any further concern.

Kilpatrick and security manager Gene Odom expressed surprise that the pilots would take the plane up with a faulty part. Once again they were assured that the airplane was safe and there was no need to be concerned. McClary guaranteed that even if one engine failed, perish the thought, the airplane could and would fly safely on the other. Since the pilot would be endangering himself as well as his passengers if there was a real danger, their concern seemed reactionary. Skynyrd's two representatives could only acquiesce to the pilot's greater knowledge of aviation and trust that he knew what he was talking about. The flight to Louisiana would take just a few hours, whereas it would take the better part of a day to drive, once another form of transportation could be arranged.

The nine members of the band and their thirteen crew members, as well as television crewman Bill Sykes, boarded the plane and attempted to relax during their trip to Baton Rouge. Some played poker, while others strummed their guitars or chatted. Ronnie VanZant was still tired from his hard work the night before. After the plane was up in the air, he decided to catnap. According to Gary Rossington, Steve Gaines sat talking to Rossington and Ronnie VanZant across the aisle from Allen Collins, Cassie Gaines, and Dean Kilpatrick. Always committed to the details, Dean had no doubt been wondering what had happened to the limousines. Evidently deciding to put the matter behind him, Kilpatrick joined Artimus Pyle in an impromptu disco bump in the aisle.

Everything went smoothly for the first part of the flight, but the plane started to labor during the last leg of the flight. Trying to compensate for the incapacitated right engine magneto, the pilots employed a procedure called "autorich"—supplying one engine with more gas than usual. Over 400 gallons of fuel were pumped into the plane's tanks before it left Greenville, South Carolina. Gray and McClary seem to have been unaware that they were creating an exceptionally rich fuel mix that would cause excess fuel consumption. They attempted to switch to alternate fuel tanks, but found that the tanks were empty. McClary then radioed to alert Houston Air Control, presumably the closest major airport, that the plane was having fuel problems.

While McClary dealt with the problem in the cockpit, John Gray entered the cabin, shaking and barely able to speak. He informed his passengers that there was a fuel problem and that McClary was going to try to set the airplane down in a field. He instructed his passengers to put their heads between their legs and "hold on tight."

"Everyone was instructed to strap into their seats . . . which they did," Kenny Peden remembered. "They were fairly calm from what I could tell. Of course they were worried, scared, but they weren't panicking." Stage manager Clayton Johnson would later say that several aboard started "cursing the airplane." For the most part, though, everyone was silent. It wouldn't be incorrect to say that many of them were praying.

Artimus later said that Ronnie VanZant very calmly walked to the back of the passenger compartment. On his return up the aisle he stopped to shake hands with Pyle. He smiled at his friend and rolled his eyes at the turn of events. Ronnie had somewhere found a big crimson pillow and returned with it to the front of the plane. He decided to lie down on the floor with the pillow under his head. So they were having engine trouble again? No big deal, he evidently thought.

No amount of preparation would have been enough. Within minutes of Pilot McClary's declaration of trouble, the plane disappeared from Houston radar. They were only ten minutes away from their Baton Rouge destination. Around 7:00 on the evening of October 20, rural residents of Amite County, Mississippi, heard what appeared to be an extremely low-flying airplane. Then the ground shook with a horrendous, metal-crushing reverberation.

The Convair had skidded across treetops for at least 100 yards and slammed into swampland eight miles south of the McComb, Mississippi, airport. The plane hit the ground so hard that luggage and clothing were later found buried deep in the mud. The forward section of the plane, where Ronnie, Steve, Cassie, and Dean had been sitting, broke away upon impact as the rest of the plane skidded into a tumultuous stop.

At first there was an unearthly silence. Then the yells and moans of passengers could be heard in the still night air. Somewhere near the rear of the plane, Artimus realized that, incredibly, the plane had crashed. He quickly surveyed the gravity of the situation. It was immediately obvious that circumstances were dire and without looking back, the drummer fled into the night through the oozing mire to get help. "My friends were bleeding and dying," remembers Pyle. "I didn't think about it, I just took off running."

Pyle, who himself had a serious chest injury, didn't stop running until he came upon a farmhouse. "Here I came, covered with blood, looking like Charlie Manson," says Artimus. He was greeted with a blast from a shotgun that pelted his shoulder. When Pyle was finally able to holler the words "plane crash," the farmer, Johnny Mote, understood. "He said, 'Is that what that was?'" recalls Artimus. (Pyle would telephone Mote nineteen years later to once again thank him for his help.)

The emergency response time was immediate. A Coast Guard helicopter quickly located the crash site. The airplane was so deep in the woods that anyone approaching it had to waddle through mud and climb over fallen trees. National Guard and Forrest County General Hospital helicopters soon aided in the rescue. Arriving by tractors, four-wheel-drive trucks, and on foot, dozens of people from the nearby cities of McComb and Gillsburg moved quickly over the wreckage to help where they could. The area was so swampy, several of the rescue vehicles became stuck in the mud. Rescue crews had to wade through a waist-deep, twenty-foot-wide creek, a tributary of the Amite River. A sandbar was eventually located to carry injured passengers across the creek.

The surviving passengers remained nearly motionless where they had fallen until the rubble could be lifted and they could be released from the metal that had entrapped them. Keyboardist Billy Powell sat speechless on what remained of the wing. His nose had been nearly severed from his face. It seemed surreal. This couldn't have happened. Only moments before they had been laughing, singing, and playing cards. This tour had promised to be the band's best yet. The band had made it, man. After all of the hard work, struggling, and bad lifestyle choices, they had arrived. This happened to others, it didn't happen to Skynyrd. Billy waited for help and he waited for news. He wasn't alone. And he wasn't dead. Hopefully everybody was O.K. and they would be telling tales about their "last moments" together on a tour bus tomorrow.

Tractors pulled away pieces of the plane to free the passengers who had been trapped inside, some piled on top of each other. "They were all in front of the plane and they were shouting, 'Get me out, get me, get me,'" Constable Gerald Wall remembered. "We were actually standing on top of some people to get others out." Injured band and crew members were painstakingly lifted and carried across the creek in the arms of the commendable folks of Amite Country. They were placed in whatever vehicles were available to rush them to McComb, University, Baptist, and Beacham hospitals as well as Southern Mississippi Regional Medical Center, where over thirty doctors attended to them. It took about three and a half hours to remove all the passengers from the plane.

Billy finally received information but it wasn't what he wanted to hear. There had been a profusion of critical injuries to almost everybody on board. And the worst was yet to come. Ronnie VanZant, Steve and Cassie Gaines, Dean Kilpatrick, John Gray, and Walter McClary were all dead. They had been killed on impact. Rescue crews ripped open the nose of the plane to remove the bodies of the pilots.

As with any disaster and anything involving entertainment personalities, there would be a lot of speculation as to what caused the deaths that night. Unfortunately, Cassie Gaines' death would later be the subject of great controversy. Billy Powell, on VH1's 1998 *Behind the Music* profile of Lynyrd Skynyrd, would tell how Cassie lay dying in his and Artimus Pyle's arms, with her throat cut from ear to ear.

Artimus Pyle says that account is a complete fabrication. "Here's Billy Powell," says Pyle. "For twenty years, Teresa Gaines . . . all of these people, thought that Cassie . . . which she did, died in the plane crash very quickly. She died on impact. She did not suffer. And she sat directly in front of me, and that's the way it happened. Billy gets on there and goes, 'Oh, yeah, her throat was cut from ear to ear . . . it was horrible . . . she was bleeding, begging to live, and she died in my arms and Artimus Pyle's arms.' It's the biggest bunch of bullshit I've ever heard in my life. I don't know what plane crash Billy Powell was at, but he wasn't at ours. It's bizarre. He's convinced himself over the years that this happened, and it did not happen. To say that without even telling anybody and going on national television . . . he ripped about twenty of Cassie's relatives' hearts right out. Judy VanZant posted her copy of the medical examiner records on the Internet to prove that [Cassie's] throat was not cut from ear to ear. The night that aired, Teresa Gaines called me and said, 'Artimus, you heard what Billy said.' I said, 'First of all, Teresa, it's not true. Secondly, Teresa, you saw Cassie's body didn't you?' And she goes, 'Yes.' I said, 'Well, was her throat cut from ear to ear?' She goes, 'No.' I said, 'Well, there you have it. Billy's just out of his mind. . . . [That] really disappointed me. I felt like calling Billy, but it wouldn't do any good. Billy is a very, very wonderful, warm, incredibly talented person, who suffers from delusions of grandeur. After all that went down, you can imagine the pain that that caused."

The FAA report clearly shows that Cassie Gaines did not have an injury to her throat. The report states, "The fourth fatality [referring to Cassie Gaines] had been seated in the center compartment and received a fracture of the right lower extremity and a small puncture wound in the left temple area." Ronnie and Steve received fractures of the lower extremities and head impact injuries, according to the report. Dean Kilpatrick died from those same injuries as well as a crushing chest injury. Judy VanZant Jenness called Powell's remarks "untrue, insensitive, and cruel."

Billy Powell's comments about other aspects of the crash were more factual. He would later tell *Billboard* magazine: "On impact, every seat belt broke. The nose cone was all the way off, a steel rod went through my arm. Leon was out cold, all his organs were shoved up into his chest, his teeth were knocked out. Here I am, trying to hold my nose on my face over here . . . .The ones up front were the most critically injured and killed. The ones in back, some of us just got out and walked around in a daze, in one to two feet of swamp mud with the sun going down and alligators and snakes everywhere."

Gary Rossington remembers the aftermath too. He told *Mojo* magazine in an article titled "The Southern Death Cult," "When you fall out of the sky and people all around you and you're in a swamp, it's like Vietnam or something, seeing all your friends and family dead and screaming and metal and flames, it's a heavy thing to lay there for hours waiting for help," he mused.

Among the passengers rushed to the hospital, Gary Rossington, Allen Collins, Billy Powell, Leon Wilkeson, Honkette Leslie Hawkins, Gene Odom, and Kevin Elson were the most seriously hurt. Several of Gary's bones were broken and the guitarist was in severe pain. His damaged leg would later require a brace. Allen had a large piece of metal imbedded in his arm, which would necessitate a bone graft upon its removal. Leon had severe internal injuries and a broken arm. In addition to the nose injury Billy had a deep gash in his forehead. Kevin Elson's leg was so seriously crushed that it was nearly severed, and Leslie Hawkins suffered a broken neck and serious facial lacerations. Roadie Joe Osborne, who had decided to fly on the Convair instead of changing to a commercial flight as he thought he might do, suffered a concussion and numerous facial fractures. Gene Odom was the only one of the survivors who was burned, but no one could figure out the cause of the burn, since there had been no fire because of the lack of fuel. Odom's left arm and face would later require months and months of extensive treatment.

Aboard the plane that day in addition to the band and the Honkettes were tour manager Ron Eckerman, soundman Kevin Elson, stage manager Clayton Johnson, security head Gene Odom, and Skynyrd's crew of techs and roadies consisting of James Brace, Joe Osborne, Mark Frank, Mark Howard, Don Kretzschman, Steve Lawler, Craig Reed, Paul Welch, Kenneth Peden and TV crewman Bill Sykes. Almost all had, at the very least, cuts, abrasions, and broken bones. The entity that had been Lynyrd Skynyrd was shattered. On that hideous night in a Mississippi swamp, the musical essence of Lynyrd Skynyrd had been silenced.

The families were notified and several immediately left their Florida homes to get to Mississippi as soon as possible on specially chartered airplanes. Judy VanZant and Teresa Gaines had been out to dinner and had just returned to Judy and Ronnie's home on Brickyard Road when Billy Powell's wife called to tell them she had heard something about a plane crash. Judy assured her nothing was wrong and several minutes later was shocked when a special report came on the television announcing that Skynyrd's plane had crashed and there were multiple fatalities.

Lacy Van-Zant had been at his home in Florida building a fence with Ronnie's brother Johnny the day of the crash. When a friend drove up to inform them that there had been a plane crash, they began to pray. When they finally heard the news of Ronnie's death, they were devastated.

The VanZant family was emotionally vanquished when they were told that Ronnie had been one of those who had died. "I really can't remember Ronnie even being buried," says youngest brother Johnny. "Not buried, 'cause he's not buried, but in a vault. I can't even remember the whole funeral. It was kind of a blur. That whole thing is just a blur to me. Actually I remember hearing that [Ronnie] was killed and that's about it . . . you know, seeing the reaction my mom took. It's all a blur. My brother Donnie, you know, we made a pact then, that we were going to stick together and carry on what [Ronnie] started."

Judy VanZant traveled immediately to McComb. Lacy Van-Zant joined her there soon after. A casket was selected for Ronnie and the two brought his body back to Jacksonville's Orange Park Rivermead Funeral Home. There was a public viewing of the casket on Monday, October 24.

Ronnie VanZant's funeral in a chapel in Orange Park, Florida, was an emotional experience for all who attended. Although Ronnie's only visible injury from the crash was a small bruise on his temple, his casket was closed to respect the often-stated wish he had expressed to his wife that people not "gawk" at his body when he was dead. There was a poignant ten-minute service, with 150 of Ronnie's close friends and family in attendance to pay their respects to the man who had indeed been one of a kind. Ronnie's favorite fishing pole and his Texas Hatters black hat had been laid in the casket beside him. David Evans, who had engineered on *Nuthin' Fancy,* had become a clergyman. He officiated at the wedding of Gary Rossington before the tour, and now gave the short service. A tape of Merle Haggard singing "I Take a Lot of Pride in What I Am" was played. Jeff Carlisi and Don Barnes played David Allen Coe's "Another Pretty Country Song" on their guitars before Charlie Daniels sang a haunting "Amazing Grace." Billy Powell was the only one of the band able to leave Mississippi in time to attend the funeral. The funeral was low-key, with fans outside paying their respects to their fallen hero.

As prominent as Ronnie, Steve, Cassie, and Dean had been in life, the funerals of all four would be subdued, mostly attended by family and friends. Steve and Cassie would be memorialized at a service in their hometown of Miami, Oklahoma. Dean would be buried in Arlington, Florida, after a Catholic mass.

Ronnie VanZant was laid to rest in an aboveground vault at Jacksonville Memory Gardens. A bird in flight decorates the marble, under his name and dates. In front of the crypt was a bench carved with a poem Charlie Daniels wrote about his fallen friend. The bench would be stolen some years later and vandals would damage the vault, making it necessary to move Ronnie's body. Yet Ronnie's little garden was comforting to his family and friends and would continue to offer solace for those who were profoundly affected by his death. Ronnie VanZant was gone, but he would not be forgotten.

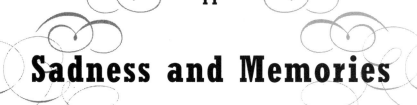

11

Sadness and Memories

THE MUSIC WORLD was greatly saddened at the tragedy that had befallen Lynyrd Skynyrd, but the crash of yet another chartered airplane with music luminaries wasn't the shock it once was. Already there had been Buddy Holly, Ritchie Valens, The Big Bopper, Patsy Cline, Otis Redding, and others. Just the month before, on September 20, music lovers were remembering singer/songwriter Jim Croce on the fourth anniversary of *his* death as a result of a plane crash in Natchitoches, Louisiana. But most importantly, those who loved rock-and-roll were still mourning their King. It had only been two short months since Elvis Presley died on August 16.

Obituaries, along with brief reports of the crash, were carried in almost all of the music publications, as well as major publications such as *Time* and *Newsweek*. Jim Jerome had interviewed Ronnie before the start of the tour for a profile in *People* magazine, which would appear on November 7, 1977. Jerome wrote, "If ever reconstructed, Lynyrd Skynyrd could not be the same. Stunned and mournful, the rock world has lost one of its most colorful and distinctive artists."

Yet it wouldn't be until Ronnie VanZant's songs were listened to in the context of the singer's death that many people actually paid attention to the music of Lynyrd Skynyrd. And the more they heard, the more they liked it. Ronnie would have felt it ironic that he had to die to have the majority of the rock-and-roll mainstream acknowledge the importance of Skynyrd. Yet dying in the field, on tour, was the stuff of music folklore. On October 20, 1977, Ronnie VanZant and Lynyrd Skynyrd became that of which they had always dreamed: legends.

As Lynyrd Skynyrd lay in ruins, the friends they left behind could not believe or comprehend their loss. This was not rock-and-roll hero Buddy Holly and the song playing in their minds was not "Bye, Bye Ms. American Pie." The compelling lyrics of Skynyrd's classic encore "Freebird" took on a poignant new meaning. "If I leave here tomorrow, will you still remember me?" was on everyone's mind. Ronnie VanZant's pointed question would be answered with a resounding "yes" by legions of family, friends, and fans. Many of those who would wonder at Ronnie's prophetic song were also engulfed in their own personal pain.

Jo Billingsley remembers hearing about the crash. "The next day [after Jo had agreed to join the band in Little Rock] some friends and I were in Memphis celebrating my return to Skynyrd when the phone rang," she recalled. "It was my mother. She was trying to tell me something, but was crying and couldn't speak. She put my brother Neal on the phone and he told me about the plane crash." Although thankful not to be on the airplane, Jo was devastated.

"I actually found out several months later that my aunt, who was a nurse, was at the hospital the night they brought them in," recalls the band's old friend Charlie Faubion. "I remember her calling and she says, 'Didn't you know these guys?' I said, 'Yeah, I sure did.' She said, 'Well, I just happened to be on duty that night when they brought 'em in.' I said, 'God, I can't believe it . . . my own aunt was right there, treating these guys.' So, it was full circle, kind of a unique deal."

The Southern music community was profoundly saddened at the loss of the four Skynyrd members and tried to rally around the survivors of the crash and their families. "After the plane crash," remembers Judy VanZant Jenness, "Robert [Nix of The Atlanta Rhythm Section] was like right there. He and Ronnie were real good friends. Robert played on one of their songs on one of their albums. He was just a really nice guy and he was right there to give me support. There are a few people that stand out at that time and he was one of them. I remember that he just couldn't do enough to help, to support me and all."

Some of the survivors would seek solace from the company of friends and those who could feel their pain at the loss of their friends. "Allen Collins came to my house when he got out of the hospital," Al Kooper remembered. "I had never talked to anyone who had survived a plane crash. He told me the whole story in six hours. It was one of the most incredible nights of my life. *We* can only imagine what being in a plane crash would be like."

The music of Lynyrd Skynyrd had been for the masses, and the masses responded to initial reports of Skynyrd's losses with stunned disbelief. People beyond the Skynyrd circle began to hear about the crash, and the news was staggering. Word spread fast and no one could believe it. The effect on many people would be poignant and everlasting. "Billy [Ray Cyrus] told me the story about how he was waiting for the school bus and he found out that Skynyrd had crashed," says Artimus Pyle. "He started crying and he walked to school and prayed for us. He let the bus go on." That moment would be recalled in Cyrus' song "The Day the Freebird Fell," which he cowrote with Pyle and Ed King.

"On October 20, 1977, I had gotten up and had planned to go to the mall and hang out with my friends," remembers fan Marianne Burrow Gray. "It was just another day. I wanted to go check out the nearby pumpkin fields for Halloween and such. But when I heard the news on the radio that Lynyrd Skynyrd's plane had gone down in Mississippi and that Ronnie, Steve, and Cassie were gone . . . well, time stood still. I had been driving to a friend's house and had to pull over. I just sat there in disbelief. How could it be? How could a thing like this have happened? With tears in my eyes I arrived at my friend's house. There were about a dozen people there. I could see by the looks on their faces, they had heard the news too. The remainder of that day and into the night we all sat there, semi-motionless, listening to the radio and any TV reports that we could. We heard the next day that everyone at [the] high school had Skynyrd on the radio and many wore Rebel flags. None of the teachers stopped them. [They] understood their grief. My younger brother was a senior and saw firsthand how badly the news hit everyone. When I was in junior high, 'American Pie' was a very popular song. Each one of us sitting in that house that night suddenly and fully understood the meaning of that song and how it came to be written. For all of us Skynyrd fans, October 20, 1977, was the day the music died."

"I lived in Pittsburg, Kansas," recalls fan Dallas Bryan. "Steve and Cassie lived just down the road in Miami, Oklahoma [in their earlier days]. Night after night we [had] opened [for Steve's band Crawdad]. My God, could Steve play and Cassie sing. A good friend told me that the plane went down and that he had talked to Steve and Cassie's brother Bob. It looked like Steve and Cassie had died. I was so in shock and hurt, and still to this day I am. My God, what a tragic loss. I think every day of Ronnie, 'the Best of the Best'; Cassie, what a beautiful [girl], so young and such a great talent; and Steve, [with] the fastest hands and what a nice guy. I mean, down-to-earth 100 percent. I live and breathe and feel them every day. Fly on Freebirds. [They] changed my life immensely and I wouldn't have it any other way. [They] touched me like no other and [they] left too quick."

"When I got the news (the day after I heard them in concert) that the plane had gone down, I was devastated," says Michael B. Smith. "It was so hard to believe. It still is. People talk about remembering where they were when they heard Elvis had died. That's the way I feel about Lynyrd Skynyrd. I heard it on television, and I sat there and cried. It was a vague report and we didn't know who had been killed for several hours. All I can say is, that plane crash will be forever with me, as one of the greatest tragedies in rock-and-roll and one of the saddest days of my life."

It wouldn't only be people in the United States who would be touched by the tragedy. "I can remember October 21, 1977, quite well still," says fan Glen Scrivener in England. "I didn't always listen to the news on the radio at that time and breakfast TV was not around in those days. I remember so many people that morning at school coming up to me and saying 'Have you heard the news? Lynyrd Skynyrd is dead.' Some thought he was a person, a bit like they think Jethro Tull is the one who plays the flute. They only knew about Skynyrd because I was mad keen about [them] and kept talking about them. Later that Friday, someone came and told me that Ronnie was among the fatalities so I knew that a lot of the magic was gone."

"I was a seventeen-year-old schoolboy in Coventry, England," remembers fan Julian Clarke. "We all had every album and we were waiting eagerly for U.K. tour dates to be announced as none of us had had the chance to see the band before. We were hanging around the school at lunchtime when a friend who had left school the previous term arrived looking very upset. He looked at us and told us 'Ronnie and Steve Gaines are dead.' Up to that point, the 'news' was something that happened out there, that didn't really impact me. This was a turning point in my life. This was the first event that happened to people I had never met, nor was ever likely to, that actually affected me. I guess it was the moment that I realized that I was part of the world."

The plane crash would long be remembered by Skynyrd fans, wherever they lived or listened to the music. Yet as much as they would remember the crash, they would remember the music of the band. "I [remember hearing] the awful news about the plane crash, not far from my home [in Louisiana]," recalls fan Mike Brinkley. "I remember going to school the next day with my Skynyrd shirt on, in mourning. Most of my classmates did not understand. But I still turn to Ronnie's lyrics for comfort."

Ronnie spoke to their souls and they would miss him. "It's twenty-four years later," says fan Robert "Slim" Rader, "and I still 'turn it up' every time RVZ tells me to in 'Sweet Home Alabama.'"

As the fans mourned, those associated with the band attempted to pick up the pieces. In the aftermath of the crash, Ron Eckerman realized that the briefcase holding the band and crew's per diem money and checks from their last shows was missing. It was later located, the lock to the case having been pried open, and $6,900 in cash and checks totaling $88,743.58 were returned to the band. Ron Eckerman claimed that an additional $1,100 was still missing. Several other items, such as cameras and personal items, were reported missing from the crash site, and representatives of the band made a plea to have the items returned, no questions asked.

According to the McComb *Enterprise-Journal,* the band had paid $5,000 in advance on the leasing of the Convair and had received contractual liability insurance. The leasing agreement stipulated $2 million liability insurance in amounts of $100,000 liability per seat and hull insurance for the total value of the aircraft. The agreement was signed by L&J president Lewis L. May, Jr. and tour manager Ron Eckerman. At least the families of those who died and those with injuries would find some of their financial needs met. In light of the fact that all of the survivors were now out of a job, any monetary recognition of their trauma was appreciated.

The official report of the National Transportation Safety Board concluded that the "probable cause of this accident was fuel exhaustion and total loss of power from both engines due to crew inattention to fuel supply. Contributing to the fuel exhaustion were inadequate flight planning and an engine malfunction of undetermined nature in the right engine which resulted in higher-than-normal fuel consumption." In other words . . . the plane ran out of gas. Most of the people who had been on board could only shake their heads in anger, frustration, and profound sadness.

Four members of the band had died but many others had survived the crash and now it was time to rebuild their physical and emotional lives. There were acute injuries to deal with and some band and crew members took years to physically recover. Yet as bad as they were, the physical injuries seemed far less than the emotional trauma. "Everybody in the band that survived was real bitter," recalls Billy Powell. "We were blaming God and everything, for destroying our careers. We were really very bitter and that was probably the heaviest drug use of our lives back then. We were just all getting drunk all the time and doing downers and stuff—just being real bitter."

Guitar tech Chuck Flowers, who had been one of the early roadies, had been fired from the band right before the crash over a minor infraction of the rules. There had been some question about a hotel bill and for some reason he and drum tech Raymond Watkins had been canned. The calamity of his friends overwhelmed Flowers. He shot himself in the head, using a rifle Ronnie VanZant had given him as a gift. Watkins was killed in a shooting a year later.

"[Chuck was a] real quiet guy," said Leon Wilkeson. "I went to school with him. Him and Raymond Watkins got fired right before the plane crash. It was some kind of a big disagreeable spat between them and Ronnie. After Ronnie died in the plane crash, from what I understand, Chuck Flowers felt that he should've been on that plane and died with him. So he took his own life with a .306 rifle, I think it was. Beautiful rifle Ronnie gave him. [And] poor Raymond. Raymond ended up getting shot by a girlfriend later on, because he was spanking her son or something like that. [Chuck and Raymond] were an important factor in Skynyrd's success. They did a wonderful contribution as well."

"[Chuck] used to live with Ronnie and me," remembers Judy VanZant Jenness. "He was a great guy. He did everything for those guys. Dean [Kilpatrick's] the same. I mean, Dean would do anything for those guys. Dean was a fun guy. Dean would do anything. He dressed flashier than anybody in the band. He was like 'Mr. Flash' when it came to his clothes. He was a good friend. He took care of Ronnie on the road. . . . And he took care of all the guys. He was a special kind of guy. Loyal. They had some loyal people working for them."

"Dean was wonderful," says Al Kooper. "He was [almost] the governess of the band. He really cared about them and really took care of them. He packed them, dressed them for the stage, [whatever needed to be done]. I'm not implying he was homosexual, he was not."

Steve Gaines (left) and Dean Kilpatrick on tour.

Regardless of the fact that his duties within the band primarily took place while Skynyrd was on the road, Dean Kilpatrick had been a close friend and confidant to everyone in the Skynyrd organization. He was missed tremendously by the members of the band and their devoted crew. "Dean was the most dedicated guy you can imagine," recalls Ed King. "He'd do anything for you and was always there if you needed someone to talk to."

The Atlanta Rhythm Section's Robert Nix remembered Dean to be "a great guy who always had time to do anything that needed to be done no matter how crazy the request may have seemed." Nix had heard about the crash on the radio. He called a friend who knew a neurosurgeon in Jackson, Mississippi, who later confirmed the deaths to him.

To his family and friends, Ronnie VanZant had held a special place in their lives, as a mentor, friend, or source of musical entertainment and fun. Ronnie's brothers and sisters were stunned. His father Lacy was hospitalized for three days after the funeral, clearly in a state of profound grief. Ironically, or maybe not, Ronnie had given his father his prized 1955 Chevy pickup truck and a lawnmower before he left on the tour. He gave his uncle EC his best black hat and a beautiful ring he had worn. Could Ronnie VanZant have known he would not be back to claim them?

Charlie Daniels would later immortalize Ronnie in the song "Reflections." "It's the song about Elvis, Janis [Joplin], and Ronnie," mused Leon Wilkeson. "I saw him doing that live. 'Ronnie, my buddy above all the rest, I miss you the most, loved you the best. And after all I thank God I was blessed, just to know you.' I saw him doing that live. Got all choked up. He almost got too choked up to sing it. Him and Ronnie were an item, man. They were close. There was some kind of compatibility between those two. And you can hear it in that song."

"I loved that guy so much, man," says Rickey Medlocke, who was back with Blackfoot at the time of the crash. "It really hurt me to the bone when the whole thing happened. It saddened me and even saddens me today to think about it. [Ronnie was] the most unbelievable storyteller and poet that I've ever seen come from the South. That guy was so dead on. He knew how to communicate stories that people understood whether they be from the North, the South, East, or West, wherever they come from, in all walks of life. People can relate to those stories that he would tell. He was just an unbelievable writer. And, I'll tell you something—the guy could sing, man. He had a style that just was unlike anybody I'd ever heard, you know, even to this day."

"[Ronnie is] almost like the James Dean of rock-and-roll," says Billy Powell. "He was just such a genuine person. He wasn't afraid of anybody. He wouldn't let anybody push him around. If Ronnie was alive today we might be millionaires, because he always did the business with the band. All we did was play. He had the business head. None of us did. One of our dreams after making it fairly big in the early days was to be able just to play the music and not have to worry about the business. Ronnie always said, 'You guys just play your instruments, think of music, and I'll do the business.' And that's the way it was. We knew we could just trust him. We knew we could count on him. We knew he had the head for it, and he did. He did all these things. He

Ronnie VanZant fronting the band.

was the father, founder, and leader of Lynyrd Skynyrd. Gary Rossington and Allen Collins had a lot to do with it too but Ronnie was the true sole leader at the time. And nobody's ever filled those shoes since his death. He was one of the most generous people I've ever met in my life."

Both the Jacksonville community and those involved in Southern rock continued to fixate on the airplane crash and its aftermath. The loss of the members of the band continued to be felt profoundly by each and every person whose lives they touched. It seemed the names Ronnie VanZant, Steve Gaines, Cassie Gaines, and Dean Kilpatrick were constantly raised and mourned.

Everyone involved with Lynyrd Skynyrd, from fans to those previously associated with the band, reacted strongly. In some cases, although the plane crash had been a shock, the fact that something so calamitous had happened to the band was not a complete surprise. "I knew something bad was going to happen to the band when I left it," says Ed King. "When my mother called to tell me about the crash, I knew Ronnie was dead. He always said he was going to die before thirty and I believed him. I wasn't surprised at all."

Ed King's reaction to the crash went beyond his involvement with the band and continued friendship with its members. Steve Gaines, in that third guitar spot, had taken Ed's place and was on board the airplane instead of King. "I was so fortunate not to be there," says King. "Steve Gaines and I had the exact same birthday. I didn't know that until I visited his grave and saw the date on his headstone. They've told me about the crash, what they went through. Those guys have a common bond that can never be broken. They experienced indescribable horror that will be with them for the rest of their lives."

"That boy [Steve] never really had a chance to really go all the way, let people know what he could do," says Rickey Medlocke. "There was a talented writer, very talented guitar player, and, from what I understand, just a hell of a nice overall guy. I really respected that in him."

"I didn't know a whole bunch about Steve," recalls Billy Powell. "I don't know if he was self-taught or what, but he was a smoker too. He was great on guitar and was a real good songwriter. He was like taking a lot of the pressure off Ronnie when he joined the band, 'cause he was sharing a little bit of singing. And he was taking some pressure off Gary and Allen. He was doing a lot of the solos. He was just an all-around good guy too. A fantastic person. About the last six months of his life, before the airplane crash, I was becom-

Teresa, Steve, and Corrina Gaines, October 1977.

ing real good friends with him. We were hanging out a lot. He wasn't around us enough for me to get any history on him. I just know he was a great guy."

"In Japan, Ronnie told me that he would not live to see thirty," recalls Artimus Pyle. "And he would go out with his boots on. [After Dean's van accident] Dean told me that he would not live out that year. I remember saying to myself, 'Well, Dean knew his destiny.' He lived, breathed, and ate Lynyrd Skynyrd. And I loved Dean . . . I loved Dean very much."

Cassie Gaines had played an important role within the structure of the band and would be greatly missed. "Cassie was simply one of the purest, sweetest people I've ever met," said Robert Nix. "I remember seeing her in airports and backstage and she always had that warm special smile for you."

"[Cassie] could make a Holiday Inn hotel room seem like home, in five minutes, with a couple of sticks of incense and a scarf or shawl here or there," says Artimus Pyle. "We'd all go down

Cassie Gaines.

to Cassie's room to smoke a dooby and you'd walk in her room and you'd think, 'Wow.' It felt like you were in somebody's house. She'd rearrange the room. Cassie and Steve and Dean and Ronnie . . . not having them around, there's a pretty big hole there."

The tragedy of Lynyrd Skynyrd would affect people who did not know the band and crew, and those who wouldn't be aware of Lynyrd Skynyrd until years later. "[Ronnie] was such a great songwriter and a great interpreter of songs," said Nix. "I hope in some way his memory and legacy will inspire some young singer/songwriter to come along and help carry on his magnificent tradition."

The absence of Ronnie, Steve, Cassie, and Dean would leave a huge hole in the hearts of those who knew them. In the meantime, those left to survive were encompassed by their need to heal, inside and out. It would not be an easy process.

As with all things rock-and-roll, the fact that the band had suffered a tragedy served to increase sales of their latest record. The cover of *Street Survivors*, with the photo of Lynyrd Skynyrd engulfed in fire, now seemed exploitive and in bad taste. MCA acknowledged a request to change the cover that had been made by Steve Gaines' widow, Teresa. They withdrew *Street Survivors* long enough to replace the photo with something less disturbing. On the original cover, Steve was pictured with his head seemingly on fire. According to MCA's Leon Tsilis, Allen Collins and Gary Rossington were surprised by the move as they really liked the cover. The art director for the cover had been George Osaki, who had also had bad luck with his withdrawn design for the American version of the Beatles' *Yesterday and . . . Today,* which was considered in poor taste because of its portrayal of the Beatles as butchers, with doll parts surrounding them.

Despite the brief unavailability of the record, the album quickly reached #5 on the charts by year's end, as well as platinum status. "What's Your Name" was #13 on the Singles chart in

November. "You Got That Right," featuring the duet between Ronnie VanZant and Steve Gaines, also made its way up the chart. "That Smell," eerie and even more autobiographical now, also received a lot of airplay.

It came to light after Ronnie VanZant's death that he had been very interested in producing records and planned to do a country-rock album. He had been talking about recording with Waylon Jennings and his hero, Merle Haggard. According to several sources, there had already been preliminary talks with the other artists, and since MCA had just signed Haggard, the label itself showed interest in VanZant's idea. It would likely have been an outstanding effort, but unfortunately no one would ever hear it. Ronnie did rework Haggard's "Honky Tonk Night Time Man" into an autobiographical song he called "Jacksonville Kid," recorded during the *Street Survivors* album. It was the last song Ronnie VanZant recorded. It wouldn't be released until the year 2000.

For the time being, though, fans anxious to hear Ronnie's latest and last music would have to content themselves with *Street Survivors*.

12

Picking Up the Pieces

SINCE *STREET SURVIVORS* was selling so well, MCA decided to release the tragically titled *Skynyrd's First . . . and Last*, in the summer of 1978, in an effort to maximize the sales of Skynyrd product. *First . . . and Last* was a compilation album that featured songs that had been recorded during the Muscle Shoals session of 1970/1971. MCA was wrong, however, that it would be the "last" record of Lynyrd Skynyrd to be released. Everyone who heard the tracks was impressed and thought the album was a terrific way to trace the band's roots and the promise that had been extinguished much too soon. The "new" album also hit platinum status, fed the fans' desire for more Skynyrd music, and sustained Lynyrd Skynyrd's position in rock-and-roll history. Yet regardless of the morbid title, *First . . . and Last* would not be the end of Lynyrd Skynyrd's story.

"Its kind of weird," says Judy VanZant Jenness. "In 1978, after the plane crash, Gary and Johnny and myself and Teresa, we all hung out. We were kind of each other's crutch. It was like right after Elvis died and it was like everybody was trying to capitalize on Elvis. We thought it was very disgusting at the time. It was like, we'll never do that. We'll never try to capitalize on the name Lynyrd Skynyrd. It was an emotional time. We were out of our heads but it made sense at the time." While a legal document attempting to put an end to the Lynyrd Skynyrd name would be forthcoming, at the time the band's business, involving royalties and rights, was in temporary turmoil due to the crash and the apparent end of the band. It would take some time to figure out where the band stood in regards to their music.

It was felt by some of the surviving members that a return to music might help the emotional scars to fade. Billy Powell was the first to take the plunge with his guest appearance on .38 Special's album *Special Delivery*. Additionally, Billy and Artimus Pyle participated in a project of Texas songwriter/pianist Leon LeBront. Honkette Leslie Hawkins replaced Etta Avery as a Williette with Wet Willie. When the others in the band observed Powell and Pyle attempting to get on with their lives, they started to sign onto projects as their recuperation permitted.

Billy Powell and Leon Wilkeson did some sessions with some old friends who had formed a band called Alias. *Contraband,* which was recorded in Orlando, Florida, was released in 1979 by Alias, whose musicians included former Honkette Jo Jo Billingsley and Jimmy Dougherty on vocals, Dorman Cogburn, Randall Hall, Barry Harwood, Derek Hess, and Billy Powell's brother Ricky. "That was just a project I did on the side to make a bit of money," laughs Billy Powell.

According to Leon Wilkeson, both Gary Rossington and Allen Collins said that they would likely return to music sometime in the future, but when they did they would not use the Lynyrd Skynyrd name. Leon said that they didn't see themselves as the remains of something that once was. Collins said that they would not cash in on the name as a recognizable entity just because they could. Yet they both felt it would be wrong to never perform again and when the time came, they would continue their music careers, as a new band. Gary mentioned to friends that there had been some preliminary talk about him and Allen playing with Gregg Allman and Robert Nix as a band. Yet the time didn't seem right.

Although they initially agreed to play on the Alias sessions, Gary Rossington and Allen Collins dropped out after some kind of dispute with the producer. Alias was featured in a nationally broadcast live radio show from the Agoura Ballroom in Atlanta on November 29, 1979, but *Contraband* failed to chart and the group disbanded.

Thoughts seemed to be constantly turning to what the surviving musicians had enjoyed with Lynyrd Skynyrd. "By the time I was doing my session work [on *Contraband*] Gary and Allen decided to retreat from the session," recalled Leon Wilkeson. "I could sense a dispute going on between them and the director of the project. I think that was the catalyst that made Gary and Allen—they're both deciders—realize how ready [to return to working together] the rest of us were. During the sessions [for *Contraband*] someone said to me, 'What are we doing here? We ought to be making our own album.'"

MCA owned the previously recorded material of Lynyrd Skynyrd and began to think of ways it could be rereleased. The creative forces at the company clashed with the marketing and sales administration on this issue. When thoughts turned to the possibility of another compilation record, there was some dissension. It was argued by some of the label executives that such a record would cut into the sales of the previously existing catalogue. They were afraid that all the best cuts would be on the compilation album and because of that the other albums would not generate any sustained interest. At this point, the members of Skynyrd didn't know what they wanted to do, although they could surely use the money from making more music together and earning more royalties. The band's MCA liaison Leon Tsilis took the matter to the president of the label. The naysayers at the label were overruled. *Gold and Platinum* was released in December 1979 and the compilation reached the Top 12 and certified platinum. The "new" album only served to generate even more interest in the band and brought new life to the Lynyrd Skynyrd catalogue. Every album went back on the chart.

The album title *Gold and Platinum* appears to have been coined by Gary Rossington and Allen Collins. One day in the winter of 1979 the two friends sat talking about the future. Rossington picked up Steve Gaines' gold-top Les Paul guitar, given to him by Gaines' widow Teresa. At the same time, he noticed an old platinum dobro leaning against the wall. Collins and Rossington had been discussing the need for a greatest hits package and "Gold and Platinum" seemed like a fitting name and tribute to the success of Lynyrd Skynyrd. Leon Tsilis says that he came up with the name while looking at the number of gold and platinum records the band had up on the wall. Regardless of whose idea, *Gold and Platinum* it was. The songs on the album were Skynyrd's gold and platinum sellers, from "I Ain't the One" to "Simple Man" to "You Got That Right." There would be sixteen songs in all. The royalties were, as usual, much appreciated.

A few Skynyrd soundalike bands began getting notice in an attempt to fill the musical vacuum Skynyrd left. Molly Hatchett was one such band. "They came in there and they tried to fill a void after the Skynyrd crash," says Donnie Van Zant. "[They] sounded a lot like Skynyrd and actually were sort of clones of Skynyrd. Personally great guys but . . . ."

Allen Collins and Gary Rossington were finding recovery difficult. Their physical injuries from the airplane crash had been extensive and it seemed to be taking forever to mend their damaged bodies. Gary had both legs, arms, wrists, and feet broken, as well as a fractured pelvis and several broken ribs. One of Allen's arms was more seriously inured than the other and it required several grafts along with extensive physical therapy to make it operational. Trying to move forward and not be victimized by the ill fate that had befallen them, Collins and Rossington focused on their music and made extreme efforts to work towards being the guitar players they once had been.

In 1980, Allen and Gary decided that they could best heal their emotional wounds by returning to the studio. Although he had been emotionally and physically devastated by the plane crash, Gary was a guitarist who needed to be able to express himself. "Gary [is] a very smooth, very talented guy in his head," says Rickey Medlocke. "[He] knows how to put things into songs [so that] you just go, 'Wow, where did he think of that stuff?' You know, 'where did that come from?' People don't give Gary a lot of credit for his guitar playing. But I'm telling you, being a guitar player and being around him, he sometimes really amazes me . . . he really does. I'm really taken aback by his playing a lot of times. Very subtle, but boy, when you hear it you just go, 'Man, was that cool.'"

The Rossington Collins Band was formed in 1979. Billy Powell and Leon Wilkeson agreed to join the two guitarists. Barry Harwood would take third guitar. Artimus Pyle said he would be interested in being involved as well. When thoughts turned to a singer, the band immediately rejected the thought of a male frontman. The idea of even attempting to replace Ronnie VanZant was just too painful.

It was decided to bring Dale Krantz into Rossington Collins as vocalist. Dale had been one of the backup singers in .38 Special. Gary Rossington evidently felt it would be difficult for people to compare a female with Ronnie VanZant. For her part, Krantz admired the band's creativity to come up with such an acceptable solution.

Dale Krantz was an Indiana native whose initial musical employment had been as a backup singer with Leon Russell. She became friends with Cassie and Steve Gaines, and that association led to her being recommended for a job with .38 Special. Because of her affiliation with the Southern band, Dale moved to Jacksonville, which is primarily how Rossington and Collins became acquainted with her.

Anytime, Anyplace, Anywhere was released in 1980 and the first single, "Don't Misunderstand Me," went gold. The song "Getaway" was also well received. The *Long Beach Telegraph*, on July 21, would like the album and say that the new band "upholds Skynyrd tradition." The Newark *Courier News*, on August 2, would also like the record while reporting that Rossington and Collins stated emphatically that they were *not* the second coming of Lynyrd Skynyrd. The album was a success. The talent of Rossington, Collins, Powell, and Wilkeson had not been terminated in October 1977.

Only Artimus was missing from the album. Very early on in the project, Artimus broke his leg in a motorcycle accident. The drummer had been in South Carolina while working on an album called *Studebaker Hawke*. Although the rehearsal dates at the band's newly purchased Jacobs Avenue studio in Jacksonville were initially pushed back for his recovery, Artimus eventually felt compelled to drop out of the new venture. He realized that the injury would not allow him to fully participate. Derek Hess, who at the time was working as a ship's chandler and looking to get back into music full time, was then called in to take Pyle's position on drums. Artimus wasn't completely out of the picture. He would introduce the band for their concert debut in Orlando, Florida, later in the year.

Although sales were good, many of those who bought *Anytime* were disappointed that the band seemed to center around Dale's vocals, rather than the guitars. "This band was totally different," says fan Stan Warren. "This should have been named the Dale Krantz Band instead of Rossington Collins. All the music centered around Dale."

Nonetheless, ticket sales were brisk when the Rossington Collins Band announced a series of shows to promote their album. Their initial appearances included Gainesville, Florida, and New Orleans. While there were some who supported a new creative effort by the musicians they had known as Lynyrd Skynyrd, most of those who planned to attend the shows were anxious to hear Skynyrd music once again. The shows weren't quite what the fans expected, but then this band was not Lynyrd Skynyrd. "There were few guitar-dominated songs like in Skynyrd," recalls Stan Warren. "Almost all of the songs ended with Dale singing, instead of a guitar solo or duet, like the old band. Allen [Collins] played in Rossington Collins, but he was no more than a backup musician. So was Gary Rossington, but at least he was about to marry Dale Krantz. It was not a good band, nothing like Skynyrd." Regardless of the material or initial reception, Rossington Collins went on to be well received and those involved breathed easier knowing that their musical careers would continue.

The majority of fans were ecstatic that the musicians they loved were playing once again. Rossington was pleased that their former fans seemed to be behind their efforts and was glad to once again be a part of a musical entity. "We're so lucky to have the people we've gathered in this band," he told Phil Kloer of the *Florida Times-Union*. "The new members inspired us, gave us strength and pulled us out of a slump. We pulled them out of a slump and we've been playing, writing, rehearsing, and recording together as a team, a family. Suddenly we had a real band and could see daylight again."

Shortly after the release of the album, Allen Collins was faced with another catastrophe. His wife Kathy, the mother of his two little girls, was pregnant with the couple's third child. While attending a movie with her daughters Amie and Allison, Kathy suffered a massive hemorrhage. "Both her daughters were there and saw her die right in front of them," says Billy Powell. "The first person who walked in after that was Judy VanZant. Neither one of them even knew they were in the theater either. You know, that's like wow. [Kathy's death] just devastated Allen. He was never the same after that." It seemed more than the sensitive guitarist could bear. He quietly withdrew from family and friends into the oblivion of alcohol-induced lethargy.

The rest of the Rossington Collins 1980 tour was immediately postponed. When Gary Rossington broke his foot it was canceled altogether. It didn't seem to be the time to return to a full-scale tour. Allen Collins wasn't much interested in the music and the band seemed to once again be encased in a shadow of ill fortune and despair.

Allen floundered, both emotionally and musically. Rossington thought that perhaps a return to the creativity found in the studio would help his friend find his way back. The band returned to recording. Regardless of good intentions, it seemed the magic that the band had encountered in the first album was grievously missing from the second. The public interest in *This Is the Way*, released in 1981, was nowhere near that of the band's debut album. The album was dedicated to Kathy Collins. The surviving members of Lynyrd Skynyrd seemed unable to dismantle the insidious gloom that had descended upon them.

Things were changing once again in the Skynyrd family. Thankfully, not all of the events were tragic. Ronnie's brother Donnie was doing very well with .38 Special. The band was selling millions of albums and playing to capacity arena crowds. "I went to a lot of .38 shows," says Judy VanZant Jenness. "I spent a lot of time around .38. But they were just up-and-coming when the tragedy happened."

Judy VanZant tried a second shot at marriage. Her new husband was Jack Grodin, the drummer with .38 Special. "Ronnie passed away and it was probably two years after that I met Jack," recalls Judy. "Then we got married about a year and a half after that. My son is his son. Jack played with [.38] from the beginning, up until [several] years ago. Then he just had enough of rock-and-roll and kind of was born again and, as we all say, flipped out."

According to Artimus Pyle, Dale Krantz had become involved with both Gary Rossington and Allen Collins, and by 1982, the two men found it difficult to work together. The Rossington Collins venture was over. Krantz married Rossington in May 1982 and the couple made the decision to temporarily give up performing and take up residence in a log house near the National Elk Refuge in the Grand Tetons.

The year 1982 would bring more disturbing news to the family of Ronnie VanZant. The inscribed 300-pound marble tribute to Ronnie was stolen from his grave in Jacksonville Memory Gardens. Police located the tablet two weeks later in a dried-up riverbed. This, unfortunately, would not be the last time VanZant's grave was disturbed.

In December 1982, MCA continued to recycle old Skynyrd product by releasing *Best of the Rest*. This latest venture was a compilation album featuring rare tracks and outtakes. There was still enough of an interest in Skynyrd to allow the record some success.

Allen Collins continued to spin wildly without any direction. He no doubt knew that the only hope he had of any kind of recovery was through his music. He formed a band called Horsepower, whose name was quickly changed to The Allen Collins Band. MCA released Collins' solo effort, titled *Here, There and Back*, in 1983. The musicians who appeared with Collins on the record were Leon Wilkeson, Billy Powell, Jimmy Dougherty on vocals, Randall Hall and Barry Harwood on guitar, and Derek Hess on drums. Allen's fans were happy to have the new music, but the low sales of the album resulted in the band being dropped by MCA.

"[Allen was] a marvelous guitarist . . . incredible guitarist," said Leon Wilkeson. "Unfortunately he had to suffer a lot. If anybody's been to the school of hard knocks, it was definitely Allen Collins, more so than anyone you can imagine. I like the way Paul Rodgers puts it in a song . . . 'if you listen to the wind, you can still hear him play.' He was a shooting star, artistically. As a matter of fact, Ronnie, Gary, and Allen helped produce the guitar solo [Bad Company's 'Shooting Star' in London]."

By the time Artimus Pyle recovered from his broken leg there was no Rossington Collins Band left to join. He decided to put together his own venture and he called it APB. MCA released two albums: *APB* in 1982 and *Nightcaller* in 1983. Pyle had proven that he was more than a drummer. He was an accomplished musician and also performed well on vocals. Included in the band were Karen Blackmon on lead vocals, John Boerstler on keyboards, Steve Brewington on bass, Russ Milner on guitar and keyboards, and Darryll O. Smith on lead vocals and percussion. APB became a popular bar band and later opened for a variety of acts. The band never received any kind of dedicated push from the record company, however.

In 1984, tragedy once again struck close to home. And once again it involved Allen Collins. One night while driving drunk, Allen drove his new Ford Thunderbird into a ravine in Mandarin, Florida. His girlfriend, Debra Jean Watts, was killed. The legendary guitarist was critically injured. After the doctors had done all they could, the news was indeed dire. Allen Collins was paralyzed from the waist down. His injuries also included limited use of his upper body and arms. Collins eventually pled no contest to DUI manslaughter. There was little else that could go wrong for the fallen star.

"He was the crazy one of the band, you know?" says Billy Powell. "He was really funny, all the time. He was an honest man and he'd do anything for you, anything he could. When his wife died of a massive hemorrhage, pregnant with his third child in a theater . . . that's what destroyed Allen. He dove into a bottle and never came out."

Gary Rossington and Dale Krantz came out of retirement in 1986 to form a new musical venture they called Rossington, playing with Tim Lindsey on bass, Jay Johnson on guitar, Derek Hess on drums, Gary Ross on keyboards, Ronnie Eades on sax, and Gary Baker doing background vocals. Their debut album was titled *Returned to the Scene of the Crime*.

Billy Powell had decided that the only way he was going to continue was with the blessings of the Lord. He joined a Christian band called Vision. "It's a long story how I got in a Christian band," says Powell. "I was in jail for DUI and that's where I met Jesus, actually. I became a Christian, and shortly after I got out of jail, I met Roger Marshall, who is the lead singer and the main songwriter of Vision. Next thing you know, I was going to church and I was in a Christian band for four years. That's where I finally just realized to learn to forgive and forget the past and just try to move on. I was probably the most humble you'd ever imagine. The most humble and nice guy in Vision you could ever imagine. I got my health back, didn't drink, drug, or anything. I just stopped cold turkey with no treatment or anything. I finally realized the past is the past and don't be bitter. Be blessed."

It took a number of years for the surviving members of Lynyrd Skynyrd to begin to pick up the pieces and rebuild their lives. Some were more successful than others during this eight-year interval. Allen Collins certainly had his problems, as did Billy Powell and Artimus Pyle. Gary Rossington had faced divorce from one wife but was happy in a marriage to the new woman in his life. Leon Wilkeson hovered somewhere in between. Yet one common element seemed to pull the individual members of the band towards recovery from the devastation they had faced: music. It ultimately would be their music that would enable the members of the once dynamic Lynyrd Skynyrd to return to productive lives and a semblance of happiness.

13

Starting Over

BILLY POWELL'S band Vision played all different kinds of music. The reception to the few Skynyrd songs the band performed was remarkable. "We weren't making any money," recalls Powell. "We were on the road, playing churches and going into bars. The Bible says, 'Go into the world and shout the lessons of Christ and to all the people,' and that's where we'd end up. We were on the road with Mark Farner, Grand Funk Railroad, the fourth year. He was a born-again Christian too. We got a bus that broke down every two days, so you wouldn't be surprised if you saw us pushing the bus down the highway trying to get it started. But to me that was God testing my faith. I was living with my mother, broke, in debt with the IRS [for] hundreds of thousands of dollars. I thought I'd be broke for the rest of my life, paying them back and living with my mother. But I was in Vision and I was happy. We'd go in and we'd play Vision music, or new Christian stuff. We'd also play a couple of

Skynyrd tunes, because I was in the band. And then we'd take about a fifteen-minute break and go up on stage with Mark Farner. We were his backup band all of a sudden—same people. And he'd play some of his new Christian stuff and then a couple of Grand Funk old songs."

Powell started to make a realization. "Every single time, every night, in between songs, people would start yelling 'Skynyrd!'" he recalls. "It was the people yelling Skynyrd is when a light bulb finally went off in my head, in 1986 . . . the latter part of 1986. Hey, you know, we got these fans who still love Skynyrd, ten years after the airplane crash. They still are rooting and just love Skynyrd."

Powell started to think about what Lynyrd Skynyrd had meant to so many people. It was a shame that audiences, who still enjoyed the band's music, were being deprived of experiencing it in concert. Powell thought about those who made up Lynyrd Skynyrd. Ronnie VanZant would continue to be missed and certainly couldn't be replaced, but the music of the band was a legacy Ronnie had left. The precarious careers of the other Skynyrd members seem to show that in their hearts they couldn't really make it without each other. Powell came to feel that the only way he and his former bandmates were likely to mend their emotional trauma and obtain any kind of musical and commercial success was by regrouping and giving Lynyrd Skynyrd a second birth. "That's when I went to Charlie Brusco," says Powell. "He was one of my managers. We needed to learn how to be blessed. Be blessed that I'm still alive and have all ten of my fingers and can carry on this music that Ronnie and Gary and Allen started. If we'd have never re-formed the band, I think that'd [have] been letting the audience down, letting our fans down, in a big way, and letting Ronnie and them down in a big way. I think our best tribute to them is carrying the music on, and letting the music live on. The legend lives on, they say now."

When Billy Powell presented the idea of re-forming Lynyrd Skynyrd as a new entity he was met with more than a little resistance. Powell had, before talking to Brusco, tried to talk to Gary Rossington about restarting the band. "[My wife and I] went to Atlanta, Georgia, when the Rossington Band was playing there one time. (Rossington and Krantz had resumed performing, now calling themselves Rossington.) I just got Gary in the limousine and said, 'Hey, this is what we need to do,' and presented the idea to him. He didn't like it at first, 'cause we'd said we'd never use the name again."

If Gary Rossington was initially hesitant about trying to recreate what had been won and lost, he was probably prudent to feel so. After the crash the surviving members of the band had signed a legal agreement stating that they would neither re-form Lynyrd Skynyrd nor use the name. It seemed only a legal exercise as there was no way emotionally that they could continue. Gary and Allen signed the agreement with Judy and Teresa after the two women verbalized discomfort with the band continuing to perform as Lynyrd Skynyrd without Ronnie VanZant and Steve Gaines. At the time, it was unthinkable to even consider re-forming the band without VanZant—the man who had been the most integral in its creation. At the time of the agreement, that was also how Gary and Allen felt.

"Back in 1978, they were doing a bunch of drugs one night and they got this piece of paper saying they'd never use the name Lynyrd Skynyrd again," says Billy. "Judy kept that for years, and then when we did the 1987 Tribute Tour, she came in and they went, 'Oops, we forgot we signed that.' I didn't sign it, but she sued our pants off. And I was mad at her. I was mad at Judy like you wouldn't believe. I thought she was screwing us. Then I realized later, she had to do that to protect Ronnie's estate from Gary and them."

Gary also had another problem. "[Gary said,] 'I got my own band. What would Dale do?' Dale was a singer in [the] band." Rossington had found some success with his band, Rossington, and wasn't particularly anxious to throw it away. Dale Krantz-Rossington was the featured vocalist and had been receiving a lot of attention.

"I thought [the idea of a new band] was a failure at that time, but then I went to Charlie Brusco," says Powell. "Charlie thought it was a fantastic idea. He's the one that talked Gary into it. The next thing you know, [Gary] called me back. Dale just really bitched me out, too, one night. [She] told me, 'Why are you trying to take my career away from me and blah, blah, blah, and take my husband away from me?' and all this. Of course to this day she thanks me now for it all the time. But Charlie finally talked to Gary about it and Gary said, 'You know, maybe this could be a good idea.'"

After some thought, a proposal was put forth. If the surviving able members of Lynyrd Skynyrd (Gary Rossington, Billy Powell, Leon Wilkeson, and Artimus Pyle) could put together a six-week tribute tour, they could debut their reunion during their friend Charlie Daniels' XIII Annual Volunteer Jam in September 1987. This would not be a formal, forever regrouping. This would just be a group of friends showing the world that the music of Lynyrd Skynyrd would never die.

"We had them to the Volunteer Jam," remembers Charlie Daniels. "But they were already back together and they decided they were going to tour."

In the band's opinion, the main issue then was not attempting to work out legal issues with Judy and Teresa. They were concerned about how they would position the band without Ronnie VanZant providing the vocals. Regardless of the familiarity of the Skynyrd survivors, the ominous hole in the band was hard to get around.

Still, there was also a positive side to the tribute as far as Judy was concerned. "For ten years, nothing was done," she says. "Then of course when the tribute thing came up, that was actually the first time there'd ever really been any talk about trying to capitalize on the Lynyrd Skynyrd name. We had no fan club, and really no contact with people. MCA had put out a couple of albums, compilations, after that and stuff. Then when they did the tribute tour that was really the first time [that the band had been focused on in some time]. Once all the legal hassles started, there's so many lawyers and people involved, to get anything accomplished, it's like a major ordeal. Everybody has their own lawyer. You have to get releases and you have to get everybody to agree. Then someone gets pissed off and they don't want to agree and they hold you up for months. It's just chaos to get anything done. We're all trying to realize that we need to be united because we have a very valuable asset here. We need to be taking care of it and developing it. We should have an awesome fan club because we have some of the best fans in the world."

A few minor fan clubs still existed to honor the music of Lynyrd Skynyrd but there had been no real effort to establish any large organization. Again, it was one of those situations where many of the fans didn't realize how important the band was to them until after it was no more. The fans had certainly responded well to the reissues of Skynyrd's MCA material and many had attended the gigs of the musician's individual efforts. Regardless, the fans were of mixed minds as to whether or not the band should give it another try using the Skynyrd name. Many were in favor of *any* formation of Lynyrd Skynyrd, whereas others were appalled that anyone could even think of a Lynyrd Skynyrd without Ronnie VanZant. Only time would tell if such a venture would be supported by the band's previous fans, and if there would be new fans to be found.

Veteran music manager Charlie Brusco had been representing Gary Rossington and he thought the reunion was a great idea. Rossington finally agreed that he could participate if only a six-week reunion were booked. Someone had the idea that as long as Ronnie was not going to be replaced in Lynyrd Skynyrd, perhaps the good-looking Johnny Van-Zant could be asked to pay tribute to his brother for this special occasion.

Johnny Van-Zant didn't readily agree. There was no way he was going to attempt to fill the shoes of his revered older brother, if even for one performance. "Hell, I was a Skynyrd fan too, so I figured Skynyrd was over with, you know?" remembers Johnny. Rossington and Powell told him that it would show Skynyrd's fans how treasured Ronnie was to them all. Johnny thought long and hard about it, discussed the matter in depth with his family, and finally came to a conclusion.

Johnny was the third son of Lacy and Marion Van-Zant and was born February 27, 1960. Johnny was as interested in music as the rest of his family. His musical tastes were a little different from Ronnie's, yet some influences were the same. "I loved Free," Johnny says. "I love Ray Charles, all the black singers. Marvin Gaye. I loved Hank Williams, Sr., Merle Haggard. I liked the Beatles, of course. Elvis. Who couldn't like Elvis? If you didn't like Elvis, you wasn't American. Paul Rodgers was always my favorite singer. It was really weird for me because I always looked up at him as a hero and actually last year he came out and opened for us. That was very cool, very cool. I love a blues feel, I love a country feel. I'm pretty versatile. We listened to everything at our house from country to . . . everything. Except for opera. They didn't have rap back then, fortunately." He remembers watching his brothers' love for music evolve into a career and

Enter Johnny Van-Zant.

thinking, "Wow, you know, that looks very cool."

The admiration of the talents of Paul Rodgers ran throughout the Van-Zant family from Ronnie to Donnie to Johnny. The influence of his vocal style was evident in the original Skynyrd and would now be again with Johnny at the microphone. Paul Rodgers was a fan of Lynyrd Skynyrd as well. "They came to the Royal Albert Hall in London," remembered Leon Wilkeson. "All of the Bad Company guys, Rodgers' people."

Johnny decided to see if music might be in his future. He tried playing the drums at first. "I kind of took to the drums," Johnny remembers. "Then of course my other two brothers were singers, so everybody was going 'Johnny, why don't you try to sing?' I was like, I don't know, I'm happy doing this. Then it just kind of evolved. Ronnie helped me get my first TVPA and [I] just started messing around, singing to records, stuff like that. [And] it evolved into this. I never actually played out in front of people on drums. By the time I was ready to go out and play I was already singing."

Since the family music business seemed to be singing, he went for that professionally. "When I first got into the business, hell I loved Nugent," says Johnny. His first musical association was with a garage-type band called the Austin Nichols Band. "[The name] was off the bottle of this distributor of Wild Turkey, the liquor," laughs Johnny. "We played a teenage battle of the bands and won it. So I went, 'Wow, this is cool. I think I want to do this for a living.'"

Johnny soon decided to form a band of his own. "I started meeting people," says Johnny. "Hey, you want to play? You want to jam? It kind of went from there, just like anybody else." Teaming with Eric Lundgren, Robbie Gay, cousin Robbie Morris, Jim Glover, and Danny Esposito, Johnny formed the Johnny Van-Zant Band. The band seemed to be onto something. They were offered a contract by Polygram Records and recorded their first album, *No More Dirty Deals,* in 1980. The poignant "Standing in the Darkness" garnered much attention.

Who else had been called in to produce brother Van-Zant's breakthrough album than Al Kooper. "Everybody went, man, you need to get Al Kooper, you need to get Al Kooper," remembers Johnny. "Al was the best. I talked to Skunk Baxter, who actually is the Doobie Brothers, [about producing the album]. But, yeah, Al was pretty involved in that [album]." Johnny would coproduce the album with Kooper and Gregory Quesnel. The younger Van-Zant's experience with the intense producer would be similar to that of his oldest brother.

"Me and Al just had our times," says Johnny. "But to be honest, hey, I learned a lot from him so looking back on it I don't think I'd probably change a thing. I had done demos and stuff like that. 'Course I had to do demos to get the deal. But Al was one of these guys who says, man, we gotta do it, we gotta do it. I did all the vocals in about five or six days so it was done, a real quick thing. I got a lot [out of] being in there, watching the cutting of it and being involved in that. But as far as real studio experience, I didn't get that much from that. I had to learn that all down the line."

It's interesting to see that sometimes time heals wounds when it comes to professional disagreements. "When me and Kooper seen each other," recalls Johnny, "there was the premiere of the movie *Freebird.* We were just hanging out, talking to each other. It was funny as hell, 'cause he goes, 'Johnny, you know what? [Since] I ain't gotta really work with you, man, I like you.' I was thinking the same damn thing. O.K. now, we kind of like each other. [But] we can't work with each other."

Johnny's second album, *Round Two,* was released in 1981 and was produced this time by Kevin Elson. "Kevin was a good friend of mine," says Johnny of the former Skynyrd soundman. "He was working with Journey at the time. There was a thing where me and Al [Kooper] wasn't getting along too well, so I felt like I needed to change. Also, the music business was changing. By the time I came around, Southern Rock wasn't real cool anymore. The record company was going, 'Man, it's not happening.' Then, you know, you gotta curl your hair and look pretty, kind of do all that thing. I was kind of caught in the tail end of all that. I think it made it a lot harder for me to actually do what I did naturally. But [making the record] was a good experience in Doraville there, the old Studio One. It was another learning experience."

Round Two would not only reflect a change in the public persona of Johnny Van-Zant, but in his musical style as well. "I've always liked different kinds of styles," Van-Zant says. "I always think that you [can] get stuck in one kind of vein. Even with Skynyrd, we go off a little bit, you know what I mean? Now we stick to what Skynyrd's about, but would kind of go off a little bit on it. Makes things interesting. It's called spice of life. It came back to, hell, where you can't do the Southern thing, you gotta try to change a little bit. I look at all those albums of the Johnny Van-Zant Band as a learning experience. I was very fortunate to have the opportunities that I have."

Although "Standing in the Falling Rain," "Yesterday's Gone," and "Cold Hearted Woman" were standouts, *Round Two* was only moderately received. Johnny was discouraged. The following year *The Last of the Wild Ones* was released, but with the exception of the title tune, "Good Girls Turning Bad," and "It's You," the album went pretty much unnoticed. "I'm the last of the Van-Zants, of the boy Van-Zants," says Johnny. "They couldn't carry on the name. It's just about learning how you get screwed in this business, just getting tagged again as a wild one."

"I quit music for about a year and a half," says Johnny. "It just wasn't fun anymore. I enjoyed playing the bars down in Jacksonville and playing all around there more than I was enjoying going out on the road. It turned into a business, and it just wasn't fun anymore. It really wasn't fun at all. I drove a truck for, God, a year and a half. I had my own truck, so I was like a lease contractor. I love driving, but I kept listening to the radio and I was going, you know, man, I could still do this shit. I just need to get it together. So I went back to writing and doing things. I just kept thinking, hey, I can do it, I can still do it. Then I met John Kalodner with Geffen Records."

Johnny would return once again to his solo career as he signed with Geffen in 1985. "Kalodner was a very hard person to work with," says Van-Zant. "It was like, hey, the man wanted me to be something that I wasn't. So I kind of got back into the same kind of boat. But I was wanting it so bad, I went for it again. Made an album called just *Van-Zant*. I had a song called 'I'm a Fighter' on there and [I] actually got to work with Marvin Hagler, the middleweight champion of the world. Before they had pay-per-view and all that, they used to have closed-circuit fights, like at Civic Auditorium, where you could go down and watch the fights. So they used that [song] for their theme song. That was him and Thomas Herne's championship fight. Hagler ended up winning it, so I was pretty happy about that when I worked with him. So that was a pretty cool thing off that album."

Johnny became known as a charismatic singer and songwriter, and eventually drew interest from Ahmet Ertegen of Atlantic Records. Johnny's new manager, Joe Boyland, had made the arrangement for Van-Zant and Ertegen to meet. "I met [with] Joe and played him some of my stuff," remembers Johnny. "He said, 'Man, I really dig this stuff. I'll tell you what. I think I know where I could take it.' And I was like, 'Oh, whatever.' You get in the music business you hear so much shit. In this business I believe half of what I hear. So anyway, he said 'I'll give you an answer in three or four days if anything's going to happen.' Sure enough, on the third day, I went to a Tom Petty concert there in Jacksonville. I was married at the time and I came home and my wife said, 'This guy, Joe Boyland, called and he needs you to call him right away.' So I called him right away, it's like 11:00 PM at night. And I said, 'Hey', and he goes, 'What are you doing Monday?' Well this was on a Friday and I said, 'Oh, nothing much. Just kinda hanging.' He said, 'Well, I'm at Ertegen's, chairman of the board that started Atlantic Records. [He] wants to come down and talk to you about doing a deal. What would you want?' So I named off a ridiculous price and just figured he was full of shit. 'Cause I mean, I done seen it all."

Evidently, Van-Zant hadn't seen it all. "We made a date at 2:00 in the afternoon, we'd be out at the airport and meet this guy Ahmet Ertegen, who I knew very little about," chuckles Johnny. "We're sitting out there, it's a private area of Jacksonville airport, where the private planes come in. This plane comes down and it's got a big Bugs Bunny on the side. Then Ahmet Ertegen gets off. So we go in the restaurant and we're talking, you know, and [Ertegen] says, 'Well, Joe tells me this is what you want, blah, blah, blah . . . who's your lawyer?' The deal was done. That was the quickest deal I ever had."

When Gary Rossington and Billy Powell approached Johnny to handle the vocals for their Lynyrd Skynyrd Tribute in 1987, Van-Zant had already agreed to record for Atlantic. "I really didn't know what to think at that time," says Johnny. "I had plans on doing another record myself. I really didn't think too much about it. Then we had a meeting down there in Jacksonville and I walked in a room of all them guys who survived the plane crash, and my brother [Donnie], and it really changed my mind. You know, these guys were asking me to be a part of something that was, God, their lives. The last thing my brother ever did with Lynyrd Skynyrd was have an airplane crash and die. The more I sat there, I figured, wow. He deserved a little bit more than this, to make what he had started carry on. My father was there with me, my dad Lacy. After we left the meeting we talked about it."

Johnny decided, after a great deal of thought, to put his solo project on hold and sign on as the temporary vocalist for the temporary tour. "It'd be a chance to kind of set things a little bit straight, instead of Lynyrd Skynyrd totally ending on a bad note," he remembers thinking. "Let's do something for the fans, do something for the guys in the band. They've been through all the hell they've been through. So, I guess it was a few months later I agreed to go into rehearsal to see how it would go. We went ahead on and started rehearsing and the more we got to rehearsing the more natural it felt."

The surviving Skynyrds were delighted to have Johnny's support. They knew that he could get the job done, even with the difficult circumstances. "I know Ronnie, Steve, Dean and all of them are very proud of us," claims Billy Powell. "And I know Ronnie's going, 'Go for it little brother! I'm very proud of you. Keep it up, keep the music going, don't let the legend die.'"

Randall Hall on the guitar.

The Lynyrd Skynyrd Tribute Band consisted of former Skynyrds Gary Rossington, Billy Powell, Leon Wilkeson, and Ed King. "Ed loved the idea, because he wasn't doing anything except teaching, I believe, at the time," says Billy Powell. Randall Hall, a guitarist who had worked with Allen Collins in The Allen Collins Band, was selected by Allen to play Collins' guitar parts. Carol Bristow and Dale Krantz-Rossington would provide backing vocals. When it came time to approach a drummer, Artimus Pyle was the first one the others thought should take the position.

Artimus had been living in Jerusalem. He and a group of friends were initiating plans to create The World Peace Center. A monumental concert was being planned to promote the new organization. "When I was going to Ohio State University, after I got out of the Marine Corps, my father was killed in a midair plane collision in Albuquerque, New Mexico," explains Pyle. "I got out of the Marines a little early because I was the sole surviving son and I [needed to] take care of my mom. I lived up in Columbus, Ohio, and I met a guy named Ron Davis and a girl named Jane Everett. I introduced the two of them. They now have eight children and live on Mt. Zion, in the old city of Jerusalem, in the old Jewish quarter. They've been living there for all these years and they asked me to come over and visit, which I did. After one visit there I realized I wanted to do something there. Now I'm a gentile . . . I'm not Jewish. I worked with them and we started this plan for The World Peace Center. I set up an offshore company out of Hong Kong so I could promote concerts in the Mideast. We were going to do this big concert. Bill Graham was going to help me. And it never happened. We were working on it but everything kind of fell through."

Lynyrd Skynyrd was still a very important part of Artimus' life. He wanted to support his friends and decided he would commute back and forth between the United States and Israel to participate in the tribute tour. He joined the band at their makeshift studio on Jacobs Avenue to rehearse.

"The wheels got turning on it and we started rehearsing," says Billy Powell. "We had a blast rehearsing and we thought, hey, maybe this could be bigger than we think. And it was. It was a lot bigger than we thought."

After years away from being on major tours, the band found that getting back among their fans was enjoyable and rewarding. The Skynyrd concert experience oftentimes is similar to that of the Grateful Dead. "Going to a Skynyrd concert, people are actually like at football tailgate parties," says Johnny Van-Zant. "It really is. I always take a bike on the road with me and get there before the shows. I'll get on my bike and actually ride out and take a crew member with me. Me and them will go riding in parking lots and I'll put my sunglasses and my hat on. Hell, I just look like any other hippie. It's a family thing, too. It's like people are out there cooking on the back of their tailgate, drinking beer, hanging out. They got their rebel flags. It's quite an event. It's not just a concert, it's an event."

Finally the night of the Tribute debut arrived in September 1987. Taking their places before a sold-out Volunteer Jam XIII was an emotional undertaking for the band. Thoughts of the historic impact of the night were not lost on them. "I was scared shitless," laughs Johnny Van-Zant. "I didn't know what the fans were going to think or do. I think we were only playing like four songs. It was actually cool 'cause it was being broadcast on the Jerry Lewis Telethon, our segment of it. I screwed up on 'Three Steps.' I actually came in on the third verse, halfway through the guitar leads. Well, I was scared."

The band did the best they could do on some Skynyrd classics. "We had a song we did called 'Good Friends Like These,'" remembers Johnny. "Ronnie wrote about the 'Hollyweird writers,' putting them down and stuff like that. Says it just doesn't make a damn when you got good friends like these. I know we did that one. Then they did 'Freebird,' of course, instrumentally, 'cause I didn't want to sing it at that particular time. 'MCA' maybe, we might've did 'The Breeze.' You know what, it's all kind of a blur."

Tribute tour drummer Artimus Pyle.

Offering the Johnny-sung Skynyrd classics and their instrumental "Freebird" homage, the band was well received as Skynyrd fans attempted to focus on the music, not the loss. The fact that this was a tribute and not a re-forming of Lynyrd Skynyrd gave the band some breathing room and they found that, all things aside, it was good to be onstage together again.

"That's when we decided, 'Wow, this is a good thing . . . let's keep it going,'" says Billy Powell. "We sold out about every place. We sold out Nassau Coliseum in New York, two nights in a row. That's a massive place. We didn't realize the magnitude of the success until it happened."

With the success of the Tribute came serious thoughts of perhaps re-forming the group permanently. The Skynyrd survivors had enjoyed performing together again and had found a certain comfort in each others' company. However there still remained an outstanding legal obligation that hung heavily over the reestablishment of one of rock-and-roll's legendary entities. When the management of the "new" band began to book dates exceeding the six-week commitment, Skynyrd widows Judy VanZant and Teresa Gaines filed suit. They demanded that Rossington, Powell, Wilkeson, Pyle, and King adhere to the earlier mandate that they not use the Lynyrd

Skynyrd name. They would be allowed to disregard the agreement only if VanZant and Gaines were cut in for what would have been their husbands' share of the profits.

"We had the first six-week leg [booked], and if Judy says it's O.K., you know?" says Billy Powell. "'Cause she still had a right to put her two cents in there, I guess, about us touring, using the name, 'cause we did sign a contract saying we'd never use the name again. She thought since Ronnie died, Skynyrd was dead forever. And we proved her wrong. Besides, Ronnie wasn't Lynyrd Skynyrd himself. We had something to do with it too. We decided to perform another tour . . . a six-week tour. We did two more of them without her permission. That's when she started suing us."

The suit was settled out of court, with VanZant and Gaines emerging victorious. An additional legal covenant was stipulated stating that if Lynyrd Skynyrd were to continue, it would only be allowed if there were at least two members of the *original band* participating. This would include Gary Rossington, Allen Collins (who was now unable to play), Leon Wilkeson, and Billy Powell. That was agreeable at the time and the tour continued.

With the lawsuit came a certain animosity. "That's why, ever since then, we've been kind of rivals [with Judy]." says Powell. "Sometimes we try to get along, but I guess we'll always be rivals now because we went on using the name. We had to go to court for months in New York. We had to agree to give her just exactly what we're making, and she doesn't have to share any expenses, either. It's really a big hassle. She won all this because we signed that piece of paper—that contract saying we'd never use the name again. We were all [at] the time hopped up on drugs . . . painkillers, and all kinds of stuff. This was right after the airplane crash when we did this. I don't know anybody came to us saying we'd never use the name. I don't even know who did it really. I don't know if it was her or what. We had no idea we'd change our mind in ten years. But we did change our minds after ten years but she didn't. She had the best dadgum New York lawyer there was. [We] had to settle out of court. And we got [less] because we didn't have a good reputation and that John Hancock did us in."

Judy VanZant Jenness has not been one to hoard the name of the band for completely selfish purposes. Whatever her reasons for making the band uphold their end of the agreement, she had a self-proclaimed mission. "VH1 (in 1998) did the most incredible piece on the band," says Judy. "It was like so overdue and they did such a great job. Lynyrd Skynyrd had never been given the credit due them. We don't get mentioned like The Rolling Stones and Led Zeppelin and U2 and the Grateful Dead. But yet, we're right up there with those people, and we have more loyal fans. Our guitar players don't get mentioned with the top 100 best guitar players. There are so many other stupid players [on the lists], but they don't mention Allen Collins, Steve Gaines, Gary Rossington, Ed King? Guitar army!! So it's like we have to help that. Our silence over the past twenty years has not helped. I've had so many people come up to me, that I would never have guessed watched VH1, people I play tennis with, people in the grocery store . . . 'You know,

I saw that special . . . I didn't know all that stuff.' It's like, that's right, because nobody's ever told you. So now people are finally getting a chance, and that's what I want to see happen. I want people to know who Ronnie VanZant was. I want people to know that this band was as good [as], if not better than, any of those other bands."

The initial dates of the Skynyrd tour were a monumental success. The tour was expanded to a thirty-two-city "Reunion Tour." The first concert would be held in Baton Rouge, Louisiana, on September 23, 1987, where the 1977 tour had so tragically ended. Another of the early concerts was in Atlanta, Georgia—a fan base that Skynyrd did not want to ignore. The show was held at Atlanta's Omni and was a massive success. "They rolled down the Stars and Bars behind the stage at the start of 'Working for MCA,' remembers fan Joe Holt. "That was really something to see. The whole Omni was filled with an energy that was hard to describe."

The night was poignant for the band as well. "At their second encore performance," recalls Holt, "Johnny said that he could not sing 'Freebird,' that we had to sing it, and [he] placed one of Ronnie's hats on the microphone. There was a gold or silver eagle on Billy's piano with a beam of light on it as they started playing 'Freebird.' I will forever remember that concert as if it were yesterday."

Allen Collins could no longer play his guitar but he naturally was anxious to somehow be a part of the activities of the band of which he was a founding member. It was decided that Collins would serve as musical director. His duties included selecting the set lists, supervising the stage, and arranging the songs. The tour provided another opportunity for Allen. A critical component of Collins' DUI manslaughter sentence had dictated that he use his fame to raise public aware-ness about the dangers of drunk-driving. Allen fulfilled his legal obligations by taking the stage in his wheelchair to sadly explain to Skynyrd fans why he could no longer play with the band he loved so much.

"[Allen] . . . he's as much a part of Lynyrd Skynyrd as Ronnie, in the sense that, Ronnie was the man, but Allen gave it that unstaged spark and energy that Ronnie needed because Ronnie didn't jump around," says Artimus Pyle.

The fans had mixed emotions about attending a Lynyrd Skynyrd concert and being unable to see Ronnie VanZant and Allen Collins perform. "I am one of those people that, when Ronnie died in the plane crash, the band was over for me," says Charlie Faubion. "The band really ended when it ended. I hate to say this, but I think the new Skynyrd . . . there's a lot of financial stuff pushing that. I can see where the guys want to stay together, and they want to carry on a tradi-tion. They want to create new music and everything, and I can't fault them for that whatsoever. But I think, initially, when they said the band would never get back together again, I think they should have left it there. Maybe gone on and maybe form another band. But call it something else—call it Gary Rossington's Starlight Band or something. You can't say, 'This is what Ronnie would want,' because no one knew what Ronnie wanted. I don't know what Ronnie would be doing today. I think he would've gotten into more of a country, Allen Jackson kind of thing. But even that, I feel ridiculous saying, 'cause it's pure speculation. People sit there and say, 'I think Ronnie would've done this . . . ' I don't know what Ronnie would've done . . . nobody knows. Ronnie didn't sit down and write down what his future evolution was going to be. He was a driving force and Allen and Gary were a driving force, but it was a joint collaboration, and when that collaboration was gone, then you don't know what they would evolve into."

The music press accepted the Skynyrd tribute performances and most reviews raised little objection to the band continuing the tour. On September 25, the *Florida Times-Union* would render their opinion that the "Skynyrd band pleases," while the San Francisco *Examiner* would proclaim, "Lynyrd Skynyrd Rides Again." The *Los Angeles Times* wrote that the "Skynyrd tour honors memories" in their article of September 26, and the *New York Post* on October 12 would pull no punches when it confirmed the band was back by announcing the survivors were "Smashed & Crashed But Still Raisin' Hell."

Ed King didn't think much new was really offered musically when it came to the re-formed band. "Skynyrd was a copy band from the moment we got back together," he says. "The people were coming to hear the old music. They weren't much interested in anything new. In that way, the tribute tour was a success. It was a good experience that I was happy to be a part of."

In light of their reception, the band members decided that this incarnation of Skynyrd was preferable to no Skynyrd at all. After all was said and done, the tour turned out to be extremely successful. Lynyrd Skynyrd was back on the boards.

14

The Price of Success

BY THE END OF 1987, MCA decided to release additional vintage Lynyrd Skynyrd product through the album *Legend*. The record was produced by Tom Dowd and contained B-sides and uncompleted and unreleased songs from the original band. Mainly because of Dowd's involvement, *Legend* turned out to be an interesting composite and not altogether a tired rehash of previously recorded material.

Legend was moderately received and the re-formed Lynyrd Skynyrd decided to record an original album to more fully explore what their current fans might want to hear from them. Because of the touring schedule there really wasn't enough time to produce an album's worth of new material, so thoughts turned to a live album on which classic Skynyrd songs, performed by the surviving band, could be presented. *Southern by the Grace of God*, a double live-recording from the tour, was released in 1988 by MCA.

Gary Rossington enjoyed participating in the re-formed Skynyrd but did not abandon his solo career. He and Dale went back into the studio and produced another Rossington album. *Love Your Man* was also released in 1988. This album featured Gary and Dale as well as Jay

Johnson on guitar, Mitch Rigel on drums, Tim Lindsey on bass, Tim Sharpton on keyboards, and Ronnie Eades on sax. Gary Rossington had no doubt learned the difficult lesson that nothing lasts forever and was hedging his bets regarding the future of the "new" Lynyrd Skynyrd.

Johnny Van-Zant was enjoying being with Skynyrd but found it difficult to fulfill everyone's fantasies about his being a clone of his brother Ronnie. Johnny was talented in his own right and had put aside his already established career to work with his brother's band. He would always be remembered for such solo classics as "No More Dirty Deals," "Last of the Wild Ones," "Hard Luck Story," "Coming Home," and "Standing in the Darkness." If he were to remain with Lynyrd Skynyrd, it was important to Johnny to create his own position in the band. He realized that the fans were not coming to the concerts to necessarily hear new music, but rather because they wanted that link to the Lynyrd Skynyrd that they loved and were used to hearing.

There were also those who didn't think that Ronnie's youngest brother had what it took to step into such a position. At least not yet. "He has great tools," said Ed King in 1999. "He has the ability to be a great singer. [But] you can't believe a word of what he sings. He seems stuck with some bad habits and is [vocally] lazy. He has no identity."

Johnny became increasingly frustrated as the comparisons to his brother Ronnie continued to roll in. There seemed nothing he could do to establish that he was *Johnny* Van-Zant, and was perfectly capable of entertaining Skynyrd's fan base. "They were some big shoes to fill," says his brother Donnie Van Zant. "I don't think I could have done it. [Johnny's] done a great job." And even if most people were coming to compare Johnny to Ronnie, there were others, some professionals, who thought that he was doing all right, just doing his own thing. "I thought [Ronnie] was a great songwriter," says Black Oak Arkansas' Jim Dandy Mangum. "That was his greatest talent. [But] Johnny actually sings better and is a better performer. The younger brother . . . but he got the accumulation and summation of all the VanZants. And he writes good too, I don't want to say [that he doesn't]. But I really think he's the nicest person."

Johnny continued to present 100 percent, but the toll of conjuring the specter of a fallen hero every night was exceedingly strenuous. He started to experience serious mood swings and sometimes behaved as Ronnie might have under the worst of circumstances. "He was almost filling Ronnie's footsteps there for awhile," remembers Billy Powell. "You know, the Dr. Jekyll and Mr. Hyde syndrome." Johnny Van-Zant's job was not an easy one, yet he continued to do what he had been asked.

It seemed that even if they tried, Lynyrd Skynyrd was discouraged from moving away from their past to produce new music. In 1989, in an attempt to squeeze every last piece of music out of the band's prerecorded catalogue, MCA released a greatest hits package, *Skynyrd's Innyrds*. There seemed to be a bottomless pit of repackageable material in the MCA vaults.

Although he had enjoyed participating in the Skynyrd reunion tour, the toll was great on Allen Collins. In September 1989 he was admitted to a Jacksonville hospital suffering from pneumonia.

He would remain there in critical condition into the new year. There would be no release for Collins. The drugs used to fight the pneumonia ravaged his damaged liver. He died there in the hospital on January 23, 1990. He was 38 years old. Allen was buried next to his wife Kathy in Riverside Memorial Garden in Jacksonville. Lynyrd Skynyrd would now proceed without Allen Collins but, like his musical brothers before him, he could never be replaced and would be greatly missed.

"When I first worked with Allen I thought he was a pretty different guitar from the [other] guys in the band," says Rodney Mills. "He was pretty flashy and everything. Ed King was that way, but with a totally different style."

"His birthday was July 19," remembers Artimus Pyle. "And mine's July 15. And we were real alike. That's why I knew him so well and loved him." Artimus has some fond remembrances of Allen's joie de vivre. "There was a time in London, England," Pyle recalls, "when Allen dumped a salt shaker on this girl from Paris. She was sitting there and Allen was always trying to see how much somebody could take. And he dumped the salt shaker on her head. She was European, French girl. She just kind of looked at him and brushed it off, like 'O.K . . . ' Then Allen has to push it. He grabs the pepper. We're in this restaurant called the 'Up All Night Restaurant' on King's Road in West London. He's lifting the pepper thing up and he was just about ready to dump it on this girl's head and she went off. I mean she started clawing, screaming, and talking in French, and she clawed Allen's eyes. Allen jumped up and ran out of this restaurant and started running full speed. He's drunk out of his mind. I tackled him after chasing him through the streets. I'm pretty quick, but those long legs, man, I was having to pump. I finally tackled his butt about six feet before we would've fallen into this pit with a bunch of spikes . . . one of those English courtyard things. He looked in front of him and he goes, 'God, Artimus, if you hadn't hit me when you did . . . ' He would've impaled himself. It was really scary. He was the one that would go, 'Artimus, you saved our life, you saved our life.' Allen was so full of life, man. I just loved that guy. But his legacy is definitely that guitar playing of his."

"It saddens me to even think about Allen," says Rickey Medlocke. "I just look at Allen and Ronnie and all of them and it just really cuts to the bone, you know? I'm telling you, Allen Collins was a very great guitar player. And I loved him dearly as a friend. He was a wild child, there's no doubt about it, but his legacy was just [as] a very great guitar player."

"He was an honest man," remembers Billy Powell. "He'd do anything for you. Anything he could. Just an all-around good guy. He was still ready to carry on after the airplane crash, without Ronnie. It devastated him, of course, him and Gary. They were all so close. But when his wife died of a massive hemorrhage, pregnant with his third child in a movie theater, that's what destroyed Allen. Then [he] suffered a car accident and killed his girlfriend in 1986 and then he's paralyzed. Then ever since he was paralyzed from the waist down, just complication after complication set in, and he drank even heavier. [But] I'll always remember him as one of the best guitar players there was. He was great."

Pyle believes that Allen Collins' decline and eventual death might have been averted had he had more support from the people around him. "I've decided to call my book 'The Curse of Lynyrd Skynyrd,' says Pyle. "One of the chapters is called 'The Murder of Allen Collins.' And it's how his friends, including me, his father, his family, his band, let him die. And he had a lot to do with it himself too. I loved Allen. A lot of people just let him go, and Gary's one of them. Dale drove a wedge between Gary and Allen like you wouldn't believe. I had to beg Gary to go see Allen the day that Allen died in the hospital. I had to beg the whole band to go over and see Allen a couple of days before he died. They were all glad that I did. I shamed them. We were at rehearsal and I shamed them into going to see Allen. He loved it, and it meant a lot to him."

Allen Collins would be missed almost as much in death, as he was enjoyed in life. He was an innovative guitarist and his guitar playing would never be forgotten. His contribution to Skynyrd was tremendous, but as they had in the past, the boys of Lynyrd Skynyrd struggled on without yet another founding member.

Johnny Van-Zant had decided that while he would continue to front Skynyrd, he needed to maintain his solo career as well. He finally realized individual commercial success with his 1990 solo album, *Brickyard Road*. The poignant title track paid tribute to Ronnie VanZant and the relationship of the three VanZant brothers. "The song evolved from the last day that me and Ronnie and Donnie actually spent together, the week before [Ronnie] passed away," explains Van-Zant. "He lived on Brickyard Road in Orange Park, Florida. It's a biographical day we spent together." The song was released as a single and brought attention to Van-Zant as it rose to place at #1 on the Billboard FM chart, where it remained for three weeks.

"I was real proud," says Johnny. "It's pretty cool because I had people underneath me that I really admired. Bon Jovi had 'Blaze of Glory' out at that time, God, Aerosmith was out . . . I got all these people underneath me. I'd have to look at the charts and see what songs that were underneath me, but it was pretty impressive."

Skynyrd fans would flock to Brickyard Road, once the home of their fallen hero. Clay County had to replace the street sign at least a dozen times. Eventually they just gave up trying to keep the street physically noted.

Yet another emotional Lynyrd Skynyrd moment occurred in December of 1990 at Sacramento's Arco Arena. The opening acts were Steve Earle and Roy Rogers. Prior to that night's concert Johnny Van-Zant had been unable and unwilling to sing his brother's words to "Freebird." The band had decreed that a solitary spotlight focus on the spot where Ronnie would have stood if he had been performing the song. The reformed Lynyrd Skynyrd would present the song instrumentally. Deciding it was time, Johnny soulfully sang "Freebird" during Skynyrd's show at the Arco.

"I tell you, that was the most moving experience of my life," recalls fan David Halliburton. "When Johnny sang the song the first time, you just knew that everyone was there—Ronnie,

Steve, Cassie, Dean, Allen. I think all of us shed a tear that night, for we had seen the before and now the after, of a big part of our lives. When Johnny sang the last note, then walked off the stage, and was hugging people on the side of the stage while the band ripped through the second half of the song, I know me for one just wanted to be there with them onstage, to be a part of the moment." It seemed in a lot of ways that Lynyrd Skynyrd had now come full circle.

The newly established Skynyrd returned to the studio to record *Lynyrd Skynyrd 1991*. Tom Dowd was asked to produce the album. New material had been written by Gary Rossington, Johnny Van-Zant, and others, and the songs worked well. "Pure and Simple," "Smokestack Lightning," and "Keeping the Faith" were songs that stood out on the album, but it seemed that some of Skynyrd's soul was sorely missing. "[The album] to me was kind of a different Skynyrd," says Billy Powell. "I don't know if it's more technical or more to it or something. Even though all the songs to me were real good."

Another good song on the album was "Mama (Afraid to Say Goodbye)" written by Ed King, Johnny and Donnie Van Zant, and Gary Rossington. Leon Wilkeson had a story to share about that particular song. "Well, my former mother-in-law passed away," he began. "I suggested that they let me play that song at the [funeral]. They said they would be honored to have that song played. So, guess what happens. I'm sitting up in the front pew, holding hands with everybody, you know, mourning, and all of a sudden I hear "Pure and Simple." I stuck the tape in backwards." He laughed. "This was the last funeral I ever wore cowboy boots to . . . I ran up and if looks could kill. I'm eyeballing this guy and I stop the tape. I don't want to get up here in front of everybody. It was just so awkward, because it was so quiet you could hear a pin drop. So I'm clippity-clopping in, Hopalong Cassidy, wearing heavy cowboy boots. And a mile-long trek seemed to turn into ten miles. I got to the tape and cued up and I bring it back and stick it in. My brother-in-law, Frank Elvis Britton, he goes, 'Well, they damn sure know who he is now.' One of the girls popped him upside the head. But 'Mama Afraid to Say Goodbye' got played in there. What an experience that was."

Although *Guitar Player* magazine would like the album and say that Skynyrd was "back with a vengeance," the reception of the album was mostly lukewarm. Both the reviewers and fans were of the opinion that they would take a wait-and-see position as to whether or not Skynyrd should be considered to be back in the game as a *real* band, rather than as a tribute band. Recognizing that they would have to prove themselves, cautious reception from the masses did not deter the band. They believed that they were perhaps on the verge of another breakthrough.

Revered manager and promoter Bill Graham expressed interest in managing Skynyrd and the band took him up on it. "He reminded me of Lorne Greene . . . Ben Cartwright," said Leon. "He was the dadburnit pa of rock-and-roll." Not much is said about it these days, but the association didn't last long. Bill Graham was killed in a helicopter crash in 1991.

Even though the tempestuous Ronnie VanZant was no longer with the band, the band continued to be victimized by the volatile personalities of its members. On tour in Paris in 1992, Ed King and Johnny Van-Zant had a fistfight that resulted in a broken finger for King. Flaring tempers and the ensuing fisticuffs just seem to be a part of the Lynyrd Skynyrd way of life.

After coming off the road in 1992, Artimus Pyle claimed that his personal goals were not compatible with the band's alleged drug use. "I left Skynyrd because they were doing the coke thing," says Pyle. "I couldn't stand to be a part of that. I'm not saying that I haven't done drugs but that was [twenty] years ago." Artimus felt that it would be best for him to quit Skynyrd and try something on his own.

Artimus was replaced by a drummer named Kurt Custer. "There's no doubt about it, the guy's a good drummer," Pyle says. Still, leaving Lynyrd Skynyrd was not an easy thing for Artimus to do. It was a bittersweet parting in Pyle's opinion. "There's not one person on this planet that can play these Lynyrd Skynyrd songs with the love [and] compassion that I play these songs," he says. "It took me so long to develop the style and the heart for these songs. What I think the band should do if they ever want to really get real, they should ask myself and Bob Burns to come back and play double drums with the band. That would be power, strength, legitimacy, heart. Everything that the band should have there. But that is not going to happen."

Artimus was soon involved in an ordeal that would rock his world. After he left Skynyrd and relinquishing his "rock star status," as he puts it, Angela, his girlfriend of several years, had him arrested on a charge of capital sexual battery. She claimed Pyle had sexually abused their three-year-old daughter while giving her a bath. Those who knew Artimus Pyle found the charges suspect from the beginning. "When Misty was three years old, her mother told her that when I was giving her a bath I was having sex with her," says Pyle. "It was that simple. The state never had a case. Their whole case was, 'we think he touched his children.' I said, 'You're damn right I did. I changed their diapers . . . I've got six kids, I mean, what would you do?' And they go, 'O.K., so you admit it. You did touch your children.'"

"Three days after I was thrown in jail, not one, but two of her boyfriends moved into my house," claims Pyle. "She gave them all of my cars. I had four beautiful automobiles. She gave them ten sets of drums that I had collected all over the world. And my home. Brand-new television set, brand-new vacuum cleaner, 'cause I had gotten a settlement from Skynyrd and I bought everything for my family. As soon as that money was spent, that's when she did this. But after you have all of that stuff taken away from you, who cares about the material stuff? None of the material stuff made a damn bit of difference, after what they did to my kids. If Angela would've wanted money and sexual freedom, all she would've had to do is just [say] it. We would've separated. I would've taken care of the children. But no, she has to charge me with a charge worse than murder."

Pyle spent nearly $500,000 on his legal defense before running out of money. He says he had little choice but to plead guilty to "touching his children." Artimus claims he innocently touched his children "as a father should. To care for them." He was placed on eight years probation with two years of counseling. "This [shouldn't] have happened," says Pyle. "When I left the band, I lost my star status, and that's when she decided to lower the boom. I put a new band together with my son and I was ready to go on. But to this girl, I wasn't a rock-and-roll star anymore. I told her, 'The truth is, Angela, I *never* was a rock-and-roll star. There are a few stars. Ronnie VanZant is a star, Jimi Hendrix is a star. I am not a star. I'm a drummer in a band that runs a bulldozer, you know?'"

Artimus felt that despite the fact that he had been an essential member of Lynyrd Skynyrd, the members of the band did nothing to support him. He claims he was financially and emotionally left out to dry. He was extremely hurt by their seeming lack of compassion. "I've been a hardworking, loyal member of Lynyrd Skynyrd for twenty-five years," Artimus muses. "I've got a room full of documentation that cost me half a million dollars through these weasel attorneys. I've got depositions, times, places, pictures, testimony, affidavits . . . I've got everything that clearly shows what happened to me. I went down and tried to talk to Gary and Johnny one day. I told them, I need to go out with the band and play a couple of shows. Just backup vocals and percussion, just so I can go before that judge and say, 'I played with my band, Lynyrd Skynyrd, that's what I do.' Because [the prosecuting attorney] was accusing me of being a ditchdigger—not making any more money as a club musician [than] ditchdiggers make. Johnny and Gary, the day I went down there, were so far out on cocaine, neither of them could look me in the eyes. I told them, 'Fellas, this is not a joke. This is a life-threatening situation. I'm facing life in prison. You told me that I saved your life in the plane crash and all that stuff. You say there'd be no band if it wasn't for me, that you owe your lives to me. I would ask a simple favor of this.' And they all, every one of them, the management, [Charlie] Brusco, they all turned their backs on me. Promised they would call me, did not call me. They've done this over the years so many times. It's not like [I'm] some little stage door groupie begging to get back and get an autograph . . . . We'll probably cross paths at some point. And I guarantee I will be able to hold my head up and look any one of them in the eye. They will not be able to do the same. I feel bad for them when that point comes."

Pyle thinks things would have been different if Ronnie VanZant were still living. "Ronnie VanZant was the man," says Pyle. "Gary should honor that. Ronnie, Allen, Steve . . . they would be appalled if they knew how the band has been done. We could be on the same level as Aerosmith or The Rolling Stones because that's the integrity that was there. The songs say it. "Simple Man," "Freebird," "I Need You," "All I Can Do Is Write about It," the list goes on and on. . . . The songs are there. Ronnie wrote 'em. And Ronnie would not have turned. . . . Unfortunately when you take the integrity of Allen Collins, Steve Gaines, Cassie Gaines, and Ronnie VanZant away from the band, you've got nothing left. But you know something? If I got a call from Gary Rossington and he said, 'Artimus, there's been a lot of shit going down, man, and I'm sorry,' if that should ever happen, I'd forgive him, the minute he said it, and it would be over."

Whether or not Artimus *felt* like a rock star, the fact was that bad things happen even to celebrities. And when a noted rock-and-roller finds himself before a judge, the public clucks their tongues and attributes the crime, real or perceived, to the rock-and-roll lifestyle. In the case of Artimus Pyle, the allegations against him would likely haunt him for the rest of his life, regardless of whether or not they were true. In this day and age, scandal sells, and much of the Lynyrd Skynyrd story is good copy for those who dwell on such things.

That the band would be relatively unaffected by the ordeal of yet another of their band members says a lot, although it would take a professional to analyze why that would be so. It could be that the surviving members of the band had become anaesthetized to pain, or simply that the pain-induced drug consumption had produced an ennui that couldn't break through the continued anguish that had been experienced over the years. Maybe it was that they simply couldn't be bothered to support their brother in his time of need. No formal statement as to whether they believed Artimus was innocent was forthcoming. Skynyrd was, and is, a band used to ordeals of one kind or another, and they are a band used to carrying on. They may have turned their back on Artimus, but carry on they would.

15

The Last Rebels

THE *LAST REBEL* was released during the twenty-year anniversary of Lynyrd Skynyrd's first album in 1973. "I think [*Lynyrd Skynyrd 1991*] along with *The Last Rebel* both should have gone gold and platinum," says Billy Powell. "I don't think they were properly promoted by our record company. I don't think the band has been properly promoted since the new band was formed, to tell you the truth."

The songs on the album were all new material and included "The Last Rebel," "Good Lovin's Hard to Find," "Kiss Your Freedom Goodbye," a song about the ills of society, "Can't Take That Away," Southern rocker "South of Heaven," "Love Don't Always Come Easy," and "Born to Run," called by *Stereo Review* an extended son of "Freebird."

Stereo Review didn't care for the "new" Lynyrd Skynyrd. Parke Puterbaugh wrote: "Although there's plenty here to please Skynyrd diehards, there's not quite enough to match former glories, and the words are all too often an out-an-out drag."

Rolling Stone reviewed the album and seemed enthusiastic that the "new" Lynyrd Skynyrd had recaptured its past, but elusive, glory: "Skynyrd was a party band in concert, but there was also a darker undercurrent in Ronnie VanZant's lyrics, one derived not just from the traditional rebel angst of the deep South. VanZant mythologized the rural American outsider, and most of his fans, from Florida to upstate New York, knew he was talking about them. Johnny takes this stance further into furious nihilism. The world he writes about in "Can't Take That Away," "The Last Rebel," and "Kiss Your Freedom Goodbye" is closer to Megadeth than to Ronnie VanZant, whose experience was defined by the Sixties. Johnny, who came of age in the Eighties, dares you to compare him to Bruce Springsteen by titling a song 'Born to Run.' But there is none of the American escape fantasy of the Springsteen epic in this tune—Van-Zant is running not to a better place or even away from a dreaded one, but into the teeth of a world he identifies as the enemy and intends to fight to the death."

With the release of *The Last Rebel*, Lynyrd Skynyrd's association with MCA would come to a close. At least as far as new material was concerned. The label would continue to hold rights to material previously released and recorded while the band was under contract to the label. The current Skynyrd didn't believe that MCA's heart was in the new material. They complained that as far as they were concerned, the label didn't promote the product as they would have liked. They wanted to associate themselves with a new label, so that Lynyrd Skynyrd would be looked upon not as a band that "once was," but as a band that "still was."

Guitarist Randall Hall had been brought in to tour with Skynyrd from 1988 to 1994. When problems arose with the original band members, Hall left the band. Whether he quit or was fired depends on whom you listen to. Hall would then sue Skynyrd for $500,000. Hall believed that he was entitled to a share of Skynyrd's earnings through tickets, merchandise, albums, and videos. Skynyrd's management claimed Hall was an employee, not an owner of the band, and thus entitled to nothing more than the salary he had been paid. The *Florida Times-Union* wrote that Hall was seeking punitive damages "to punish his former friends for breaking contracts." Hall's attorney claimed that he had been denied the opportunity to perform for the past three years because of the problem. Skynyrd comanager Joe Boyland was quoted as saying, "I'm not saying that Randall Hall didn't perform well for Lynyrd Skynyrd. I'm saying there's a lot of things that go into being in a concert band, and when [the other band members] asked him to make some adjustments in 1993, he quit. The band never understood why." Boyland claimed the adjustments that Hall was asked to make centered on being on time and having a more positive attitude. Hall seemed to think that the issue was more money-oriented.

"It's Randall's fault that he got fired," says Billy Powell. "He brought that on himself. But anyway, that's another story. They get in a band and they get fired. Then, O.K., well, I better think of some way to make a living . . . I better sue 'em to get the money."

"Allen was a great friend and guitarist and the reason for me playing in the band," says Randall Hall. "If Allen and Ronnie were living today, things would surely be different in that band. I did the tribute tour in 1987, became a partner, and was treated as an equal partner and shareholder until 1994. Then all of a sudden, I was told my equal partnership share was being cut in half. I could take it or leave it. I refused it, of course. When it came time to tour, I was not

Lynyrd Skynyrd, 1993. Left to right: Randall Hall, tour guitarist Tim Lindsey, Ed King.

contacted. I enlisted a lawsuit which has since been settled out of court."

The lawsuit was a problem for the Sknyrd organization, but they continued to look for a record label that would understand their special circumstances. Phil Walden decided that he wanted to give Skynyrd a shot. In 1994, Lynyrd Skynyrd signed with Phil Walden's newly re-formed Capricorn Records, and released an entirely acoustic album titled *Endangered Species*. Again, the new material was good but the magic of Ronnie VanZant's writing was obviously absent.

In 1995, the documentary film *Freebird . . . The Movie* premiered at the Fox Theater in Atlanta. Chronicling the lives, times, and tragedy of Lynyrd Skynyrd, the film was Judy VanZant's project, which both MCA and Lynyrd Skynyrd supported. Jeff Waxman directed the interviews with some of the members of the band, past and present. The film also contained concert footage from the Knebworth concert as well as selections from other concerts and various home-movie clips. "One of the most incredible things about *Freebird . . . The Movie* is you could see how much everybody loved, respected, and admired each other," says Judy VanZant Jenness. "It shows on the stage, it shows offstage. It's just something real special. [But] it took us nine years to get that movie made."

"I just got through watching the *Freebird* movie a couple weeks ago," remembered Gov't Mule's late bassist Allen Woody of the movie, now on video. "The band that I saw there, like with Artimus and Steve Gaines and those guys, they were just . . . I think the memory that I have of them is that they were absolutely musically at their peak when the plane went down. 'Cause they were really rockin', man. They were playing so good, it's not even funny. Ronnie VanZant was becoming a more prolific writer. I think the last memory I have of them would be seeing them play material right before the plane crash—I'm talking about in the movie. They had a hell of a band going. They were very, very, very tight. Tight as Ronnie's hatband."

One eerie aspect of the film was the inclusion of footage shot by roadie Craig Reed of the band and crew boarding the plane that crashed, just a few days before the tragedy. The band is also seen playing cards and relaxing inside the plane. The final scene is a view from the front windshield during one of the Convair's takeoffs.

An event dubbed "Freebird Fest" marked the premiere and it culminated in an impressive jam by many of the musicians who had participated through the years in Skynyrd, along with the survivors of the original band. It was evident that Skynyrd still had a lot of friends in the music industry. They still knew how to draw a crowd.

A CD of the *Freebird . . . The Movie* soundtrack was released by MCA in 1997 and was very popular with both those who had seen the film and those who had not. "The disc highlights Skynyrd at its peak," wrote Tony Green in the *Florida Times-Union*, "with Ronnie VanZant out in front of the deadly triple guitar of Gary Rossington, Allen Collins, and Steve Gaines, whose energy (he joined the band just two months before the Knebworth performance) spurred the two veterans into some of the best playing of their careers. For that alone, along with the chance to hear VanZant's trademark growl soaring over it all, *Freebird . . . The Movie* is a keeper."

In addition to recording new material, Skynyrd continued to play before audiences as often as they could be booked. The venues may not have been as large as the stadiums they once played but the audiences were, for the most part, as enthusiastic. Those who believed Lynyrd Skynyrd had "died" in 1977 stayed home. Those who didn't subscribe to that theory rocked on with the survivors. Skynyrd would continue to be a road band, as it always had been.

In 1995, Ed King caught a severe cold while on the road and an infection settled in his heart. He went into congestive heart failure. King said the treatment for his condition is basically a heart transplant. Yet Ed wasn't anxious to take that drastic step anytime soon. He continued to enjoy his life and decided to wait until a transplant was inevitable.

Even though the tempestuous days of in-house fighting among the band members had, for the most part, passed, once in awhile ugliness would rear its head while Skynyrd was on tour.

It seems that Leon Wilkeson was having some trouble with his girlfriend Rhonda, and the other band members resented the fact that Leon was often drunk and allegedly allowing Rhonda to conduct his business. In 1994, Wilkeson's wrist had been slashed, allegedly by Rhonda. He was left with no feeling in his little finger and damage to his ring finger. One night after a particularly bad Nashville gig, Ed King woke up and while walking to the front of the bus noticed blood dripping from Wilkeson's bunk. Leon's throat had been cut. Leon claimed that he stumbled and must have cut himself, but the other band members didn't buy it. Later that year, Leon assaulted Rhonda and was sentenced to three months in prison.

Skynyrd affiliated itself with the CMC record company and more new material was released by that label on *Twenty*, an album dedicated to the twentieth anniversary of the plane crash, in 1997. The album was produced by Josh Leo, engineered by Ben Fowler, and recorded at Muscle Shoals Sound. "*Twenty*, I think, was one of the closest [albums] to our roots," says Billy Powell, "as far as musically, since the new band formed in 1987. We're just really trying to get back to our roots and get back to the old style. Sticking to our roots with the raunchy sound that Skynyrd's always been known for. I think as long as we can do that, the band is going to be around for a long time. I figure The Rolling Stones can do it, we can do it. Ever since the airplane [crash] we're twenty years older, twenty years wiser, twenty years better, and twenty pounds heavier."

Artimus Pyle claims that Gary Rossington had asked him to return to the band in order to participate on the album. Pyle says he agreed to sign on, but he never heard from Rossington again.

Owen Hale had been brought in to play drums for the album. Kurt Custer was no longer with the band. "They eventually fired Custer because he couldn't play high on cocaine," says Artimus Pyle. "It was very sad. I've watched him do big gaggers before he goes on stage, and then I've watched him, like a little brat, like a little spoiled child, complaining about the tempos after the show was over. And I say, 'Cus, I watched you do enough cocaine, before you went out there and played, to kill a horse. [And] you're complaining about tempos. Oy vey, you know?'" Others in the band believe that rather than having been fired, Custer quit. Regardless, Lynyrd Skynyrd is a hard band to be a part of, even in the best of circumstances.

Anxious to show that the band had not been defeated, Rossington, Wilkeson, and Powell hired their old friends Rickey Medlocke of Blackfoot and Hughie Thomasson of The Outlaws to bolster the strong guitar-driven Skynyrd sound.

Rickey Medlocke had been with the band in the beginning and was welcomed back with open arms in April 1996. Although he had played drums the last time he was with Skynyrd, Rickey had made a name for himself as a primo guitar player with Blackfoot and later on his own. With Allen Collins gone, that critical guitar spot was empty and the band was quite comfortable filling it with Medlocke. "When I went to see the world premiere of the movie with these guys [*Freebird . . . The Movie*] I was invited to take part in that," says Medlocke. "We jammed onstage together and the camaraderie was so electric, and I love entertaining anyway . . .

I'm a high-energy person. Gary called me up and he said, 'I don't have Allen with me anymore, and you're about as close to the money as far as guitar playing and stuff as I can get. You're that rock side and I would really like to see if it would work out.' He came down, I played one song for him. He asked me to learn "I Ain't the One," "Saturday Night," "That Smell," and "Freebird," note for note. He says, 'Hey, I'll give you $1.50—you're in the band.' And you know what . . . I never regretted the decision. I love being here with these guys. You never know how much you miss playing with people that you used to play with until you've been gone from them for a while, you know? It just feels wonderful, it really does."

"Rickey is the new electricity of the band," claims Billy Powell. "He brings a whole new feeling of energy to everybody. He reminds me of Allen. Allen was the one who did all the high jumping and dancing around and going nuts on stage a lot, where everybody else just kind of did their own thing. Rickey's a showman like that, too."

Medlocke readily admits that he pays tribute to Allen Collins' playing with his own guitar work. "I gave [Gary] my word that if I got the job, I would play Allen's stuff note for note," says Medlocke. "Mine and Allen's styles was very similar, technique and stuff. Actually we played the same guitars as each other, ironically. I play 'Freebird' every night. They're trying to recreate that feeling, that energy . . . . But what happened is, I didn't have to purposely, consciously recreate it, because it was already there. All I had to do was just enhance it. That's all I had to do. It took me no time in learning all the material and Allen's parts, note for note, because it was a part of me. His style and my style was so similar. I just fell right into it naturally. I mean people come up to me and they go, 'Man, you played "Freebird" and it's like we can close our eyes, and it's Allen standing there playing it.' Well, I guess I did my job."

"Rickey Medlocke . . . " muses Donnie Van Zant. "Mr. Showman. Great guitar player, great, great singer. Just one of the best showmen that's around. He can get an audience going. He offers an awful lot to Skynyrd."

Medlocke was certainly a product of his musical environment. "Being with the [Skynyrd] guys in the early days, I'll tell you, it's interesting enough," Medlocke claims. "I have been so fortunate, in my life, to have been around some very, very incredible and talented musicians. The Blackfoot guys, you know, Jakson and Greg and Charlie, right on through all the guys in Lynyrd Skynyrd. I grew up around all that kind of stuff. I look at a lot of people nowadays that never really get a chance to really hang with people like that, much less play with them and have success with them and successful records and things. Boy, I guess I've been very fortunate and very blessed in my life to have had the opportunity."

Rickey Medlocke brings more than just his showmanship to Lynyrd Skynyrd. He is a consummate guitarist. When he talks about his influences he doesn't hesitate. "I loved, absolutely just adored and loved, Jimi Hendrix," says Medlocke. "Jimi Hendrix . . . right next to him was Clapton and with a little bit of Beck thrown in there and with the icing on the cake, for the

Met Park. Left to right: Rickey Medlocke, Gary Rossington, Billy Powell.

sweetening of it, was Billy Gibbons. First of all, I thought Hendrix was the most innovative thing I'd ever heard in my life. I heard the blues in his playing, I heard the Delta blues in his playing, the R&B in his playing. I mean, everything, the rock in his playing. I mean, he made it rock and he was very innovative. What an imagination. I'm part Native American [Chautauqua on his mother's side, Kota on his father's], so I'm a very spiritual person in the first place. And I believe this guy was not from this plane and he was only here for a little while. I believe that's the way it was meant to be, to give us something that we could remember forever and still play today. Those guys in my teenage years [were] my greatest influences."

Yet as good a guitarist as Medlocke is, he is probably even more noted as a performer. That, and his great love of the music, also goes back to his early influences. "I got to see Elvis Presley when I was seven years old," Medlocke remembers. "My parents bought me a transistor radio when I was five . . . one of the very first transistor radios. I used to fall asleep listening to old rock-and-roll songs on a radio station in Jacksonville, Florida, called WATE. I pitched a fit when he was coming to Jacksonville—had to see him—so my parents took me down. He came one time in 1955, but I didn't get to see him. Then the next time he came was in 1957 at the Jacksonville Baseball Park. They took me to see him and I was probably, oh, I think we were somewhere around the seventh or eighth row, center. I got to see the King when he was really the King. Interestingly enough, when I was on my way home, my parents used to tell me that I kept saying to them, over and over again . . . 'That's what I want to do. I want to do that, that's all I ever want to do.' And from there on the guitar was really probably steady in my hands almost all the time. The whole stardom thing—the rock-and-roll stardom trip—really wasn't the essence of why I wanted to do this. I wanted to do this because of the love of the music, and today it's still why I do this, because of the love of the music. I eat it, sleep it, drink it, breathe it. It's everything that I could ever imagine making me as a person."

"Rickey, with just three-quarters of one lung, I don't know how he sings like he does," says Billy Powell. "When he was a little kid, he had one of his lungs removed, or three-quarters of a lung removed. I don't know what it was . . . some disease or something, but he's just always amazed me. He's the most talented in the band and he's got the most energy. He's definitely got leadership qualities."

And now Rickey Medlocke was once again a member of Lynyrd Skynyrd. "I wish a turn of events would have been where I could've actually played guitar with the guys [back in the days when he had been Skynyrd's drummer] and been the third guitar," Medlocke says. "But it wasn't to be. Actually now that I'm in the band, Gary and I talked about it. He goes, 'Rickey, it wasn't meant to happen that way. It was meant for you to be here now.' I really believe that everything happens for a reason. And it was meant for me to come later and be a part of the band now, to make the band go forward by all my energies. My devotion and dedication is really dedicated to these guys now, you know? I love being where I'm at and I don't plan on leaving. They'll get a big fight out of me [if they ever suggest it]." Medlocke laughs.

The other new guitarist is anxious to make his mark on Lynyrd Skynyrd too. "I'd like to do the best I can do," said Hughie Thomasson, one of the driving forces behind the highly successful Outlaws. "Be the best I can be and bring out the best in everybody else I'm playing with. I hope that's what I can do with this band. To make them better, in return, they make me better. Most of all we have a good time. We have fun doing it. The music is fun to play."

"Spells his name H-u-g-h-i-e," said Leon Wilkeson. "I call him Hug-hi. Absolutely [I think that Rickey and Hughie have added some revitalization into the band]. And I think the band has added some revitalization into them as well."

Like Rickey Medlocke, Hughie Thomasson grew up in a musical family. "I was born and raised along the southern coast of Florida to Virginia, so I had a lot of bluegrass when I was young," says Thomasson. "Then the Beatles came along and then Jimi Hendrix and The Allman Brothers. [It was] kind of a melting pot, so to speak, because I like all kinds of music. My folks played a lot of gospel music when I was young. Mama said, 'Get the guitars. You're gonna play, your sisters are singing.'"

Thomasson's family moved to Tampa, Florida, when he was eleven. Hughie really took to the guitar and by the time he was twelve, he had replaced the lead guitar player in a band called Dave and the Diamonds. He played with other bands throughout his teens, such as Rogue and Four Letter Words.

Hughie went to high school in Tampa, "when I wasn't getting kicked out for having long hair," he laughs. "Yep, same old story. Anybody that had long hair either had to slick it back or apply some grease on it and try to hide it, or else just get thrown out of school. Funny thing is, I ended up playing at my junior high prom and my high school prom. I couldn't go to 'em, but I could play at 'em. I figured that was good enough."

Thomasson began playing occasionally with a group known as The Outlaws, which was led by Frank Guidry in 1968. The band included Herbie Pino and Dave Dix (of the Diamonds) and Thomasson's good friend, drummer Billy Jones. When Thomasson and Jones learned that The Outlaws were looking for a full-time guitarist and drummer, Thomasson and Jones asked for and got the jobs. Two weeks later Guidry broke up the band and Thomasson and Jones asked permission to continue on using the same name. Guidry gave them his wholehearted support.

In 1974, the new Outlaws opened a show in Columbus, Georgia, for Lynyrd Skynyrd. It was a fortuitous move. "We had actually been turned down by several labels before Clive [Davis] came to see us," says Thomasson. "We needed a good show to show off the band when Clive came to see us. Through mutual friends, kind of like doing us a favor, the Skynyrd guys were kind enough to say, 'Yeah, sure, we'll let you open the show for us.' We had a really good show and within a couple of weeks after that, we were signed to Arista Records."

The Outlaws were the first act signed to the newly formed Arista Records label. All eyes were

Guitar army in 1999. Left to right:
Hughie Thomasson, Rickey Medlocke,
Gary Rossington, Leon Wilkeson.

on Clive Davis' debut act. "There Goes Another Love Song," an unaffected, somewhat inconsequential song by Hughie Thomasson and Monte Yoho, grabbed everyone's attention when it was released as a single.

The Outlaws enjoyed years of popularity with songs such as "Green Grass and High Tides," "Hurry Sundown," "Ghost Riders in the Sky," and others. Although The Outlaws had a variety of personnel changes and never achieved the radio popularity that had been theirs with "Love Song," they continued to be a favorite on the touring circuit, playing small- to medium-size venues, fairs, and festivals. Hughie Thomasson remained with the band he had cocreated until that fateful call from the boys in Skynyrd to participate on *Twenty*.

"They called and said that they needed a guitar player," Thomasson remembers. "I had played with Skynyrd off and on over the years. When The Outlaws toured with Skynyrd, I was always invited to come and jam and play with the band. And I did. It seems like I always ended up playing on a couple of songs. It was kind of a natural thing when they called and said, 'Why don't you come and play in the band?' It took me about that quick to say 'yes,' 'cause there's not another band I would've done this with, to be honest with you. I was perfectly content having The Outlaws and doing what I was doing, and I really mean that. I wouldn't have done this with any other band. But I did it with Lynyrd Skynyrd because of our history and because of the music, and because they're great people, and it's a lot of fun, and it's also something different for me, too. I've been playing Outlaws music and my own stuff for so long, that was really a refreshing change, believe it or not."

As had happened when Steve Gaines stepped in all those years ago, the new recruits dug right in and quickly became notable additions to Lynyrd Skynyrd. "I'll tell you what, boy," said Leon Wilkeson. "Good call for Gary Rossington, recruiting Rickey Medlocke and Hughie Thomasson."

"It's too bad they don't use their vocal talents more," says Ed King of Thomasson and Medlocke. "They would really have something interesting. It wouldn't be Lynyrd Skynyrd but it would be really good."

In selecting Medlocke and Thomasson, however, it seemed Gary Rossington had once again overshadowed his own guitar playing. Rossington is certainly excellent, but always seems to be in the shadows of those with whom he shares the stage. His name does not seem to be mentioned much when talk turns to stellar guitar work and that's a shame because he does stand head and shoulders above many professional players. "Toy [Caldwell] and Allen . . . ," muses Artimus Pyle. "Look at it this way . . . Gary was all that. If he was a genuine [person with] integrity, wouldn't Gary be out there, being named with the Eric Claptons of the world? Wouldn't he be getting the recognition? Well, there's a reason he's not. I'm sure he gets recognition every once in a while, you know, he'll get in a *Guitar Player* magazine or something like that. But not the way it should be, if he were to change his ways a little bit. He doesn't get respect because he doesn't earn it, like Toy and Allen."

Dale Krantz-Rossington and Carol Chase were now providing backup vocals. "Dale is just a wonderful person," says Billy Powell of the new Honkettes. "And so is Carol Chase from Nashville. They both look real good, and they both work together real good, and they both have beautiful voices. Dale has always been one of my favorite female singers. Up there with Janis Joplin and people like her, and Aretha Franklin. She's got a wonderful voice and they [contribute] a lot to the band I think."

The recording of *Twenty* was important to the members of Lynyrd Skynyrd for a variety of reasons. It kept the band in the game as it reflected their past and attempted to demonstrate why the band was important all these years later. The band was pleased with the material, feeling that it offered their fans a fine helping of the music that they had helped develop over the years.

Twenty was special in another, very poignant, way. The album provided Johnny Van-Zant with an opportunity to "sing" with his brother Ronnie on the song "Travelin' Man." Rickey Medlocke had at one point mentioned the Hank Williams Sr./Jr. digitally blended recording of "There's a Tear in My Beer" and thought it would be interesting to apply the same technique to enable Ronnie and Johnny to sing a duet together. Johnny at first resisted the idea. Ronnie's widow, however, liked the concept. "They came to me and asked me about it first," says Judy. "I thought it was a kind of cool idea."

"Rickey Medlocke brought that up to me," Johnny remembers. "We were out in Wyoming, riding. Gary lived out there in Jackson Hole. [The idea was] maybe doing something like Hank Williams, Jr. did with his dad, Natalie Cole [did with hers]. Whenever he brought it up to me, at first I thought it might be a little cheesy. So I ended up talking to the producer and the engineer, Josh Leo and Ben Fowler. They kind of reassured me that we could do it pretty cool. Then the band actually started playing it in the studio, man, and I was singing along and I thought about where Ronnie could sing and stuff. The more I thought about it, the more I got into it. In the end, I'm really proud that we did it, you know? Especially live, man, just to hear the audience go crazy when Ronnie's picture come up on stage. Ronnie actually sang it with me, live. It was a very cool thing. Rickey Medlocke was the demon of that seed. But it came out great."

It's hard to imagine the affable Medlocke the "demon seed" of anything. Although his long locks are pure seventies hard rocker, there is an important spirituality to Rickey. The dual images he conjures are not lost on the guitarist. "I have two different tattoos on each arm," he reveals. "The one on my left arm is an eagle with Crazy Horse imprinted over the top of it. There's a warrior on my right arm that kind of looks like both [a guy or a girl], the man and the woman together, symbolizing one spirit, one unity."

Medlocke did seem to influence a continued unity within the band, both old and new, by his suggestion that Skynyrd's deceased singer sing a duet with its current frontman. The combination of the multiple incarnations of the band, both through personnel changes and the music, was what Lynyrd Skynyrd was now all about. Owen Hale again provided drums but would be replaced in May 1998 by Bill McCallister.

"Travelin' Man" worked on the album, and when it was sung in concert, with a huge video presentation of Ronnie singing the song twenty years earlier, the audience was ecstatic. The album also contained several other songs that would become popular with the fans: "Bring It On," the ballad "Home Is Where the Heart Is," the Cajun-accented "Voodoo Lake," rowdy "O.R.R.," and the boogie-beat "Talked Myself Right into It." With the exception of "Travelin' Man," all of the songs were original.

Gary Rossington cowrote seven songs. It was almost as if Rossington felt freer to nurture his own musical ideas than he had in the past. "He pisses me off sometimes," says Billy Powell. "He's so natural. I had to struggle to write a song, but they just come to Gary. They're just so easy. They just come natural to him. Gary would just come up with these rhythms. Out of nowhere he'll just come up with a different rhythm and then present that to the band. Everybody would just start following, playing around it, and then everybody in the band would start putting their part in and then it would start slowly forming into a song. But Gary, he is just the most natural at it as anybody I've ever known."

Johnny Van-Zant emerged as a new songwriting force for Skynyrd with his ten cowritten songs. Donnie Van Zant would sit in on the songwriting for "How Soon We Forget" and "Talked Myself Right into It," and Rickey Medlocke and Hughie Thomasson also had a hand in seven of the songs. Only "None of Us Are Free" was composed by someone outside the band— the talented Barry Mann, Cynthia Weil, and Brenda Russell.

The record was met with substantial media acceptance. "The songs' recipes have a lot of the Jacksonville band's trademark Southern seasonings: guitarist Gary Rossington's silky slide work and impeccable, overdriven solos spiced up with plenty of red-hot guitar accents by Rickey Medlocke and Hughie Thomasson," wrote the *Florida Times-Union*. "The tasty stew is supported by Leon Wilkeson's driving bass and Billy Powell's wide-ranging piano, from classical flourishes to honky tonk, barroom pounding. Singer Johnny Van-Zant's fine-grained sandpaper vocals work well in the mix, even if the voice does seem a little forced on some pumped-up choral refrains." Carol Chase, Vicki Hampton, and Kimberly Fleming provided background vocals with Dale Krantz-Rossington.

Lynyrd Skynyrd was asked to perform at one of the annual record industry events after *Twenty* was released. The band was delighted to see that Skynyrd could still get people off their feet. "We went to New York and did a BMG conference," remembers Johnny Van-Zant. "I thought [it] was going to be the suckiest ass thing in the world. The president of BMG got up first. We came out gangbusters. There was about 300 to 400 people there, industry people, that worked for BMG. There might've been more than that. By the middle of the first song we rocked. We had one of the best times, as far as something intimate like that, that I've ever had in my life. [The president] was wonderful. He jumped up. I don't know, maybe it was other people [thinking] . . . oh shit, if he jumped up, I gotta jump up too. We had girls on stage, we were bringing 'em up on stage. It was funny as hell. We had guys up there. We just had a great time."

Ed King had enjoyed playing with the "new" Skynyrd. "The set list was so diversified that it was always pretty entertaining," he remembers. King acknowledged that the lyrics seemed to have a common thread, but the music was different, reflecting the different styles of the guitarists and writers.

As much as he enjoyed being a part of the band, King soon found his playing hampered by his health problems. It became necessary for King to curtail his involvement with Skynyrd in order to tend to his enlarged heart. Ed's last gig with the band was on September 20, 1995, in Asheville, North Carolina. Based on his long-term involvement with the band, King asked his friends in Skynyrd for financial assistance. King says his request was denied. "They promised to take care of me and I had agreed to work on the anniversary album," says King. "Next thing I knew, the management is telling me I won't be needed and Gary isn't returning my calls."

King, like Artimus Pyle before him, felt betrayed by his friends and filed suit. "They'll say it's sour grapes," believes King. "I don't know why the whole thing had to happen that way."

"I still love him, even though [he sued] us," claims Billy Powell. "I didn't really have anything to do with his being gone. That was not my decision. That happened without my knowledge and I'm still pretty disappointed about it. But he had to quit the band because of doctor's orders. He had a bad heart. It was really enlarged. He's grouchy on the outside [but] he had a heart of gold on the inside. He had a big heart. He's a good guy too, actually."

King's suit against Lynyrd Skynyrd would be settled out of court in 1999. For the time being, Ed is feeling fine, thanks to his team of doctors in Nashville.

Those who have been involved with the band over the years find the exclusions and lawsuits sad, and injurious to the future of Lynyrd Skynyrd. Artimus Pyle is not one to mince words when it comes to what he believes to be true. "All of Lynyrd Skynyrd's power and glory and strength goes so that Gary Rossington's wife and other unbelievably untalented, undeserving people can go out and have a shopping spree," says Artimus Pyle. "It's very pathetic at this point."

Something positive happened in 1997 to boost Ed King's spirit. In 1987, King's 1959 Gibson Les Paul guitar had been stolen at gunpoint from his home in New Jersey. King was most anxious to find the guitar, but multitudinous calls to guitar and pawnshops all over the country provided no result. King had begun to feel that he'd never see the guitar again when he stumbled across a book, *The Beauty of the 'Burst*, at a guitar show in Dallas, Texas. While thumbing through the book, King recognized his stolen guitar. King's Les Paul had a distinguishing red blemish near the toggle switch. King believed the guitar pictured in the book to be his. When he checked the serial number of the missing instrument against the one in the book, he was certain.

King enlisted the assistance of the New Jersey police but the statute of limitations had expired and the department could be of no help to him. The guitar in the book had been collected by Perry Mergouleff. King tracked down Mergouleff with questions about the $40,000 guitar. Mergouleff told him that he had bought the instrument from Voltage Guitars in Hollywood, California, and then had traded it to a friend. The friend turned out to be billionaire Dirk Ziff. After much red tape involving insurance companies and attorneys, Ziff offered to either return the guitar to King or purchase it from him. King asked the guitar be returned to its rightful owner and so he was happily reunited with his Les Paul. "I view [the return of the guitar] as an omen of good things to come," says King.

Another happy event took place within the extended Skynyrd family, when Steve and Teresa Gaines' daughter Corrina married John Biemiller on June 15, 1997, in Amelia Island, Florida. Teresa had married musician Barry Rapp several years after Steve's death. Barry had grown up with Teresa and Steve in Oklahoma. Corrina is a beautiful and accomplished young woman who graduated from Orange Park High School and attended St. John's Community College. Judy and Melody VanZant have remained close to Teresa and Corrina, having been through the same trauma.

Ronnie and Judy's daughter Melody had by now graduated from high school as well and, also in June 1997, bought the Brickyard Road property, which had belonged to her parents. Some time after divorcing Jack Grodin, Judy married musician Jim Jenness, to whom she remains married today.

Touring for Lynyrd Skynyrd was somewhat different than in the past. For the most part, groupies were replaced by wives and children. Some members of the band were sober now, and planned to stay that way. The days of destroying hotel rooms were a thing of the past. "In those early days we had a reputation for being a real rowdy band," says Billy Powell. "But at least we grew out of that. We're kind of family people now. As a matter of fact, everybody in the band's straight now, too. None of us really do drugs anymore and only one of us really drinks. Those brain cells finally started regenerating."

Some people questioned that the band is 100 percent clean and sober at that time. "When somebody tells me that, I really do have to laugh," says Artimus Pyle. "Because if they're not doing that, they would be making better decisions at this time."

After the lawsuit was filed by Randall Hall, other suits were filed against the band. "That's the thing to do this day and age," says Billy Powell. "Sue Skynyrd." One night Skynyrd's new guitarist Rickey Medlocke aggressively showed a former "associate" of the band to the door and told him his "services" were no longer welcomed. "This cocaine dealer came out to Jackson Hole, Wyoming, where we were out there doing a benefit," says Billy Powell. "See, everybody stopped doing coke. It's at least two years now. And he tried to sell us some. Our guitar player, Rickey Medlocke, wouldn't tolerate it. He almost got in a fight with him, kicked him out, wouldn't let him in the show, and all that." The former associate filed suit against Medlocke and the band, claiming he had been assaulted. "In order for us not to rack up a ton of lawyers' fees, we just went ahead and settled and gave him a couple thousand dollars," claims Powell.

It was evident to all that Lynyrd Skynyrd was no longer one big happy family. "Anybody that can think of the littlest reason to sue us, they try to do it," says Billy Powell. "We were a family back [in the beginning]," says Judy VanZant Jenness. "It's not like that anymore. It's all business now."

With their alleged newfound sobriety, Lynyrd Skynyrd was perhaps truly enjoying the music for the first time in a long time. The previous few years had their share of continued tribulation but also their share of triumphs. Skynyrd was back on its feet and totally committed to continuing its legendary music. What the future would bring was anybody's guess.

16

The Beat Goes On

WHILE LYNYRD SKYNYRD continued to play auditoriums, amphitheaters, and state fairs, many friends and family of the band acknowledged the twentieth anniversary of the plane crash by gathering to dedicate Ronnie VanZant Park on October 20, 1997. First, though, a memorial service was held in Jacksonville Memory Gardens at the graveside of Ronnie, Steve, and Cassie. Steve and Cassie had been cremated and their ashes had been placed in a twin vault, steps away from Ronnie VanZant's tomb.

"There was a thousand people at the graveside that morning," remembers Artimus Pyle. "Robert Nix [formally of The Atlanta Rhythm Section] spoke, and Jeff Carlisi [formally of .38 Special] spoke, and Judy [VanZant] said something. I spoke—she asked me to say a few words. Melody VanZant read a poem that she'd written for her dad. Corrina Gaines, Steve's daughter, tried to speak . . . she couldn't say anything, she just squeaked. I put my arms around her. I said, 'Honey, you didn't say a word and everybody here knows exactly what you meant.' There was a tour bus sitting there. Ronnie would've loved that, you know? About 200 beautiful Harley Davidsons. It was a beautiful day. The sky was blue. It was a gorgeous Jacksonville, Florida, day.

Grave of Ronnie VanZant on the twentieth anniversary of the plane crash, 1997.

It was just perfect. And where was the band? Where was Gary? Where were they for that weekend? They should've been there meeting and greeting people from all over the world, from Japan and France and Italy, who had come there to celebrate Ronnie's life and the music of Lynyrd Skynyrd. And what did the management do? They had the band sitting over in Barcelona, Spain, playing a concert . . . probably for people that enjoyed it, but what were they doing in Spain? They should have been in America, man."

In the late nineties, Judy, Melody, and Ronnie's eldest daughter Tammy donated a large sum of money to Clay County, Florida, in order to buy land and establish Ronnie VanZant Park. The park is a ninety-acre recreation area with a fishing pond, softball fields, tennis courts, and a large children's playground. "I think it's wonderful," says Johnny Van-Zant. "I have people all the time saying, 'my kids and me go out there.' Anytime you drive by there on a Saturday or Sunday there's a lot of people out there. So, I think its pretty cool. I think Judy's done a good job there with that. As long as it had kids involved in it, I think Ronnie would've been very proud of it."

Those who wanted to share in the celebration of Ronnie and his bandmates gathered at Ronnie VanZant Park to participate in the park's dedication. "There was 1,500 to 2,000 people that came to the Ronnie VanZant Park," recalls Artimus Pyle. "Lacy Van-Zant was there, and I

APB
All Points Bulletin

Promotional photo of Artimus Pyle for the APB.

signed autographs and we dedicated the Ronnie VanZant Park 'Freebird' sign—the beautiful wooden sign with the Freebird on it. It's beautiful and the park is incredible. Everybody accuses Judy of ripping off [the band] and doing this and doing that. Judy has taken every penny, plus some of her own money, and put it into that park. It's a ninety-acre park. It's one of the most beautiful children's playgrounds. It was so cool-looking, I ran over and wanted to play on it. I wanted to climb and slide and swing. If I passed away, I'd be really wanting my wife to do something like that, to have a park for children and families that's a beautiful facility and with my name on it. And Judy even named [places in the park after the band members]. There's the Artimus Pyle Softball Field, the Steve Gaines Fishing Pond, the Allen Collins tennis courts . . . and I think it's the Gary Rossington commode. I'm not quite sure."

Others of those who had been touched by Skynyrd's music began to think of ways to honor their musical heroes. Skynyrd fans Mary and Brian Nash have sent a proposal to the United States Post Office in an attempt to have that organization issue, either a Ronnie VanZant, or a

Lynyrd Skynyrd stamp. They feel that helping to get Ronnie the recognition he deserves is a priority. Maybe one day, their efforts will pay off.

As with any fallen hero, there are those who seek to make their own statement as to whether or not they should be honored. On a not-so-pleasant note, on June 29, 2000, the graves of Ronnie VanZant and Steve Gaines were vandalized at Jacksonville Memory Gardens. Sheriff's deputies found Ronnie's damaged casket on the ground after being called at 3:00 AM. Nearby was Steve's urn, with the plastic bag containing his ashes torn. No arrests were made and no motive was concluded. Naturally, the families were quite upset and soon decided to relocate Ronnie's body and Steve's ashes to an undisclosed burial site. The mausoleums will remain at the Memory Gardens, so that Ronnie and Steve's fans may continue to visit and pay their respects.

Artimus Pyle continues to attempt to overcome the complicated and devastating events of his past. He has experienced both the highs and lows of being a rock star. For a short time, he played with a band called the Truth. Things didn't work out for the drummer. "I found out that two members of the band were smoking crack," Pyle says. "So I pulled the plug on the Truth the day I found that out. I confronted them and they were all in denial. I said, 'Look, I left Lynyrd Skynyrd because they were all cokeheads and they were liars. Do you think I'm going to stay with this penny-ante deal?'"

Pyle reestablished APB (Artimus Pyle Band this time) in 1998 with Tim Lindsey, Mike Estes, and Greg Baril. Estes had toured with Lynyrd Skynyrd on guitar from January 1994 to April 1996 and played on two of their albums. It was interesting for Pyle to be reunited with musicians who had the shared experience of playing with Skynyrd.

Lindsey toured with Skynyrd on bass for the Last Rebel tour and the tribute tour. He was also a member of the Rossington Band. "He actually went out with Skynyrd, when Leon was too drunk to play," says Pyle. "Then they realized that they have to have Leon in the band otherwise Judy won't let them play." Lindsey left the band in August 1999 because he wanted to spend more time off the road. He teamed with Randall Hall in a band they called Caliber. Baril is also a veteran player. "Greg is no spring chicken," says Pyle. "He's probably in his late thirties, but he has played with B.B. King, he has played with Stevie Ray Vaughn. I would say he is in the same category as a Stevie Ray would be."

Pyle likes playing with APB and expects to be with the band for some time to come. "We are honest with each other and everything is open and aboveboard, on the table." he says. "It's the best band I've been in. We do a lot of Skynyrd stuff and it's fun. We do it better than they do. It's insane how good this band is. Everywhere we play, people are just amazed because we can do any Skynyrd song, and we do it with zest and zeal and heart, and our vocals are strong. I sing some of the vocals. What we are is we're rocking Southern blues. I actually sing better than Johnny VanZant. I have a better voice. I sing more in key and I have a hell of a lot more stage presence than that man does. I don't mind at all singing these songs. If I couldn't do it, if it sucked, I would not honor the song . . . but people come up and they say, 'man, we love hearing these tunes.'"

APB is an extremely popular band that continues to play continuously to sell-out club crowds in both the United States and Europe. "I'm going for Steve Gaines and Allen Collins and Cassie. I mention their names every time I play. It's not because I'm getting paid a bunch of money to do it. It's not because a bunch of managers are squeezing me to do it. It's because it's from the heart. I loved these people. I learned a lot from these people. I'm not gonna let that go in one ear and out the other."

Artimus still lives the life of a musician, but life is a bit calmer. For starters, he lives in a lovely beach cottage in northern Florida that was once the home of William Faulkner. Artimus married Kerri Hampton in 1998, and the couple welcomed son River on July 2, 1999. Music, however, is always a priority. "You know, I'm [fifty-three] years old," said Artimus, "and I play drums every night, better than I've ever played in my life. People come up to me and they go, 'God, man, you're playing really good.' It's 'cause I love it. And so I want to do the best I can. I won't go to a gig drunk and play. I won't do a bunch of cocaine and get up on stage and think I'm playing good, but really sound like shit. I don't do that."

The two surviving Honkettes have been successful in getting on with their lives after the demise of the original Lynyrd Skynyrd. Leslie Hawkins continues to sing with Wet Willie, when they make their appearances, and also with Molly Hatchett.

Jo Jo Billingsley's life after Skynyrd wasn't always a good one. She sang at various times with Molly Hatchett, Billy Jo Royal, and The Atlanta Rhythm Section. It was during a gig with the Rhythm Section in December 1980 that Jo was raped and beaten by a roadie. Recovering from that attack, she decided that would be the end of her singing career. "I said then, 'If this is what music is all about, I don't want any more part of it,'" she said. She went on to marry Timothy White and have children and now travels the South, testifying through her own personal ministry and, once again, singing.

As the reformed Skynyrd continued to play various venues and entertain fans, both old and new, Judy VanZant continued to feel the need to immortalize the legacy of Ronnie VanZant and the original Lynyrd Skynyrd band. Although Judy had twice remarried, her ties to Ronnie would be eternal. Along with their daughter Melody and Ronnie's daughter Tammy, Judy established the Freebird Foundation in 1996. The foundation operated successfully until March 1, 2001, when Judy felt she no longer had the time or desire to devote to the endeavor. "The Freebird Foundation [was] a nonprofit organization set up in honor of Ronnie and, of course, Steve and Cassie and Dean and Allen, all the people who are no longer with us," says Judy. "The idea came to us probably [six or seven] years ago. I was on the planning commission here in Clay County, [Florida], and was talking to a man about how Skynyrd had influenced him. He suggested we get some kind of permanent tribute to Ronnie in Clay County. So this park came to mind. We decided to do the park and it was like we needed a way to help raise funds to build the park,

At the Freebird Foundation picnic, 2000. Left to right: Fan Brian Nash, Johnny Van-Zant, Melody VanZant, Judy VanZant Jenness.

because recreation's very low on the agenda for [county] funds. So it was like, O.K., what can we do to help? We thought through rock-and-roll and the various people we know in the business, we could probably help build the park. So, we purchased the land, myself and Ronnie's two daughters. [We actually] donated the money to Clay County and they purchased the land. It's a county-maintained park, so they take care of it, and we help in various ways to fund it, and do different things at the park. So the foundation was basically set up for that purpose, to help build the park."

Being involved with that successful venture gave way to thoughts of other projects. Judy and Melody started to think of other ways to honor VanZant and the others. "[It] kind of evolved into other things," says Judy. "We [had] four scholarships that we [granted]. We also help[ed] sponsor local baseball teams, soccer teams, things like that."

Among other philanthropic activities the foundation funded were financial need scholarships. "The first scholarship was established in memory of Allen Collins. Since then we have run into problems with his father, who has told us he doesn't want to do the scholarship in his name anymore," Judy explained. "So we decided, O.K., that's fine, [but] we've already awarded this scholarship so it's going to last for four years, whether you like it or not, because our scholarships are for four years. So, we changed the name to the Ronnie VanZant Scholarship." The recipients of the scholarship were awarded $2,000 a year for four years. Corrina Gaines established a similar scholarship in Steve and Cassie's names. During a twentieth anniversary event in October 1997 the Freebird Foundation raised some money and established an art scholarship in Dean's name. The criterion for all the scholarships was financial need. Foundation officers felt that honor students receive the lion's share of available scholarships, and wanted their scholarships to go to students who didn't have the opportunity to be awarded the scholarships they really needed. "Without our funds they probably wouldn't be able to go to college," says Judy. The foundation also participated in a massive food drive for Jacksonville's hungry for several years.

The foundation took quite a bit of Judy's time but she felt it was worth it for the years it operated. "You'd get a little discouraged and then you'd get a phone call or a letter from a fan," she said. "They're so appreciative and they love Lynyrd Skynyrd and Ronnie and all the guys so much. It's like you kind of feel you owe it to them. We got great fans—we got some of the best fans in the world." The foundation provides a website, still in service, that dispenses information about the band, past and present. The address is www.skynyrd.com.

In 1999, a state-of-the-art recording studio, called Made in the Shade Recording, was opened by the foundation. The studio offers special recording programs for musicians who need financial assistance. The studio is located in Jacksonville Beach, Florida. That same year, Judy opened the Freebird Cafe, a full-service restaurant and music club. The cafe is decorated with Skynyrd memorabilia and is located in Jacksonville Beach. It has become quite the north Florida hotspot, as many established musicians, as well as talented up-and-comers, play the club.

In 1997, a Steve and Cassie Gaines memorial was spearheaded by Larry Gower in the Gaines' hometown of Miami, Oklahoma. The memorial, by sculptor Nick Calcagno, includes a bronze bust of Steve and Cassie with biographical information on the outer columns of a display podium. In between the two is a center podium featuring a bronze plaque of the brother and sister, together with a dedication written by the Gaines family. The memorial is on display at Miami's Garden Club Park.

Lynyrd Skynyrd did yet another benefit concert on May 8, 1998. This time funds were raised and donated to Skynyrd guitar tech Gary Smalley, who had been diagnosed with cancer. Profits raised went directly to Smalley and his family to help with expenses incurred from his illness.

In 1998 Johnny and Donnie Van Zant turned to a project very near and dear to their own hearts. Johnny still fronts Skynyrd and Donnie remains with .38 Special, but the brothers decided to combine their talents on an album they would call *Brother to Brother*. "I had written songs with [Johnny] back when he had his Johnny Van-Zant Band," says Donnie. "He had a record deal when he was about seventeen years old. Very young. I helped him back then on songs and stuff like that all through the years. He actually helped me write a song on [.38 Special's album *Resolution*] called 'After the Fire Is Gone.' I helped him write a couple of songs on their record *Twenty*."

"I was young back then when Ronnie died," says Johnny. "I'd just started writing songs. Me and Donnie were actually messing around, writing songs. Donnie pretty much kind of taught me how to write songs—what a verse was, and what a bridge was, chorus line, a hook, all that. So over the years, we've just wrote tons of songs together. We've had so many people go, 'Why don't y'all do something together?' We were always like, well, I got my own thing . . . he's got his own thing. It just never had evolved or been the right time. On the *Twenty* album, me and Ronnie had sung a song together—the 'Travelin' Man' song. I started thinking, now's the time to do something with me and Donnie. I actually have a friend over in Europe, Reiner Hensler, who owns a company there. I was over there doing promotion about the same time I was thinking this. I asked Reiner, 'Man, would you be interested in maybe doing something with me and my brother?' He said, 'Let's start it tomorrow. What do you need?' I said, 'O.K., well, let me go back and talk to Donnie.'"

Donnie thought the idea was a good one, so the brothers decided to proceed with testing the waters. "We had been writing a bunch of songs with other people, so we knew we had the material," says Johnny. "This was an opportunity to put it out. So Reiner gave us a deal for Europe and we were just going to stick it out in Europe. Then Tom Lipsky, who Skynyrd's on over here, CMC International, got word of it. He said, 'Hey man, do you have a deal in America yet?' No, we hadn't even thought about that. He said, 'Let me come in and listen to some stuff.' He came in and liked it and it evolved into getting a deal here in America."

Johnny and Donnie Van Zant viewed the album as an opportunity to enjoy both each other's company and each other's talent. "It was just a blast to do to begin with," says Donnie Van Zant. "We had the most fun. We had total freedom to do whatever we wanted to do. What a sweet deal. It's something that we've been wanting to do for years and years. The only thing I could've wished for us is that Ronnie would've been with us—all three of us could've done it. But it was a record that was just so much fun."

"Over the years we hadn't been able to spend much time together," says Johnny. "To be able to do that record really gave us an opportunity to. We shared a two-room suite kind of thing at this Residence Inn in Nashville. So we lived together and man, we just had a blast. Hopefully we'll get to do it again. People have asked me, are we going to go tour and stuff like that. We don't have any plans to do that, [but] that would be fun one day, I'm sure."

The album was so personal to both brothers that there may have been times that they regretted the emotional intensity. But the overwhelming sentiment was positive. "[The album] is a blessing," says Johnny. "That's a dream come true. We had a great time doing it. I don't know if we'll ever do another one . . . who knows? [They would.] But, hey, we had a great time doing it. It's a very moody record. It's a very different kind of record."

"I actually would have to put it in a style of .38 Special's record, *Resolution*," says Donnie. "I don't think it's what most people think of Johnny and Donnie maybe as being. And that would be just a Southern Rock sort of sound, whatever that may be. It's got a lot of songs on there with a lot of integrity to 'em."

One of the songs on the album that Johnny is quick to categorize as moody is "Rage." "Maybe [God] can try to get to people through a song," says Johnny. "Look at TV, just take a

Johnny Van-Zant looks to the future.

look at TV. Look at all the rage in the world today. There's a lot of inner rage in people in general. [The song's] basically saying, 'now I got to bury you and find something else to do. Don't be caught up in that. Go fishing, do something. Let the rage out of you, but not in a violent way.'"

"The song is about the desire to be set free from rage—the frustrations and angers that just fill the world today," says Donnie. "You hear about the mass shootings that happen all the time and then you hear about even road rage, which affects us all every day. But the song also acknowledges that we offer some hope here too, encourage freedom from it. It's pretty heavy stuff. There's some pretty heavy stuff on that."

The songs included on the album were well chosen. It was noted in the accompanying booklet that "Right Side Up" was inspired by Stevie Ray Vaughn. "That Was Yesterday" and "Black Bottom Road" seem to relate to the brothers' shared childhood experiences. "I'm a Want You Kind of Man" and "Downright and Dangerous" show that both Donnie and Johnny know their blues. There is a poignancy in "Friend," "Can't Say It Loud Enough," "Livin' a Lie," and "Brother to Brother" that demonstrates the fraternal and musical bond that the two share.

Brother to Brother initially was meant to be a one-time-only Van Zant collaboration. "It's just a once in a lifetime thing here," said Donnie after the release of the album. "We're both very dedicated to our bands and what we're doing and want to put our energies into that too. It was great to have the opportunity and we're proud of it, no matter what. Johnny said the other day, he was talking to somebody, he goes, 'Well, I don't care if it sells but one or it can sell a million. It don't make no difference to me.' I told him he was crazy. But when it comes down to it, that's about the truth."

However, *Van Zant II* was released in March 2001 to fairly good reviews. There were ten original songs and the album showcased rock, pop, and blues numbers. There were songs about love, having fun, fans, and society, among other things. A couple of standouts were "Imagination" and "Is It For Real." Russ DeVault for the *Atlanta Journal-Constitution* wrote, "What we have is a couple of formerly wild-eyed Southern rockers competently having at it."

Johnny Van-Zant continues to think that music should be positive. "I guess to the culture listening to [rap], I guess maybe it means something," he says. "But there's so much violence in that too, with the death of what's-his-name, Tupac, or whatever it is. I think Will Smith kind of said it, 'if you're going to do it, do it in a positive way.' Whenever you hear 'kill the cops' and all this shit, that's not a good thing. 'Cause some of the kids take this shit literally. It affects their whole life. I mean we got rowdy fans too, but you know what? That's their time to be rowdy. We've stopped shows because people were fighting. I'll go, 'Hey, you know, we're not here to fight, we're here to have a good damn time . . . if you want to fight, take that shit out of here.' That's not what it's all about."

Donnie Van Zant holds the same philosophy about musical content to which his brother Ronnie adhered. "I think what really lacks in music today is just truthfulness," says Donnie. "It just seems like there's so much negativity. Not a lot of hope and the doom and gloom and all that. I think [Ronnie] just said it the way the working man would say it . . . the blue-collar person would say it. That's how you try to write songs. That's where he was from. It was a blue-collar town here and he just offered truth here. And people believed that. He was just real. There was no fakeness to him whatsoever. What you see is what you got. He was just a real person. I think that people see that. If there's anybody that should be in the Rock and Roll Hall of Fame, it should be Lynyrd Skynyrd. I think one of the main reasons why is Ronnie VanZant."

Although Lynyrd Skynyrd was eligible for induction into the Rock and Roll Hall of Fame in 1999, they have yet to be inducted. This doesn't sit well with most of Skynyrd's fans. Rocker Courtney Love, in fact, demanded that the Rock and Roll Hall of Fame return all of the memorabilia belonging to her and her late husband, singer/songwriter Kurt Cobain. "How dare you fools not put Lynyrd Skynyrd, Patti Smith, or AC/DC in your Hall of Fame," she demanded, according to *New York Times* writer Neil Strauss on December 21, 2000. "Damn you to the darkest belly of the underworld," Love was said to have written in a telegram to the institution.

While he doesn't dwell on it, Johnny Van-Zant does give thought to the future of popular music. "It's kind of hard, whenever you hear shit on the radio and you go, 'Man, the guy can't even hold a fucking note," he says. "It's kind of hard to appreciate that. But that's not for me to judge. My kids turn me on to a lot of stuff. I have three daughters and they turn me onto stuff all the time. I'll think, well, maybe I won't like it. It's like Alanis Morissette. It's kind of down and out, but the more I listened to it, the more I liked it."

Johnny also addresses the issue of Skynyrd's fans being alcohol-fueled much of the time. "We'll all take a drink," he muses. "I love to take a drink, but you gotta know what your limits are. We've all went through the drinking and the drugs and all that stuff. We've finally come to the conclusion that it's not worth it. But there's nothing wrong with a social drink or something. There's nothing really wrong with that. It's just when people let it get the best of them. 'Cause hell, I love to see an audience go crazy as hell. I love to see 'em rock with us. We feed off that."

Although the brothers' two albums were moderately successful, they both swore allegiance to their respective bands. "[Donnie's] heart's in .38 Special and mine's into Skynyrd," says Johnny. "I love doing Skynyrd. It took me a long time to come into my own and I'm finally at home with Lynyrd Skynyrd. I'm at peace with myself, too, with it. 'Cause a few years there I didn't know for sure. There was so many lawsuits, and this one and that one. Sometimes you just start doubting yourself, whether it's the right thing to do. Then I'd go out and I'd sing and the fans would be just going nuts 'cause they'd love that music. I always say Lynyrd Skynyrd's bigger than the people that's in it. The name and the music of Lynyrd Skynyrd will live on long after the whole band's gone. I believe that."

Donnie Van Zant's .38 Special continues to release new material. Brother Johnny is very supportive of Donnie's musical career. "[Even] as a kid, there's never been any kind of a competition thing," says Johnny. "It's always, hey man, I want you to do good, you know?"

After some critically dismissed albums, record sales are on the rise for Lynyrd Skynyrd. *Lynyrd Skynyrd . . . Lyve from Steeltown,* released on CMC in 1998, was a compilation double CD of "live" Skynyrd classics, along with five songs from *Twenty.* The album was recorded at a Pittsburgh concert some months before the April 1998 release, and was produced by Lynyrd Skynyrd and Ben Fowler, who had been the engineer on *Twenty.* The tracks weren't necessarily live, as some were spiced up in the studio. The songs include Skynyrd classics "Freebird," "Sweet Home Alabama," "Gimme Three Steps," "I Know a Little," "Simple Man," "That Smell," "You Got That Right," "On the Hunt," "What's Your Name," and "Saturday Night Special." Also included were some Van-Zant/Rossington/Medlocke/Thomasson cowritten songs, such as "Voodoo Lake," and, with Rossington and others, "We Ain't Much Different" and "Bring It On." Rossington's poignant song for the guitar named after his recently deceased mother, "Berneice," was included, as well as the dual Van Zant "Travelin' Man."

It was fun for Skynyrd to do another live album. "We're there to play for our audience," says Hughie Thomasson. "For a crowd, for fans. We feed off that. They give it back to you, they get it back ten times over. They're part of the show. We had a really good show in Pittsburgh. Everything was great. We went in and mixed [the album] in Nashville."

Rickey Medlocke remembers the thrill of recording the *Lyve* album and accompanying video. "We were all over there listening to us play on the tape and on the video and everything," he says. "Johnny looked at me and I says, 'You know what? This is one heavy ass band. The band is rockin'. It sounds great, we're so tight, and so dead spot on it, man.'"

Recording a live album can be a very difficult project. Many times live albums need to be "sweetened" in the studio after the fact, which often includes a bit of rerecording and overdubbing. Not everybody associated with Skynyrd thought the *Lyve* album was a true representation of Skynyrd live. "There's nothing live on it but the crowd noise," says Artimus Pyle.

"To me it's just another dadgum live album with the songs rearranged in different order. I'm getting tired of all these live albums coming out, but if people are going to buy it, you know . . . I think the only people that'll buy this [album] would be just like the real diehard Skynyrd fans," says Billy Powell.

The band enjoyed being filmed for the *Lyve* video. It was apparent that they had finally found a comfort level with one another. They now could let down their defenses and have a little fun with one another. "I stand on that stage every night," says Rickey Medlocke, "and I play those songs. In doing so, I made a promise to Gary. I want to give you my 110 percent effort, every night, every day for this band. [During the production of the *Lyve* video] we were standing in the studio watching the video and I'm looking at myself up there, and they're laughing at me. They're laughing because unconsciously I make all these faces and stuff while I'm playing. I'm very high-energy onstage. I go for it. Like Johnny will tell you, 'Rickey goes for it every night.'

Well, the thing about it is, I looked in there and I looked around at Gary and the guys and I said, 'I gotta tell you guys something. There is no place on earth that I would rather be than right here . . . . My dad was like that, his dad before him, and me. There's no place I'd rather be than standing on that stage doing what I'm doing right there. If I died on that stage, if I fell over from exhaustion, keeled over and died right then, guess what? I went out doing exactly what I love to do."

Lyve received mixed reviews. After releasing a video to go with the new album, the band accompanied the release with another national tour. Lynyrd Skynyrd continued to be well received. Thanks in large part to the exposure given the band from VH1's *Behind the Music* profile in 1998, Lynyrd Skynyrd summer tours in 1998 and 1999 were some of the most successful since the airplane crash. Although the album they were touring to promote initially, *Lyve from Steeltown*, initially achieved only minimal sales, the band's earlier catalogue jumped seventy-five percent in 1998. The band's manager, Charlie Brusco, told *Rolling Stone* in the July 9–23, 1998, issue that while the band was on tour, scores of people had come up to tell him they had seen the VH1 feature.

"I've had so many people come up to me and say that they were doing pretty good until the one part [in the program] when I said this one thing and then they just broke down," says Artimus. "And I [say] 'Well, I guess you'll notice that I broke down too.' The girl from VH1 asked me, 'Why do you come here?' I was sitting in front of Ronnie's grave and Steve and Cassie's place. I said, 'I come here to thank these people for being in my life.' And when I said that, all of a sudden, I felt like I was hit by a board, by a two-by-four. My chest heaved, my heart came up in my throat. I literally could not finish my sentence. I thought surely she would not use that, because it was really a hard moment."

There were other noteworthy aspects of the documentary. Gary Rossington, Artimus Pyle, and Billy Powell were interviewed for the first time on national television. It was interesting to hear their tales on such topics as the band's beginnings, their multiple tribulations, the airplane crash, and their success.

In August 1998 MCA Records (who still owned the material of the original band) announced that they were celebrating Lynyrd Skynyrd's twenty-fifth anniversary with the CD release of *The Essential Lynyrd Skynyrd*. The album was a twenty-five-track compilation of a sampling of the band's recordings, newly remastered from the original source tapes. The album was produced and compiled by Andy McKaie and Ron O'Brien and also included a twenty-page booklet. The concept and content were very similar to the Lynyrd Skynyrd Box Set that MCA had released in 1991. MCA was making money with their multitudinous Skynyrd releases, but not everyone thought that the approach was what the fans wanted. "The sound on that box set was an abomination," says Al Kooper. "MCA knows it and never have repaired it and it's ten years and counting. The endless reissues all have notes by their resident lynyrdophile Ron

O'Brien, who collects press clips and prints whatever they say in them without checking to see if they're accurate or not. It's a sorry state of affairs over there for Skynyrd fans. They had live two-track tapes of a radio concert from 1973. I owned the sixteen-track masters, which could have been remixed quite a bit better than their two tracks. I did [the mixing] originally live on the air, and [the tracks] were lacking in balance due to the spontaneity of their performance and my lack of knowledge of the new material. Because of not wanting to do business with me, [MCA producer Andy] McKaie just slapped out the old two-track masters and never considered remixing it—a big loss for the fans, I'd say."

Ed King remembers that Andy McKaie at least tried to get the band's participation for the liner notes on the box set. "I was, sadly, the only member of the band to get a 'thank-you' on the liner notes, because I was the only one who would cooperate. What a surprise."

Whether or not the cooperation and quality were there, MCA continued to release old material. In 1998, *Lynyrd Skynyrd Solo Flytes* was also released. The album is a nice sampling of some of Skynyrd's band-related offshoots. While primarily consisting of music from Rossington Collins, there are also songs from APB, Steve Gaines, The Allen Collins Band, and the Rossington Band.

Also released in time to cash in on the anniversary were remastered versions of *Nuthin' Fancy* and *Gimme Back My Bullets*. Each contained three previously unreleased bonus tracks. Later in the year MCA released *Skynyrd's First: The Complete Muscle Shoals Album*. This CD featured the tracks recorded in Alabama in 1971 and 1972. The following year *Skynyrd Collectibles*, a two-CD compilation of rare material and outtakes from *One More ~~For~~ From the Road,* was released. There was still a lot of unmined gold in the Skynyrd archives. And MCA was going to be sure to mine it.

Although all the reissues seem redundant, most of Skynyrd's albums continue to sell well. The "old" fans enjoy many of the reissues, and the newer fans go to the original albums to familiarize themselves with how Skynyrd intended their music to be heard. The band's concerts continue to be well attended and have actually grown in size in recent years. Skynyrd may not sell out arenas like they used to do, but the music is almost as popular as it was back in the heyday.

Despite his health problems, including liver function concerns and emphysema, Leon Wilkeson continued to enjoy being a player in the Lynyrd Skynyrd band. Sometimes living the high life resulted in his having to accept a substitute bass player on those nights when he couldn't perform up to snuff. "He [pulled] some crazy stunts sometimes, but we [called] him 'bassist extraordinaire,'" said Billy Powell. "He [was] a bass player's bass player."

Leon lived life on the edge, but he seemed to have a great time doing it. He was married several times and continued to enjoy the camaraderie found in bars and clubs. He loved his sixteen-year-old son Lee, and his family, friends, and fans were always important to him. "Leon [was] my lifelong buddy," says Billy Powell. "He's the one I've known since third grade. He never tamed or toned down at all. That's how he never gained weight. He [was] always going, going, going, doing something."

Leon Wilkeson with fan Mary Nash, 2000.

By July 2001, forty-nine-year-old Leon Wilkeson had evidently stopped drinking to excess. Not an easy task for someone who had enjoyed alcohol since he was a teenager, and who worked in the rock-and-roll industry. Having just done a show in Wisconsin on July 22 for their summer tour, Skynyrd was home for a few days before resuming the tour in California.

On Tuesday, July 24, Leon enjoyed a visit to the Freebird Cafe in Jacksonville Beach. He had dinner with Teresa Gaines Rapp and her husband Barry on Wednesday night. On Thursday he would tell a friend that he felt the best that he had in years. Yet something went terribly wrong. On Friday, July 27, Leon was found dead in his room at the Marriott at Sawgrass Resort in Ponte Vedra, Florida.

Authorities didn't believe foul play was involved in Leon's death, but because he was so young, an autopsy and toxicology test were performed. The St. John's County medical examiner determined that Leon died of complications from emphysema. Drug intoxication and cirrhosis of the liver were contributing factors. Leon had various prescriptions for drugs. He took oxycodone for chronic pain and diazepam for anxiety and insomnia. The medical examiner believed that too much oxycodone combined with the diazepam may have caused Leon to fall asleep face down on his pillow. Coupled with his breathing problems, the result was fatal.

Leon was dedicated to his Christian faith and carried a Bible with him on tour. It was said that his favorite verse was Psalm 33: "play skillfully with a loud noise." His memorial service, which was open to the public so that his fans could participate, was held at Evergreen Cemetery where he would be buried in the St. Mary's section of the memorial park.

Leon would be greatly missed. Artimus Pyle said, "Leon gave us a chance to appreciate life and all that it has to offer." Artimus explained that those present at the memorial service "stood tall for a man that never lost his childlike wonderment. Leon wore many different hats on stage, and he now has a new hat . . . a halo."

Al Kooper would remember Leon with fondness and amusement. "The last time I saw Leon, years and years ago, I was mentioning a photo I had of him," Kooper recalled. "He wanted a copy. I told him to write down his address so I could send it. He gave me his driver's license! I handed it back saying he might need this soon. He said, 'Keep it. I got a few of those.' I did and I still have it."

Ed King believes that Leon was an extraordinary bass player. "I never write a bass line for a tune without first asking myself, 'What would Leon play?'" says Ed.

Skynyrd's fans would be heartbroken at Leon's passing. He was known for his variety of hats and his high jinks and would be sorely missed in concert. "Leon was one of our last links to the original Skynyrd band," fan John Eastwood stated. "His easygoing attitude, quiet demeanor, laid-back personality made him one of the easily approachable members of that band. My wife [Robin] and I will always remember the 1996 backstage experience we had with Leon. He showed us his hat collection, his tribute tattoo of his fallen friends, he took time from his busy schedule to talk with us, take pictures with us, and laugh. We will always remember the soft-

Gary Rossington, original founding member of Lynyrd Skynyrd.

spoken, almost shy man with the most soulful eyes we've ever looked into. True, Leon had problems, as we all do. I think a part of him died in that crash along with parts of his childhood and dreams. It seems, tragically, that the crash not only claimed six victims but it also claimed scores of survivors. Leon will always live on in our hearts, memories, and prayers."

According to the *Florida Times-Union* on August 8, Gary Rossington issued a statement saying that the rest of the tour would be dedicated to Leon's memory. "We're all crushed," Gary's statement read. "Leon's death was, and is, a shock. Lynyrd Skynyrd is a band of survivors, though. It was hard to pick back up and play again as Lynyrd Skynyrd in the 1980s and it's hard now. But that's what we're all about."

The paper also reported that Gary Rossington was unable to attend Leon's service because of "a death in the family," yet Johnny Van-Zant and Billy Powell also were apparently not in attendance. Once again it seems the Skynyrd musicians would be mysteriously unsupportive of one of their own. Lynyrd Skynyrd did, however, cancel eight shows, and resumed their tour on August 11. Ean Evans was brought in on bass. Evans had pinch-hit for Leon before. For the time being, Ean Evans was Skynyrd's new bass player.

Gary Rossington is now technically the only original founding member of Lynyrd Skynyrd. The years have been hard on Gary but he continues to play his guitar in an attempt to bring the music of Skynyrd to the fans. "People don't give Gary a lot of credit for his guitar playing," says Rickey Medlocke. "But I'm telling you, being a guitar player and being around him, sometimes he really amazes me, he really does."

Johnny Van-Zant, after years of internal struggle, feels that he finally has been granted the opportunity to develop his own Skynyrd style rather than merely appearing as a stand-in for his older brother. "He's straightened out, I mean totally, completely" says Powell, "He's doing great and he's a hard worker. I don't really hang out with him or anything like that, but we get along great and he's just a real nice guy. If anybody was to fill in Ronnie's place, it's definitely Johnny, 'cause he looks like him and he sounds like him. Even if he doesn't like to be tagged as copying Ronnie or anything like that, it's just natural, you know? He can't help it. It's a natural style. I don't think anybody else could have filled Ronnie's shoes, except maybe Donnie or Johnny, but not even Donnie. I think Johnny has always had the best potential of being a better singer than both of them. But he's never really been disciplined, taken vocal lessons or anything like that." Johnny has penned some exceptional songs and will likely someday be recognized for his own abilities.

"I wish I took vocal lessons when I started taking piano lessons," says Powell. "I really do wish that, 'cause I cannot sing a lick. I believe if I could sing, I could be a much better songwriter. Billy Joel, he sits down at the piano and sings and plays. I just can't do that. But Johnny's kind of like Ronnie. He's just natural. The only difference was, Johnny has to write the words down to the song. Ronnie just never wrote a lick down, never wrote anything down. Just instantly memorized those lyrics in his head. I don't know how he did that either. But Johnny still has to write the lyrics to 'Freebird' on a piece of paper. He writes about four or five songs. He's got it all down there. It's kind of funny, actually. We make fun of him about it, but sometimes you just get these mental blanks and forget the words, and then he'll put the microphone out there [to] the audience, like *you* sing it. He gets caught sometimes, but it's pretty funny. He pulls out of it good. He's a fun guy to have in the band. A great guy to be around, and we all love him too."

"Lynyrd Skynyrd's the real thing," says Johnny Van-Zant. "The lyrics are about real people. It's the working-class people. It's the people who made America, made the world. You don't have to just be an American either to understand Lynyrd Skynyrd. It's good music. I think it's going to live on long after we're all gone. I think that's a blessing. I think God gave a gift and [you have to] use your gifts to the best of your power."

And the fans keep comin' . . . "We got like second-, third-generation fans," said Leon in 1999. "Because of parents getting their little drape apes in front of the stereos and getting them to sing 'Sweet Home Alabama.' Kids were literally just reared on Skynyrd. I like to look at it as the timeless factor. Skynyrd music is timeless. Made by Americans, played by Americans, for Americans. That kind of thing. Can you imagine how many Harley Davidsons are driving around with 'Mr. Breeze' written on the side?" Leon laughed.

Leon paused to think of Ronnie VanZant's contribution to all of this. "I'll tell you," he said, "Ronnie used to say this quotation. I'm not exactly sure what it is, but it was one of his favorite quotations 'cause it said so much. He'd look at me and say, 'Leon, ain't no God in New York City in the way you'd understand. And cross the Mason Dixon line make a hell of a fool out of a man. If I hadn't seen the sunshine or Lord, worked to curse this rain. And if my feets could fit a railroad track, I'd rather be a train.' That song's the best answer I can think of to come up with."

You may have to be a Southerner to understand Ronnie's quote, if it's meant to be understood at all. The first two lines of the quote might refer to Ronnie's love of the South and his lifelong dedication to its people and ideals. The reference to New York City might pertain to his distaste for the "corporate" music fostered by New York and Los Angeles. Ronnie wrote several songs about traveling and railroads. It's evident in his lyrics, culminating in "Freebird" itself, that Ronnie felt free to traverse the world, making and sharing his music. Lynyrd Skynyrd, Ronnie's own band of gypsies, apparently adhered to his philosophy as well. As much as the band loves their homeland, they love their music and are dedicated to travel wherever it is their audience needs them to be. Lynyrd Skynyrd, past and present, is a traveling, ever-evolving, band.

17

Coming Home

SO LYNYRD SKYNYRD continues to travel, evolve, and entertain. The musical contribution begun in the 1960s continues to be important and appreciated by audiences worldwide. Still, as popular as the band is today, its roots and continued success remain firmly planted in the influence of Ronnie VanZant. Johnny Van-Zant thinks that his brother's contribution to music not only was important, but will also stand the test of time. He believes that Ronnie's achievements with Skynyrd were unique and special. While Ronnie inspired and nurtured the band, he also encouraged each member of the band to make his or her *own* unique contribution to Skynyrd's sound. "That's why they call it Lynyrd Skynyrd," he says. "It wasn't Ronnie VanZant, it was called Lynyrd Skynyrd. That's the difference between an artist and a band. It takes a band. Of course Ronnie was a great lyric writer but he was a very basic lyric writer. [His lyrics were] almost like reading a story. If you listen to Jim Croce, some of your best artists, it's just a basic thing. Telling a story where the common person can understand it. You don't have to be a damn brain to understand it. I think music is emotion, if you can hit someone in the heart with it. It even says that in the 'Brickyard Road' song. It says, 'Brother do you realize what you've done? Touched the hearts of everyone.' He was just a fore-sighter, too. He could see what the hell was going to happen in the future."

Talk of the immortal Ronnie VanZant is interesting because of the artist's early demise. There has been talk that Ronnie knew, and told others, that he would not live beyond thirty. "That's what everybody told me," says brother Johnny. "He never told me that personally. But I'll tell you, if I could switch places with him I'd do it in a second. Anytime you could be on this earth and touch people like he did. . . . *All* the guys in Skynyrd. To touch people like they did, I think it's almost like a gospel. God uses you in different ways. Some preachers preach to people that go to church on Sunday, and I think musicians can preach to people who don't maybe go to church on Sunday. I don't want to say brainwash, but you can actually get to a person through a song. Them songs come from somewhere. If you sit down and try to write one, they usually don't come. But when He puts His hand on top of you and goes, 'O.K., I want you to do a song,' He gives it to you. It even says, 'God giveth and He taketh away.'"

Throughout the 1990s and into the new century, MCA and its various and sundry vanity labels continue to release mostly tired, but occasionally insightful, product from the original band through their repackages and reissues: *What's Your Name* (a slightly different song list); *The Essential Lynyrd Skynyrd* (a two-CD set of classic Skynyrd with a previously unreleased, original version of Johnny's "Coming Home"); *Twentieth Century Masters: The Best of Lynyrd Skynyrd* (Millennium Edition with the original recording remastered); *Double Trouble* (with no new material); and *All Time Greatest Hits* (with at least a slight variation to "Swamp Music"). There has even been a tribute album dedicated to Skynyrd with Skynyrd songs covered by artists such as Hank Williams, Jr., Travis Tritt, and the Black Crowes.

Other labels, such as BMG and Asin, have released Skynyrd-related special product in the past several years, including *Classic Live Performances, Vol. 1* (which includes "Freebird"); *The Hits of Lynyrd Skynyrd* (karaoke); *Extended Versions: Encore Collection* (which at least offers up some material original to the current band); *Pickin' On Lynyrd Skynyrd* (part of the Pickin' guitar series); *Southern Rock Essentials* (which includes Skynyrd, Johnny Van-Zant, and Rossington Collins Band, among others); *Winning Combinations* (half Allman Brothers, half Skynyrd); *The Blues Tribute to Lynyrd Skynyrd, Yesterday and Today* (same vintage Skynyrd); and *The Complete Lynyrd Skynyrd Live.*

Skynyrd music continues to find its way onto the soundtracks of major motion pictures. Lynyrd Skynyrd songs have appeared or been mentioned in *Con Air, Kalifornia, Almost Famous, Blow,* and *Forrest Gump,* among others. Brad Pitt's seedy "Kalifornia" killer identified with "Freebird." Not only does the music appear in other films, but some of the on-screen characters are directly influenced by the personalities of members of Skynyrd. Scott Rosenberg, the screenwriter of *Con Air,* said that the Nicolas Cage lead character, Cameron Poe, was inspired by Ronnie VanZant. "Poe *is* that guy. He's Ronnie VanZant," Rosenberg claims. Cameron Crowe, director and screenwriter of *Almost Famous,* has said that a great deal of his development of that movie was based on his relationship with Ronnie and the members of Lynyrd Skynyrd. As for *Forrest Gump,* Leon Wilkeson was delighted that both "Freebird" and "Sweet Home Alabama" were included on the soundtrack. "I'm just proud we taught Forrest Gump to dance," he said. Skynyrd will continue to be a presence in film. In 2001, a film titled *Sweet Home Alabama* went into production.

Lynyrd Skynyrd still enjoy appearing before sell-out audiences. Their presence as opening act for ZZ Top in the summer of 1999 caused a great deal of controversy. The tour got off to a rocky start when Johnny Van-Zant developed throat problems and the start date of the tour had to be postponed. Yet by the time they got into the swing of the tour, Skynyrd was rockin' as usual. The band's fans, many of them faithful for twenty-five years or more, were indignant that Skynyrd was opening for a band that, in their opinion, was past their prime. Many of them left after Skynyrd's set. It was decided by fans that they would not support Skynyrd opening for ZZ Top in the future. Skynyrd was flattered and very touched by the fans' loyalty.

"We even like being the underdogs now, which we haven't been for God knows how long," says Billy Powell. "We were supposed to do some fairgrounds in England this summer. But we got canceled. We were going to do them with Deep Purple and Van Halen. I don't know if we'd have headlined or not. But we like being the underdogs because the way we figure, who's gonna want to get up on stage after 'Freebird?' Hank Williams, Jr . . . we used to play with him and he'd headline. After our set, during his set, [people would] leave left and right. We kind of chuckled about it. He gets mad, but we don't go around saying, 'hey, we blew these people off.' We didn't have to. There are a lot of good bands out there, a whole bunch of good ones. Bad Company is one of [my favorite] bands to deal with. Them and .38 Special, I like dealing with them, too. Doobie Brothers are good too. With .38 and Bad Company, we have this fun thing. Who's going to be better tonight? We're gonna blow *your* doors off . . . no, we'll blow your doors off. But it's just a fun thing."

"I'm a little partial to the original band," says Judy VanZant Jenness. "That's the music you hear on the radio. That's the legacy of Lynyrd Skynyrd, from what I get from all the fans. They'll send you letters and say Lynyrd Skynyrd has helped me through this crisis in my life, or that crisis in my life and so and so and so. I think they can relate to the music and the songs and their lyrics. It's part of their lives. They feel they're a part of Lynyrd Skynyrd music and therefore they're dedicated for life. Their kids are dedicated, because their kids hear only that. The kids grew up on the music. We've got fans from sixty years old to eight years old, so it's pretty amazing. It's best for us to be around for awhile, I think."

Steve Gaines' widow, Teresa Gaines Rapp, found the interest in her husband's music so overwhelming that she launched a Steve Gaines website in 2000 (www.stevegaines.com). The site is dedicated to preserving the memory of both Steve and his sister, Cassie. One of Teresa's projects, in conjunction with Steve's father Bud, was to make available two excellent CDs of Steve's music: *Okie Special* (featuring cuts from Steve's bands Detroit and Crawdad, released independently by Steve's widow Teresa) and *I Know A Little—Live* (also released by Teresa and featuring live cuts from Steve's early years).

Lynyrd Skynyrd continues to have support from others in the music industry. "They're still great," says friend Charlie Daniels. "They're still wonderful."

Regardless, the joy derived from playing both their classics and their newer material remains with each member of the band. Lynyrd Skynyrd plans to be around awhile longer. "Nothing's going to break this band up, unless there's another tragedy," said Billy Powell in 1998. "God forbid." Yet even with the recent death of Leon Wilkeson, Skynyrd has regrouped and headed back out on the road.

If Johnny Van-Zant has anything to say about it, the music will continue to make a statement. "When you have a kid come up and go, you know, "That Smell" or something touched me, it got my life straight . . . if it's just one person, what a big influence," he muses. "That's why I'm so concerned about some of the music these days, 'cause it's so depressing. It's very depressing, if you listen to some of it, really deep, especially lyric-wise. I think a lyric can be a powerful thing. But Skynyrd wasn't all about trying to preach to people. It was about, hey, O.K., we're going to have some fun too. It still is to this day. I try to go out and take people's minds off their worries for an hour or two. And that's what it's all about."

"Our gimmick has always been our music, not our lights, not our sound system," said Billy Powell. "Not really necessarily that much of a visual thing as a musical thing. People come to hear us for our music, not for any other reason. Like some bands are famous for their light shows. Pink Floyd or whoever, they're just famous for their light shows and their massive productions on stage, their visual thing. Well, our gimmick is our music, and that's one thing I'm real proud to say."

"Lynyrd Skynyrd is timeless," says Rickey Medlocke. "I believe that there'll never be a time that you won't hear it on the radio. I don't think there's ever going to be a time that somebody won't want to listen to it on CDs and hear it in their car. Even today, with the younger audiences. They can remember where they were the first time they ever heard 'Sweet Home Alabama,' or 'Gimme Three Steps,' or 'What's Your Name,' or 'Freebird.' It brings back memories. It is beautiful to me, because that to me means that the music is timeless."

In the Skynyrd tradition, the band continues to tour extensively. After all, it's what they always have done. But that's not necessarily a bad thing for the boys in the band. "I actually grew up on the road," laughs Rickey Medlocke. "My dad would travel during the summer [and] he would take my ma and me with him. I kind of grew up sleeping in dresser drawers as a kid and stuff. I guess that's how it got into my blood. And still today, I just love to tour. If I had my choice, I'd probably be on the road eleven months out of the year, and one month at home. If I had my rathers, that's what I'd rather be doing . . . I just love the freedom—the openness of being able to be on the highway and travel. I actually get more rest when I'm on the road than I do at home. When you're settled down and you're in one place, you're always finding something that's got to be done. Or this person calls, that person calls, or da da da da da. But when I'm on the road, every night when we get on the bus, we sit and have a good chat. People laugh and we have a good time. It's like a big family. And then all of a sudden everybody's in their bunks and you go to sleep. You get a good eight or nine hours worth of sleep on the bus. You wake up and you're in the next town, and you check in, and all of a sudden that night you're playing music. I look forward to that hour and forty-five minutes every night. That's what I live to do, every day."

Medlocke, and some of the others it seems, don't consider a time when they would want to leave the road. "Johnny and I were talking one day," laughs Medlocke. "Johnny goes, 'What's gonna happen one day when we are no longer like touring, or whatever? When we're older people and we're off the road and basically at home and this and that and the other.' I got to really, seriously thinking about that. I said, 'You know, as much as I love to travel and be on the highway and stuff, what in the heck am I going to do, you know?' I think I've got it figured out. I'm just going to take all my money and just buy a bus myself. I told Johnny I would pick him up and we'd alternate taking turns driving. Like I'd drive into one city, he can check out the hotels, act like he's going to do a gig that night. And that night we'll just travel to the next town or whatever. I've often wondered to myself, in my lifetime, how many miles I've actually traveled in my life. It would be a very interesting thing to really know, 'cause I know it's probably millions."

"We'd have to get us one of those RV things and just drive around," laughs Johnny. "It's just imbedded in us. I love it. There's something very romantic about getting on a tour bus. It's like a sweet lady. Once you've done it all your life, it's imbedded in you. There's even something about a hotel room. I know what it is. I don't have to clean up afterwards. But there's something very romantic. When you're in music, it's kind of like being in love. Once you find her, it's hard to let her go. Hopefully, you don't have to."

Although Johnny has had his share of problems in the romance department, having been divorced more than once, he finds his family bond with daughters Lindsay, Kristen, and Harmony, as well as his extended family, most comforting. Unfortunately, Johnny's mother, Marion "Sister" Van-Zant, died suddenly on April 8, 2000. Her absence would be greatly felt by the family she left behind.

The current, and possibly last, line-up of Lynyrd Skynyrd is feeling good about their music these days. Gary Rossington, Billy Powell, Johnny Van-Zant, Rickey Medlocke, Hughie Thomasson, and new bassist Ean Evans, along with the recently recruited drummer Michael Cartellone, formally of Damn Yankees, continue to entertain and make their living as Lynyrd Skynyrd. No public statement has been made about the "three original members in the band" clause in the agreement with Judy VanZant Jenness and Teresa Gaines Rapp. Perhaps Rickey Medlocke is considered an original member as, even if he didn't appear on Skynyrd's first MCA album, he did appear on the first Skynyrd recordings done in Muscle Shoals. The band says that not only are they making it a priority to get their music out to their fans in concert, they are also looking forward to continuing to release new, original material. "Think about it," says Medlocke. "Grateful Dead faded on out of here. It's almost like Lynyrd Skynyrd is the Grateful Dead of the South or something. We're not like them but it's like the popularity of the band has become kind of like that. The music of Lynyrd Skynyrd on the radio is never ending. The music has said it all. The music is the bottom line. You can have all the rock stars you want, you can have all the big lights, and the big amps, and the production, and the popularity, and the press . . . what's really going to hold you steadfast is those almighty songs."

"You go out and see them guys play . . . " says Donnie Van Zant. "They still have got more fire and desire than most bands will ever, ever have. I don't know if there's an obvious difference [between the new Skynyrd and the old Skynyrd], 'cause there's different players now. They sound fantastic to me. I love the line-up that they have with Rickey Medlocke from Blackfoot and Hughie from The Outlaws. I think it's the best line-up I've heard since the old days. They're very impressive." Yet Thomasson hasn't given up on the Outlaws altogether. That band released a brand-new album titled *So Low* on Asin Records in 2000.

As to brother Johnny, "He's a very multitalented guy," says Donnie. "He's really strong when it comes to melodies. He's another underrated songwriter. He's very good at what he does. I think he'll go on as long as he wants to go on."

Yet thoughts continue to return to Ronnie VanZant. A lot of the continued success of Lynyrd Skynyrd is owed to the initial association with Ronnie VanZant and his continued musical presence. "Ronnie, fortunately, achieved a lot of notoriety and a lot of commercial success," says Charlie Faubion. "And that's what he wanted. It's a tragedy, like anybody's, that his life was cut short, but he was headed doing what he wanted to do . . . ."

Ronnie lives on through his daughters, Tammy and Melody, and his four granddaughters: Ashley, Amber, and Courtney (Tammy's daughters) and Aria Ronni Marion (Melody's daughter). Yet for those who don't know his family, the music remains. "The messages in [Ronnie's] songs," says Judy VanZant Jenness, "that seems to be the key. Everybody can tell you what that song means to them. Of course 'Freebird's' one of the biggest ones. But I guess it's the message he left in the songs and in 'Freebird.' He left a big message in all the other ones too. The songs are timeless. They're not about certain periods. They're just songs that people can relate to for years and years and years. We still sell over a million records a year with MCA. There's still material that hasn't been released. It's not new material, but it's different versions of stuff that's been out. There's a lot of stuff. It's not like we're at the bottom of the well. We still have footage, unreleased stuff. We have a lot of stuff."

"There would've been no Lynyrd Skynyrd if it wouldn't have been for Ronnie," says Artimus Pyle. "There would've been no band. There could have been any number of musicians play with Ronnie, and it would've been Lynyrd Skynyrd, or it would've been something special. But if Ronnie hadn't have been there, it would've been a very different story for Mr. Rossington and a few others. You gotta look at it. None of the incarnations have been anywhere near as successful as Lynyrd Skynyrd. None of the incarnations have had anything. It was all given to them by Ronnie VanZant. Unfortunately, they don't honor that."

Pyle has a few thoughts of his own as to the future of the band. "If there would have been integrity and character within the band, and strength and stage presence, the band would be able to raise money for cancer and AIDS and Eric Clapton would be jamming with us," he says. "There'd be all kinds of specials on television, like Aerosmith was able to enjoy, because they kicked their drug habit and they turned to the task at hand. With Skynyrd, drugs, cocaine, alcohol, lying, cheating, thieving, that was more important than the music."

Yet Lynyrd Skynyrd does continue to make an effort to stay involved with their community. After the tragic terrorist attack on the World Trade Center on September 11, 2001, the band donated $10,000 to the Red Cross Relief Fund. They also participated in the "Volunteers for America" benefit (again for victims of the WTC disaster) held in Atlanta on October 20, 2001, along with Bad Company, Styx, Journey, John Waite (formally of The Babys), and others. The band also participated in a concert and motorcycle run sponsored by the Alabama Music Hall of Fame, in conjunction with the "Trail of Tears" commemoration on September 15, 2001, with Leon Russell. Artimus Pyle and his wife Kerri, along with the APB, held a "Celebration of Life" concert on October 20, 2001, the twenty-fourth anniversary of the plane crash. The purpose of the concert, which benefited the St. Augustine Amphitheatre, was to honor the lives of Ronnie VanZant, Steve and Cassie Gaines, Dean Kilpatrick, Allen Collins, and Leon Wilkeson.

Although Skynyrd is still popular, there are many fans who reject the current band and remain fiercely loyal only to the pre-October 20, 1977, Lynyrd Skynyrd. They believe that Skynyrd does not truly exist without founder and frontman Ronnie VanZant. "There are dozens of reasons why the pre-1978 Skynyrd is the 'real' thing and 'the only Lynyrd Skynyrd band'" say fans Brian and Mary Nash. "But all of these reasons mean nothing to anyone who doesn't care about truth, honor, dignity, loyalty, or friendship. The people that these things *do* have meaning for, and [who] are knowledgeable about the history and lives of the band members, all agree on one simple fact: The reason the pre-1978 band is the only true Lynyrd Skynyrd band is Ronnie VanZant."

With the loss of Allen Collins in 1990, many of those who were inclined to agree but reluctant to take a stand finally felt compelled to believe that a Skynyrd without Ronnie VanZant and Allen Collins (and now Leon Wilkeson) is not a Skynyrd at all but rather a band attempting to cash in on the glory of a musical legend.

"[Lynyrd Skynyrd is] one of the greatest rock-and-roll bands of all time," says Hughie Thomasson. "That's it in a nutshell. They paved the way for a whole lot of people. Just the way they are has made them who they are. Their fans love them, are dedicated, it's like nothing I've ever seen before. Hardcore Skynyrd fans is what we call 'em, and there's lots of 'em. Playing with this band I see a second generation sometimes even a third generation. Their parents bring their kids with them to come and see Skynyrd. The same folks that came to see Skynyrd when they were teenagers. And now they're bringing their kids to see us and it's very cool, especially to see like a twelve-year-old kid up front that knows the words to all the songs. It's like, wow, you know? These songs have stood the test of time, and stood it very well. It's the band's reputation for playing live, being an awesome band . . . a band no one wants to open for."

Lynyrd Skynyrd, past and present, influences bands as well as musicians. "Skynyrd came up with their style and everything and it definitely had an influence on a lot of bands at that time," says Rodney Mills. "And still does, to a certain extent. Any musician that sits around and listens to Skynyrd cannot help but be influenced by those guys."

"I'm real proud of the music the band has produced in the last twenty to twenty-five years," says Billy Powell. "And [me] still being a part of it and still carrying on the music is just a real good feeling. Instead of giving up and throwing in the towel. It took a lot of work to get it going, a lot of struggling to get it back again. We still have conflicts here and there with lawsuits and stuff, but that's not going to ever stop the music. Nothing will stop it."

"We're going to go forward," says Johnny Van-Zant. "We're carrying on something that we need to do and want to do. As long as the fans want it, we'll be there. There's a whole new generation of Lynyrd Skynyrd fans we haven't even got to yet. So, we'll be out there going for it."

Lynyrd Skynyrd has sold over thirty million records. It's amazing to think that the opening act for the *Quadrophenia* tour would eventually outsell even The Who. According to BMI, "Freebird" has been played on the radio more than two million times. On the VH1 poll for the 100 best songs in rock-and-roll, "Freebird" placed fourth. In 2000, fans enjoyed the fictional characters depicting Skynyrd in the Cameron Crowe movie *Almost Famous,* and Skynyrd's appearance on the PBS program *Austin City Limits.*

Lynyrd Skynyrd would surprise everyone, including their fans, when BMG/CMC released a, gasp, Lynyrd Skynyrd Christmas album in 2000! *Christmas Time Again* featured Christmas songs, from Billy Powell's instrumental "Greensleeves" to Johnny's rendition of "Rudolph the Red-Nosed Reindeer." A poignant and memorable "Mama's Song," written by Gary Rossington and Johnny Van-Zant with Rickey Medlocke and Hughie Thomasson, is sure to become at least a country station Christmas classic. Charlie Daniels and .38 Special also contributed songs to the album. Who would have thought it, but Lynyrd Skynyrd's *Christmas Time Again* is as good a Christmas album as most, if not better.

The boys keep their name in the public consciousness. Skynyrd decided to demonstrate their appeal to both of their audiences, country and rock-and-roll, by appearing in Nashville one night with Travis Tritt and the next with Gov't Mule. Lynyrd Skynyrd even put in an appearance performing at the 2000 Republican National Convention.

On August 23, 2001, Lynyrd Skynyrd was honored during a hometown performance in Jacksonville for two distinctions. Their 1998 CMC album *Lyve from Steeltown* was certified gold by the Recording Industry Association of America, and MCA joined in the celebration by honoring Skynyrd for reaching twenty-three million units in their MCA sales career. It was a poignant moment for several of the band's children, including Ronnie VanZant's daughter Melody, Allen Collins' daughter Amie, Leon Wilkeson's son Lee, and Artimus Pyle's son River.

Skynyrd seems able to overcome any tragedy, any challenge. Those who remain loyal to the original band would like to see Skynyrd "retired," and choose to remember them from their records and personal experiences in concert. Those who are unwilling to give up the band still flock to their concerts, all over the country and all over the world. No matter where or how they do it, fans continue to find ways to listen to the music and experience what was, and is, Lynyrd Skynyrd.

 # Selected Discography

Lynyrd Skynyrd

1973	*Lynyrd Skynyrd (Pronounced 'Leh-'nerd 'Skin-'nerd)* (MCA)
1974	*Second Helping* (MCA)
1975	*Nuthin' Fancy* (MCA)
1976	*Gimme Back My Bullets* (MCA)
1976	*One More ~~For~~ From the Road* (MCA)
1977	*Street Survivors* (MCA)
1978	*Skynyrd's First and . . . Last* (MCA)
1979	*Gold and Platinum* (MCA)
1982	*Best of the Rest* (Uni/MCA)
1987	*Legend* (MCA)
1988	*Southern by the Grace of God* (MCA)
1989	*Skynyrd's Innyrds* (MCA)
1991	*Lynyrd Skynyrd* (Box Set) (MCA)
1991	*Lynyrd Skynyrd 1991* (Atlantic)
1993	*The Last Rebel* (Atlantic)
1994	*Endangered Species* (Capricorn)
1996	*Southern Knights* (MCA)
1997	*Freebird . . . The Movie* (MCA)
1997	*Twenty* (CMC)
1997	*What's Your Name* (MCA Special Markets)
1998	*Lyve from Steeltown* (BMG/CMC)
1998	*Skynyrd's First: The Complete Muscle Shoals Album* (Uni-MCA)
1998	*The Essential Lynyrd Skynyrd* (Uni/MCA) [2-CD Set]
1999	*Edge of Forever* (BMC/CMC)
1999	*Best of Lynyrd Skynyrd Millennium* (Uni/MCA)
1999	*Gimme Back My Bullets Remastered with Extra Tracks* (Uni/MCA)
1999	*Twentieth-Century Masters: The Best of Lynyrd Skynyrd* (MCA)
2000	*All Time Greatest Hits* (Uni/MCA)
2000	*Double Trouble* (Universal Special Products)
2000	*Christmas Time Again* (BMG)
2000	*Lynyrd Skynyrd Collectibles* (MCA)
2000	*Then and Now* (BMG/Sanctuary)
2001	*One More ~~For~~ From the Road Deluxe Edition* (Uni-MCA)

Rossington Collins Band

1980	*Anytime, Anyplace* (MCA)
1981	*This Is the Way* (MCA)

APB

1982	*APB* (MCA)
1983	*Nightcaller* (MCA)
2000	*Live From Planet Earth* (Last Resort Records)

Allen Collins Band

1983	*Here, There and Back* (MCA)

Alias

1979	*Contraband* (Mercury)

Vision

1984	*Vision* (Dunamis)

Steve Gaines

1988	*One in the Sun* (MCA)
2000	*I Know A Little* (Private Issue)
2000	*Okie Special* (Private Issue)

Rossington

1986	*Returned to the Scene of the Crime* (Atlantic)
1988	*Love Your Man* (MCA)

Johnny Van-Zant
1980   *No More Dirty Deals* (Polydor)
1981   *Johnny Van-Zant* (Polydor)
1981   *Round Two* (Polydor)
1982   *The Last of the Wild Ones* (Polydor)
1985   *Van Zant* (Geffen)
1990   *Brickyard Road* (WEA/Atlantic)
1994   *The Johnny Van Zant Collection*
         (Uni/Mercury)

Johnny and Donnie Van Zant
1998   *Brother to Brother* (BMG/CMC)
2001   *Van Zant II* (BMG/CMC)

Selected Special Product:
1995   *Classic Live Performances: Vol. 1*
         (MCA Special Markets)
1998   *Hits of Lynyrd Skynyrd* (Karaoke)
         (Sound Choice)

1998   *Pickin' On Lynyrd Skynyrd* (CMH)
1998   *Extended Versions: Encore Collection*
         (BMG Special Projects)
1999   *Solo Flytes* (MCA)
1999   *Southern Rock Essentials* (Uni/
         Hip-O-Records)
2001   *Winning* (Universal Special Products)
2000   *Blues Tribute to Lynyrd Skynyrd* (CMH)
2000   *Yesterday and Today* (BMG)
2000   *Country Tribute to Lynyrd Skynyrd*
         (Cleopatra)
2001   *Winning Combinations: The Allman
         Brothers Band and Lynyrd Skynyrd*
         (Universal Special Products)
2001   *Complete Lynyrd Skynyrd Live*
         (Calamari)
2001   *"Sweet Home Alabama":
         Tribute to Lynyrd Skynyrd* (CMH)

 # Bibliography

The quotes throughout the book are taken from the following author interviews and secondary sources.

Author Interviews
Buddy Buie: November 4, 1997.
Jeff Carlisi: March 30, 1998.
Danny Chauncey: February 6, 1998.
Charlie Daniels: March 17, 1998.
Charlie Faubion: January 6, 1998.
Doug Gray: February 2, 1998.
Paul Hornsby: January 7, 1998.
Judy VanZant Jenness: February 5, 1998,
    March 5, 1998.

Harriet Kilpatrick: March 26, 1998,
    August 5, 2001.
Ed King: November 7, 1997, June 17, 1998,
    October 29, 2001.
Al Kooper: November 25, 1997.
Dru Lombar: November 10, 1997.
George McCorkle: November 11, 1997.
Jim Dandy Mangrum: April 1, 1998.
Rickey Medlocke: March 10, 1998,
    March 11, 1998.
Rodney Mills: April 10, 1998.
Billy Powell: March 10, 1998.
Artimus Pyle: March 20, 1998, May 8, 1998.
Hughie Thomasson: April 8, 1998.

Donnie Van Zant: January 22, 1998.

Johnny Van-Zant: March 11, 1998.

Leon Wilkeson: April 7, 1998.

Allen Woody: February 13, 1998.

Author's Correspondence

Diana Berryman to author: November 2, 1997.

Andy Blake to author: October 21, 1997.

Jimmy Darrah to author: October 30, 1997.

Larry Gower to author: July 10, 1998.

Marianne Burrow Gray to author:
    August 27, 2001.

C.E. Dallas Bryan to author: August 27, 2001.

John Eastwood to author: July 28, 2001.

Randall Hall to author: September 22, 2000.

David Halliburton to author: April 16, 1998.

Carla Harrington to author: October 22, 1997.

Richard Hawkins to author: October 7, 1997.

Joe Holt to author: October 22, 1997.

Harriet Kilpatrick to author: August 28, 2000.

Ed King to author: November 11, 1997,
    January 3, 1998, April 20, 1998, April 22,
    1998, May 22, 2000, September 8, 2000,
    September 6, 2001, October 5, 2001.

Al Kooper to author: September 22, 2001.

Tim Lindsey to author: July 30, 1999.

Pat Matthews to author: December 12, 1997.

Andy Mc Kaie to author: July 17, 1998.

Brian and Mary Nash to author: October 7, 2001.

Steve Powell to author: October 10, 1997.

Kerri Pyle to author: July 5, 1999.

Bob "Slim" Rader to author: August 25, 2001.

Teresa Gaines Rapp to author:
    September 11, 2000.

Rob Scherini to author: October 13, 1997.

Michael B. Smith to author: August 28, 2001.

John Stucci to author: January 11, 1998,
    January 13, 1998.

Rick Thomson to author: October 7, 1997,
    October 22, 1997.

Jason Toone to author: October 20, 1997.

Stan Warren to author: April 29, 1998,
    April 30, 1998.

Books

Ballinger, Lee. *Lynyrd Skynyrd: An Oral History.*
    New York: Avon Books, 1999.

Brant, Marley. *Southern Rockers: The Roots
    and Legacy of Southern Rock.* New York:
    Billboard Books, 1999.

Kooper, Al. *Backstage Passes and Backstabbing
    Bastards.* New York: Billboard Books, 1998.

Van-Zant, Lacy. *The Van-Zant Family: Southern
    Music Scrapbook.* Self-published, 1997.

Magazine Articles

Charlesworth, Charles. "Caught in the Act:
    Skynyrd, Southern Fried Boogie."
    Melody Maker, December 21, 1974.

Cohen, Scott. "We Want This Hit Bad,
    Say Skynyrd." *Circus Raves,* April, 1975.

Collette, Doug. "Lynyrd Skynyrd, No Flash
    or Frills." *Pop Top,* August/September, 1975.

Costa, Jean-Charles. "Gimme Back My
    Bullets." *Hit Parader,* August, 1976.

Cristgau, Robert. "Lynyrd Skynyrd:
    Not Even a Boogie Band Is as Simple
    as It Seems." *Creem,* August, 1975.

Dupree, Tom. "Lynyrd Skynyrd in Sweet
    Home Alabama." *Rolling Stone,*
    October 24, 1974.

E. B. "Why Are Lynyrd Skynyrd One of the
    Season's Hottest Tickets?" *Rolling Stone,*
    July 9–23, 1998.

Edmonds, Ben, and Jaan Ulhelski. "The
    Southern Death Cult." *Mojo,* 1998.

Esposito, Joe. "Lynyrd Skynyrd—The 100-Proof Blues." *Creem,* October, 1975.

Friedland, Nat. "Lynyrd Skynyrd: 3 Gold LPs in Row." *Billboard,* October 11, 1975.

Glazer, Mitchell. "Lynyrd Skynyrd Fight Rock-and-Roll Civil Wars with Nuthin' Fancy." *Circus,* June, 1975.

Ingram, John. "Lynyrd Skynful." *Sounds,* October 25, 1975.

Jerome, Jim. "The Rock Road Claims Another Tragic Victim: Ronnie VanZant of the Lynyrd Skynyrd Band." *People,* November 7, 1977.

Joseph, Susan. "Lynyrd Skynyrd: Not Just Another Saturday Night Special." *Gig,* October, 1975.

Keel, Beverly. "Back in His Arms." *Nashville Scene,* August 28, 1997.

"Lynyrd Skynyrd in Turmoil—VanZant on Redneck Rock." *Circus Raves,* September, 1975.

"Lynyrd Skynyrd Return." *New Musical Express,* October 25, 1975.

"Lynyrd Skynyrd: 'Saturday Night Special.'" *Sounds,* May 31, 1975.

Makowski, Pete. "A Tale of Two Skynyrds." *Sounds,* November 16, 1974.

Makowski, Pete. "Lynyrd Skynyrd." *Sounds,* December 21, 1974.

Makowski, Pete. *Sounds,* November 27, 1974.

McConnell, Andy. "Ronnie VanZant Kicked His Scotch Habit: It's Wine Now . . ." *Sounds,* May 21, 1975.

McConnell, Andy. "Sleazy Riders." *Sounds,* October 18, 1975.

McGee, David. "Gimme Back My Bullets." *Rolling Stone,* March 25, 1976.

Mitchell, Tony. "Superstars—By the Skyn of their Teeth." *Sounds,* October, 1975.

Moore, Bob. "Lynyrd Skynyrd." *Concert News,* November, 1974.

N. C. "Lynyrd Skynyrd—Gimme Back My Bullets." *Stereo Review,* April, 1976.

Point, Michael. "Hard Rock Nation, Land of Contrasts." *Performance,* April 25, 1975.

Puterbaugh, Parke. "Lynyrd Skynyrd: 'The Last Rebel.'" *Stereo Review,* June, 1993.

"Random Notes." *Rolling Stone,* November 7, 1974.

Robinson, Lisa. "Ronnie VanZant Talks about Skynyrd's Music and Politics." *Hit Parader,* January, 1976.

Scoppa, Bud. "Nuthin' Fancy—Lynyrd Skynyrd." *Rolling Stone,* June 19, 1975.

"Second Helping—Lynyrd Skynyrd." *Rolling Stone,* November 7, 1974.

Simon, Kate, and John Ingham. "What's Sillier Than a Four-Month Tour of America." *Sounds,* February 26, 1976.

"Skynyrd's Own Rainbow Show." *New Musical Express,* December, 1974.

"Southern Sounding." *Rolling Stone,* May 20, 1975.

Stewart, Tony. "I See the Bloodbath That Was Hamburg." *New Musical Express,* October 25, 1975.

Swenson, John. "Lynyrd Skynyrd: The Billboard Interview: The Crash." *Billboard,* December 11, 1998.

"The Last Rebel—Lynyrd Skynyrd." *Rolling Stone,* May 27, 1993.

Walker, Billy, and Pete Makowski. "Southern Fried to Roasting." *Sounds,* November 23, 1974.

Walker, Billy. "Nuthin' Special." *Sounds,* April 12, 1975.

Newspaper Articles:

Anderson, R. Michael. "Van Zant, Gaines Remains Moved." *Florida Times-Union,* July 12, 2000.

Anderson, R. Michael. "Van Zant's Tomb Defaced." *Florida Times-Union,* June 30, 2000. *Atlanta Constitution,* July 4, 1976.

"Band Released Album Just before Plane Crash." *Florida Times-Union,* October 19, 1997.

Bell, June D. "Guitarist: Lynyrd Skynyrd Pushed Me Out." *Florida Times-Union,* date unknown.

Brumfield, Patsy. "Skynyrd Representative Asks Return of Items." McComb *Enterprise-Journal,* October 27, 1977.

Cagle, Lisa Marie. "Singer Trades Stage for Pulpit with a Musical Ministry." *Decatur Daily,* June 14, 1992.

Cain, Scott. "Dixie's Darlings Live High on Hog." *Atlanta Journal,* July 8, 1976.

Carter, John. "Airplane 'Just Flat Ran Out Of Gas,'" *Florida Times-Union,* October 19, 1997.

Carter, John. "Beginnings." *Florida Times-Union,* October 19, 1997.

Carter, John. "Chronology." *Florida Times-Union,* October 19, 1997.

Carter, John. "Remembering Lynyrd Skynyrd." *Florida Times-Union,* October 19, 1997.

Carter, John. "Twenty Points Up Difference in Bands." *Florida Times-Union,* October, 1997.

Davis, Rachel. "Fans, Family Remember Lynyrd Skynyrd Bassist." *Florida-Times Union,* August 2, 2001.

Davis, Rachel. "Bassist Couldn't Breathe." *Florida Times-Union,* September 8, 2001.

Davis, Rachel. "Public Memorial Set for Musician." *Florida Times-Union,* July 29, 2001.

De Lorenzo, Kris. "Oh Clive, Clive, Please Don't Do This to Me." New York City newspaper, unknown, April 11, 1976.

Eldredge, Richard L. "'Free Bird' to Fly at New Arena." *Atlanta Constitution-Journal,* July 23, 1999.

Elwood, Phillip. "Rough, Rowdy, Ribald Rock." San Francisco *Examiner,* March 6, 1976. *Florida Times-Union,* October 19, 1997.

Fukuyama, Bob. "Lynyrd Skynyrd— Keep It Basic." *Los Angeles Free Press,* September 26, 1975.

"Gillsburg Plane Crash Kills Hurts Twenty Including Rock Singers." McComb *Enterprise-Journal,* October 21, 1977.

Glad, Peggy Malloy. "Sound of South Lacks Spark." *Milwaukee Journal,* May 21, 1975.

Green, Tony. "Skynyrd Soundtrack Showcases Band at Its Best." *Florida Times-Union,* September 6, 1996.

Kloer, Phil. *Florida Times-Union,* 1979.

"Lynyrd Skynyrd to Play." *Pensacola Journal,* March 29, 1975.

"Lynyrd Skynyrd." *London Daily Express,* December 13, 1975.

Makowski, Pete. "U.S. Sextet's Biting Back." *London Daily Telegraph,* October 28, 1975.

Marino, Nick. "Lynyrd Skynyrd Death Continues Legacy of Loss." *Florida Times-Union,* August 5, 2001.

"Music Reviews, Rock, Van Zant II." *Atlanta Constitution-Journal,* March 9, 2001.

Oppel, Pete. "Skynyrd Draws Crowd into Spell." *Dallas Morning News,* April 23, 1976.

"Randall Hall." *Macon Telegraph,* January 8, 1997.

Richter, Greg. "Ex-Skynyrd Member Now Wife, Mom Singing for Lord." *Daily Mountain Eagle,* April 26, 1991.

Robbins, Wayne. "Transcending Their Regional Identity." *Newsday,* April 12, 1976.

Rockwell, John. "Southern Rock Stirs Up Rebel Yells." *New York Times,* April 13, 1976.

Rohter, Larry. "Southern Boogie." *The Washington Post,* January 21, 1975.

Rudis, Al. "Skynyrd Snatches Rock Evening from Jaws of Disaster." *Chicago Sun Times,* April 4, 1974.

Russell, Woody. "The Music Stopped and the Fight Started—16 Arrested 1 Hurt at Lynyrd Skynyrd Concert." *Jacksonville Journal,* July 6, 1975.

Sabulis, Thomas. "Skynyrd Sparkles." *Boston Globe,* April 9, 1976.

Soergel, Matthew. "Remember? 'Freebird' Takes You Back in Time." *Florida Times-Union,* September 6, 1996.

Van Matre, Lynn. "Southern Rock—Loud and Gutsy." *Chicago Tribune,* April 5, 1976.

Williamson, Mike. "$100,000 Plus Recovered from Crash." McComb *Enterprise-Journal,* October 31, 1977.

Williamson, Mike. "Airplane Crash Probe Continues." McComb *Enterprise-Journal,* October 24, 1977.

Williamson, Mike. "Officials Tell of Stealing at Crash Site." McComb *Enterprise-Journal,* October 26, 1977.

Williamson, Mike. "Plane Crash Questions Linger Unanswered." *McComb Enterprise-Journal,* November 3, 1977.

Williamson, Mike. "Skynyrd Crewman Nearly Nixed Plane." McComb *Enterprise-Journal,* October 25, 1977.

Internet Material

All Points Bulletin Home Page.

Freebird Foundation, Biographies of Allen Collins, Billy Powell, Artimus Pyle, Steve Gaines, Gary Rossington, Ronnie VanZant.

Freebird Foundation, FAX page

Freebird Foundation, Judy's Letter to the Fans, November 4, 1997, November 12, 1997.

Freebird Foundation, Lynyrd Skynyrd Biography.

Freebird Foundation, Skynyrd History Lessons: "Talkin' about the Big Boys," "Gimme Three Steps," "Gold & Platinum," "Name Changes and Ten Dollar Gigs."

Freebird Foundation, Story of the Week: November 5, 1997, November 21, 1997, December 27, 1997, January 3, 1998, January 6, 1998.

Freebird Foundation, Tour Jacksonville.

Freebird Foundation, Treasure of the Week, June 18, 1998.

Hot Grits, April 3, 1999, "The King of Southern Rock," by Michael B. Smith.

Ed King Official Website.

Al Kooper Official Website, Al Kooper Biography.

Mr. Showbiz, June 10, 1997, "The Making of Con Air."

Rockin' Websites, Teresa Gaines Rapp Interview, August 15, 2000.

Radio Interviews
WZZQ radio interview with Kenneth Peden, October 23, 1977.

Reports and Documents
Mississippi State Department of Health, Vital Records, Certificate of Death, Cassie LaRue Gaines, October 24, 1977.

Mississippi State Department of Health, Vital Records, Certificate of Death, Steve Gaines, October 24, 1977.

Mississippi State Department of Health, Vital Records, Certificate of Death, Dean Arthur Kilpatrick, October 21, 1977.

Mississippi State Department of Health, Vital Records, Certificate of Death, Ronnie VanZant, October 21, 1977.

National Transportation Safety Board, Aircraft Accident Report, L&J Company, Convair 240, N55VM, Gillsburg, Mississippi, October 20, 1977, Report Number NTSB-AAR-78-6, January 16, 1978.

Post Mortem Death Report, Victims of October 20, 1977, Convair 240 N55VM Aircraft Accident.

 # Photo Credits

Index